Praise for *Vi*

MW00563678

"Old-timers and newcomers to this subject as formally addressed here will not be alone in recognizing a need for a book like this. Every day, hour, and minute, as well as personal experience and media demonstrate the incivility of public discourse in moral, political, and religious life. Not content merely to report on the public scene, these essays demonstrate the values of curiosity, attentiveness, open-mindedness, intellectual carefulness, and intellectual thoroughness.

So what? What can be done? *Virtue and Voice* attends not only to public discourse but to St. Augustine's definition of virtues as 'right-ordered affections.' The authors also remain concerned about finding 'common ground' in community and public life. Since they can be judged in respect to one of the virtues which receives much attention here, humility, it would be out of place for them to advertise themselves as titans on the international scene. Instead, they naturally and systematically deal with the provinces they know best and in which they can help make the most difference: education—whether in academies, forums, or ad hoc community gatherings, where uncivil argument comes easily. Civil discourse can make a refreshing difference. *Virtue and Voice* creatively dedicates itself to such discourse, and readers of this book who put any of its contributions to work in the larger society will find fresh ways to be intellectually virtuous."

—Martin E. Marty
The Fairfax M. Cone Distinguished Service Professor Emeritus,
The University of Chicago

VIRTUE
AND VOICE

VIRTUE AND VOICE

HABITS OF MIND FOR A RETURN TO CIVIL DISCOURSE

EDITED BY GREGG TEN ELSHOF
AND EVAN ROSA

Abilene Christian University Press

ACU PRESS

ISBN 978-1-68426-170-3

Printed in the United States of America

Library of Congress Cataloging-in-Publication Data

Names: Ten Elshof, Gregg, 1970-editor.
Title: Virtue and voice : habits of mind for a return to civil discourse /
Gregg Ten Elshof and Evan Rosa, editors.
Description: Abilene, Texas : ACU Press, 2019.
Identifiers: LCCN 2019016252 | ISBN 9781684261703 (pbk.)
Subjects: LCSH: Virtue. | Political culture—United States. |
Courtesy—Political aspects—United States.
Classification: LCC BV4630 .V59 2019 | DDC 172/.1—dc23
LC record available at https://lccn.loc.gov/2019016252

Cover design by Bruce Gore | Gore Studio, Inc.

Interior text design by Westchester Publishing Services

For information, contact:
Abilene Christian University Press
ACU Box 29138
Abilene, Texas 79699
1-877-816-4455
www.acupressbooks.com

19 20 21 22 23 24 / 7 6 5 4 3 2 1

Contents

Introduction
Seeking Intellectual Virtue for the Sake of Civil Discourse 1
Gregg Ten Elshof and Evan Rosa

Chapter 1
Intellectual Virtues, Civility, and Public Discourse 9
Jason Baehr

Chapter 2
It's Good to Be Humble: An Empirical Account 33
Peter C. Hill

Chapter 3
Civil Discourse at the Table of Reconciliation 43
Christena S. Cleveland

Chapter 4
Rationality and Rightly Ordered Affections: C. S. Lewis on Intellectual Virtue and Civil Discourse 57
George M. Marsden

Chapter 5
Respect as an Intellectual Virtue 69
Adam C. Pelser and Ryan West

Chapter 6
Humanity as Common Ground: Tolerance and Respect as Ideals in Communicative Discourse 93
Robert Audi

Chapter 7
The Virtues of Pride and Humility: A Survey 113
Robert C. Roberts

Chapter 8
Intellectual-Virtue Terms and the Division of Linguistic Labor 135
Linda Zagzebski

Chapter 9
Virtues and Vices of Civility 153
Michael Pace

Chapter 10
Cultivating Intellectual Humility and Hospitality in
Interfaith Dialogue 175
Richard J. Mouw

Notes 187

Selected Bibliography 217

Introduction

Seeking Intellectual Virtue for the Sake of Civil Discourse

Gregg Ten Elshof and Evan Rosa

Civil society is losing its civility—especially in the realm of public discourse about political, moral, and cultural issues. What hope is there for healing the broken state of public discourse in our nation and world? How can we respond with intellectual virtue to ideological disagreements? What is intellectual virtue anyway? What does it mean to say that there are virtues of the mind? And how might these virtues be acquired and applied to matters of public policy debate, educational reform, interpersonal reconciliation, and character development? What is the role of intellectual virtue in a life of flourishing, and how can it help us communicate about the issues that matter most?

The contributors to *Virtue and Voice* represent a compilation of viewpoints from philosophical, theological, psychological, historical, and sociological perspectives, aimed at providing an analysis of intellectual virtue and vice as well as exploration of their application to specific problems in contemporary society. In acknowledging the current climate of civil discourse, one often marked by heated disagreement and uncivil contention, this work explains how a more robust understanding and application of virtue might impact both personal and public domains of discourse. Furthermore, the authors seek to establish the particular virtues of humility, pride, respect, and tolerance as being foundational in the exploration of how virtue ethics might be applied to more productive civil discourse. The authors survey various sociological phenomena, ethical and epistemological theories, theological and religious factors, and psychologically informed literature to develop a rationale for the implementation of intellectual virtues for a more civil public discourse.

Recent surveys produced by the Associated Press-NORC Center for Public Affairs Research reveal that 74 percent of Americans think public manners and behavior have deteriorated in recent decades (March 2016), and 84 percent consider the country as being divided on our most important values

(October 2018).[1] A June 2018 study by Weber Shandwick, Powell Tate, and KRC Research found that 93 percent of Americans identify a problematic deficit of civility in the workplace and public square—with 69 percent classifying a lack of civility as a major problem.[2] And a November 2018 survey conducted by PBS Newswire, NPR, and Marist Polls just prior to U.S. midterm elections found that 79 percent of citizens, across all political parties, generally agreed on at least one point: they were concerned or very concerned that negativity and incivility in national politics would lead to physical violence or terrorism.[3]

Democracy and cultural progress require robust civility in public discourse if they are to be successful endeavors. Whereas politeness and niceness may only conceal and perpetuate division, a civility that facilitates respect, honor, and kindness toward ideological opponents is what our sharply divided world is in great need of. But how can this be achieved?

As the moral category of virtue has come back into vogue over the past sixty years, many contemporary scholars have noticed that understanding and cultivating the intellectual virtues may contribute to restoring civility in public discourse. However, there is a wide chasm between this literature and the public figures—both religious and non-religious—through whom change might realistically be effected. Furthermore, the literature that exists on the topic is often tucked away in complex philosophical tomes that are far removed from the spheres of cultural influence. It is rare to find penetrating analysis and the integration of both virtue and the nature of civil discourse that is not limited to an audience of specialists in one academic field or another. Thus, the authors of this volume push for ways in which we can remedy our culture's inability to engage in truly civil discourse about the issues that matter.

In Chapter One, Jason Baehr undertakes the application of virtue epistemology to our understanding of the state of public discourse and what might be done to improve it. Virtue epistemology is an approach to the philosophical study of knowledge that focuses on intellectual virtues and their role in the life of the mind. Intellectual virtues are strengths of intellectual character like curiosity, attentiveness, open-mindedness, intellectual carefulness, and intellectual thoroughness. Baehr begins by arguing that virtue epistemology provides a conceptual and linguistic framework that makes possible an illuminating diagnosis of the deficiency in contemporary public discourse. According to this diagnosis, public discourse is deficient largely on account of how frequently and pervasively it manifests intellectual vices like narrow-mindedness, intellectual arrogance, intellectual dishonesty, dogmatism, and closed-mindedness. Baehr goes on to argue that virtue epistemology contains important resources for addressing this problem. It does so, first, by offering a robust account of the antidote to these vices: intellectual virtues. It also speaks meaningfully to how these virtues can be fostered, including within an educational setting. Growth in intellectual virtues is a central and important educational aim. Therefore, one way of improving the quality of public discourse is to "educate for intellectual virtues," which is an exercise in applied virtue epistemology. After addressing several possible objections to his argument, Baehr concludes by sketching practical suggestions for those interested in engaging in public discourse marked by greater civility or intellectual virtue.

Social psychologists have long documented the extent to which people view themselves positively. A significant amount of research indicates that many individuals are prone to self-enhancing biases; however, a growing body of literature also suggests that some individuals are able to maintain a non-defensive sense of self by accepting their finitude, which includes recognizing personal limitations and making mistakes while respecting the strengths and wisdom of others. Because literature on humility as an intellectual virtue is sparse, a review of literature pertaining to humility as a general dispositional characteristic is provided, to supplement other epistemological approaches in our understanding of intellectual virtue. Peter Hill's inclination is to consider humility holistically, as a general construct, and to view intellectual humility as a subset of this broader characteristic, and particularly of the intellectual domain. In Chapter Two, Hill lists some key findings regarding humility that are well established in the literature. In attempting to relate current findings to the discussion of intellectual virtue, he lays out the various conceptualizations of intellectual humility so as to consider various psychological implications.

Christena S. Cleveland notes that one need not be a social scientist to notice two patterns in our diverse society. In less than an hour of flipping through cable news channels, one can gather evidence of the first pattern: that disagreement (both intergroup and interpersonal) is often characterized by incivility and mutually uncharitable perceptions. And in the course of one short drive from the suburbs into the city center of the nearest metropolitan area, one can observe that our society is organized around segregation rather than integration. But do these two patterns have anything to do with each other? In Chapter Three, Cleveland argues yes. She presents social-psychological research that confirms that when different social groups are separated from each other, they will inevitably (albeit, non-consciously) perceive each other through the lens of hostility. As such, in a segregated society, even well-intentioned attempts at discourse are often marred by hostility. However, converging social-psychological research shows that discourse between groups who enjoy healthy contact with each other is more likely characterized by a willingness to listen, interdependence, forgiveness for past wrongs, and repentance. Integrating this research with trinitarian theology, she introduces the table model, a practical psycho-theological model of reconciliation—centered on common identity, mutuality, equality, sociological imagination, and solidarity—with which leaders can begin to reorganize their group's relationship with an estranged group and begin to forge a pathway toward a more civil discourse across difference.

In Chapter Four, George M. Marsden notes the intellectual virtues that C. S. Lewis cultivated that are helpful for promoting civility. Lewis sought to follow the example of Augustine in defining virtues as "right-ordered affections" that need to be nurtured. Intellectual virtues should operate within the framework of these other virtues. So rather than seeing rationality as objective, Lewis sees it as needing to operate in the context of properly ordered affections. In *Mere Christianity*, he appeals to the imagination of his audience as much as their reason. Marsden recognizes that Lewis's quest for timeless truths is another intellectual virtue that leads him to find common ground with diverse audiences in perennial human nature. Historical perspectives also helped Lewis appreciate how much modern people's views need to be re-enchanted. While his presentations have a winsome personal dimension, they ultimately point not to himself but to the realities that he sees as answering perennial human needs.

For Adam Pelser and Ryan West, another key missing ingredient from much of public discourse is respect. The term "respect" can refer to an attitude, a judgment, a manner of behaving, a feeling, or a virtue—a family of concepts, the unifying theme of which is "the esteem of excellence or worthiness." In Chapter Five, they offer a sketch of the intellectual variant of the virtue of respect. Their analysis begins with Stephen Darwall's distinction between two species of broadly moral respect: "recognition respect" and "appraisal respect."

Whereas all people deserve recognition respect in virtue of their equal moral worth, one's worthiness of appraisal respect depends on the comparative value of one's excellences and achievements. Similarly, Pelser and West distinguish two kinds of intellectual respect: equal basic respect for all thinkers and special comparative respect, the latter of which is properly reserved for subject-matter experts, the intellectually virtuous, and the otherwise intellectually excellent. The person with the intellectual virtue of respect is intelligently disposed, in action as well as in emotion, to both egalitarian and comparative intellectual respect. The authors consider the two kinds of respect in turn, exploring how each is relevant to the intellectual virtue of respect. Along the way, they note some connections and differences between intellectual respect and related traits, such as open-mindedness and intellectual humility, and develop several narrative examples to illustrate what intellectual respect and disrespect look like in a variety of contexts of discourse, from policy discussions in the Oval Office to elementary school classrooms to social media posts. Their conclusions reflect on some behavioral, contemplative, and social practices that might help the less-than-virtuous to approximate the ideal of respect more closely and encourage others to do likewise.

In Chapter Six, Robert Audi suggests that many disagreements in discourse, whether in politics, education, or personal life, arise because there is a lack of clarity about the common ground of human experience. This chapter takes elements including birth, growth, success, and failure seriously, suggesting that the common ground of such human experience provide a place from which mutual understanding and tolerance can grow. Audi contends that certain ethical standards should be more widely recognized as part of our common ground than they are, that they support tolerance and humility as virtues important for both public and private discourse, and that they enable us to deal civilly and rationally with much of the disagreement that is inevitable in a pluralistic democracy. His chapter offers a partial account of both tolerance and humility, considers their bearing on disagreement, and formulates ethical principles that can contribute to achieving civic virtue.

Chapter Seven explores pride and humility. Though these traits are often presented as being in opposition—with one in the role of virtue, the other in that of vice—with the help of a more precise vocabulary, Robert C. Roberts offers a fresh sketch of both. In his new schema, he explores the vices of pride as well as the vices of humility, suggesting that pride's virtuous qualities be respected alongside the virtues of humility. The virtues of pride and humility, far from excluding each other, actually stand in more positive relation to each other, the virtues of humility supporting or enhancing the virtues of pride and vice-versa.

In Chapter Eight, Linda Zagzebski extends her work in developing a moral theory she calls Exemplarist Virtue Theory, in which a "good person" functions semantically in the same way that natural, kind terms function in the theories of linguistic meaning developed by Hilary Putnam and Saul Kripke. She proposes that individuals discover the meaning of "good" as we read or watch narratives of paradigmatically good people, admiring certain patterns of emotions, perceptions, ends, and behaviors. This approach to virtue, she suggests, excludes natural talents from the category of virtues, but it includes a wide range of traits acquired through human agency, including intellectual virtues. Her focus on the division of moral linguistic labor and the semantics of these terms illuminates the use of virtue theory for the practical purposes of moral education and civic discourse, and it explains some of the particular challenges that arise in the use of the intellectual-virtue terms.

Michael Pace's chapter offers a philosophical account of civility that makes sense of the truth in these competing attitudes. Rules of civility, Pace argues, are socially established norms that allow us to communicate respect or disrespect for others. Though Pace considers different ways that civility can be morally and epistemically valuable, he focuses on some less-than-obvious ways that it can be dangerous. Some of these dangers arise from the fact that rules of civility are often determined by social convention. Norms of civility can be skewed, even to the extent that they require intellectual vice and prohibit displays of intellectual virtue. Pace also argues that even rules of civility that are morally adequate can have bad epistemic consequences, hindering—rather than helping—us in getting at the truth.

In Chapter Ten, Richard Mouw develops a Christian theological approach to an intellectually virtuous pursuit of the truth. He bases his comments on Simone Weil's suggestion that "If one turns aside from [Christ] to go toward the truth, one will not go far before falling into his arms."[4] To that end, Mouw recommends the cultivation of humility and hospitality in our intellectual quest. He criticizes St. Augustine's encouragement of Christians to reappropriate the truth found in "heathen" thinkers, just as the Israelites reappropriated Egyptian wealth for "better" use. Using examples of Augustine's own reliance on Plato, Mouw offers an alternative approach to regarding non-Christian contributions to philosophy, theology, spirituality, and more—appreciating and respecting it for what it is. For positive examples, he cites John Calvin's regard for the "admirable light of truth shining" in non-Christian sources and Herman Bavinck's suggestion that we not limit Christian interreligious dialogue to "dogmatics and apologetics." Mouw points out the distasteful habits of mind present in the evangelical community, regarding what can or cannot be learned from engaging non-Christian thought and cultural contributions, and he offers practical recommendations for cultivating intellectual humility and hospitality in contexts of religious disagreement.

We wish to thank these contributors, along with many other supporters, including President Barry Corey and the administration of Biola University, without whose support the work of the Center for Christian Thought (CCT) would be impossible. Thanks also goes to Tom Crisp, Steve Porter, and Laura Crane of the CCT. Working as a team with these people is and has been a joy. Finally, special thanks is owed to the John Templeton Foundation for its generous support and funding of research on "Intellectual Virtues and Civil Discourse" for the 2014–2015 academic year.

Chapter 1

Intellectual Virtues, Civility, and Public Discourse

Jason Baehr
Loyola Marymount University

> [O]pinion ought, in every instance, to determine its verdict by the circumstances of the individual case—condemning everyone, on whichever side of the argument he places himself, in whose mode of advocacy either want of candor, or malignity, bigotry, or intolerance of feeling manifest themselves; but not inferring these vices from the side which a person takes, though it be the contrary side of the question to our own; and giving merited honor to everyone, whatever opinion he may hold, who has calmness to see and honesty to state what his opponents and their opinions really are, exaggerating nothing to their discredit, keeping nothing back which tells, or can be supposed to tell, in their favor. This is the real morality of public discussion.
>
> —John Stuart Mill, *On Liberty*

Mill's description of the "morality of public discussion" marks a sharp contrast with the present state of public discourse in the United States and beyond.[1] Specifically, it calls attention to a familiar and problematic deficiency of civility. Of course, incivility in public discourse is nothing new. In certain respects, public discourse is more civil today than it has been in times past.[2] Nevertheless, the quality of public debate and disagreement remains poor. And questions about the nature of the problem and what can be done about it remain worthy of consideration.

Later in the chapter, we will look closely at the sorts of uncivil actions and attitudes that comprise the deficiency of civility in public discourse. However, to orient the discussion, I briefly note two examples:

> Lenar Whitney is a member of the Louisiana House of Representatives. In connection with her recent bid for a seat in Louisiana's 6th Congressional

> District, Whitney released a video titled "Global Warming is a Hoax," in which she describes belief in global warming as a "delusion" and as "perhaps the greatest deception in the history of mankind." She claims that "any ten-year-old can invalidate [the global warming] thesis with one of the simplest scientific devices known to man: a thermometer."[3]

Whitney's rhetoric here is marked by problematic and uncivil exaggeration, oversimplification, and distortion of the truth.

> In a *New York Magazine* article titled "Why I'm So Mean," Jonathan Chait criticizes a column by Veronique de Rugy in which the latter argues that the U.S. tax code is more progressive than those of most other countries. Chait describes his ensuing exchange with de Rugy as follows: "I wrote a response, noting that this reasoning is completely idiotic. . . . De Rugy's reply is an incoherent collection of hand-waiving that does not come close to addressing this very simple and fatal flaw with her claim. She introduces a series of other fallacies. . . . It's a simple case of her making up false claims based on extremely elementary errors."[4]

De Rugy is a nationally syndicated columnist with a PhD in economics. While she is on an end of the political spectrum opposite from Chait, the assertion that her reasoning is "idiotic," that her response to Chait was "incoherent," and that she is simply "making up false claims based on extremely elementary errors" seems like a clear case of the kind of uncivil name-calling, exaggeration, and mental inflexibility that regularly undermine the quality of public discourse.[5]

In this chapter, I undertake the application of virtue epistemology to our understanding of the state of public discourse and what might be done to improve it. Virtue epistemology is an approach to the philosophical study of knowledge that focuses on intellectual virtues and their role in the life of the mind.[6] Intellectual virtues are strengths of intellectual character like curiosity, attentiveness, open-mindedness, intellectual carefulness, and intellectual thoroughness.[7] I argue that virtue epistemology (1) provides an illuminating diagnosis of the deficiency of civility in contemporary public discourse and (2) contains important resources for addressing this deficiency.

Readers already acquainted with virtue epistemology may find the claim that it contains resources for diagnosing and addressing the state of public discourse obvious, perhaps even trivially true. Accordingly, part of my aim in the chapter is to show why my thesis is significant and substantive. Readers unfamiliar with virtue epistemology present a different challenge. They may have little sense of what intellectual character or intellectual virtues are and thus be ill-equipped to follow or appreciate the argument. For this reason, I begin with an overview of the concepts of intellectual character, intellectual virtues, and intellectual vices. I then turn to defend the two claims noted above. Next, I respond to several other possible objections to my argument. Finally, I offer some practical suggestions concerning intellectual virtues and public discourse.

Intellectual Character, Virtues, and Vices

A person's character (*simpliciter*) consists of a nexus of dispositions to act, think, and feel in various ways. Virtues are excellences of personal character, and vices are deficiencies of such character. Thus, a person who is disposed to tell lies (action), think uncharitable thoughts about her neighbors (thought), and be pained by the accomplishments of her peers (feeling) possesses various character defects or vices (e.g., dishonesty, unkindness, envy), while a person who is disposed to speak the truth (action), think well of others (thought), and take pleasure in the accomplishments of her peers possesses various character excellences or virtues (e.g., honesty, charity, selflessness).

We can think of a person's intellectual character as the character she has as a thinker, learner, or inquirer. Alternatively, it is the nexus of her dispositions to act, think, and feel in various ways in the context of thinking, learning, or inquiring. A person possesses intellectual virtues to the extent that she is disposed to act, think, and feel well in this context, and she possesses intellectual vices to the extent that she is disposed to do so poorly.

To unpack the concepts of intellectual character, intellectual virtues, and intellectual vices in a bit more detail, it may be useful to take a step back and consider a broader question: What are the requirements of successful inquiry? More specifically, what qualities or strengths would we expect an ideal inquirer or truth-seeker to possess?

Several things come naturally to mind. One is general intelligence or raw cognitive aptitude. An ideal inquirer would be intellectually gifted or talented; she would be naturally "smart."[8] Second, an ideal inquirer would also have an adequate knowledge base, particularly with respect to the field or fields of inquiry at issue. One cannot be a good scientific inquirer without knowledge of science, a good historical inquirer without knowledge of history, and so on. Third, an ideal truth-seeker would also possess a wide range of intellectual skills. These include general intellectual skills like reading, writing, and logical inference. They also include certain domain-specific skills, for example, the skills necessary for operating a microscope, doing statistics, or analyzing a historical text.

This suggests that being an excellent inquirer is a matter of general cognitive ability, knowledge, and intellectual skill. While these are no doubt of central importance, they are not sufficient. To see why, we need only observe that a person can be highly intelligent, knowledgeable, and intellectually skilled while also being intellectually lazy, arrogant, aggressive, careless, hasty, superficial, closed-minded, fearful, dishonest, and quick to give up. If a person is strong in the former areas but also manifests the latter sorts of qualities, her excellence as an inquirer will be seriously limited.

Good inquiry, then, has a characterological dimension. Intellectual virtues, as I am thinking of them, are the traits that comprise this dimension. Intellectual vices are the traits that mar, disrupt, or detract from it. Intellectual virtues include qualities like curiosity, attentiveness, intellectual humility, intellectual autonomy, open-mindedness, intellectual thoroughness, intellectual tenacity, and intellectual courage. And intellectual vices include qualities like intellectual laziness, inattentiveness, intellectual arrogance, dogmatism, intellectual dishonesty, intellectual hastiness, narrow-mindedness, and closed-mindedness.[9]

Vices, Virtues, and Public Discourse

In this section, I argue for two main claims. The first is that intellectual-vice concepts provide an illuminating diagnosis of the breakdown of civility in public discourse. The second is that intellectual-virtue concepts suggest a promising antidote to this problem.

Before getting to these arguments, a few qualifications are in order. First, I am not concerned with every manifestation or variety of civility or incivility but, rather, with these phenomena as they manifest in the domain of public discourse—and especially in the domain of public debate and disagreement, whether in politics, traditional media, social media, or related spheres. Second, even in this domain, I am not attempting to specify an exhaustive or comprehensive diagnosis or antidote. My claim is not, for instance, that intellectual-vice concepts shed light on all that is uncivil in the context of public debate, or that intellectual-virtue concepts point in the direction of a complete solution. As these points illustrate, my thesis is fairly modest. Nevertheless, I hope to show that the bearing of virtue epistemology on "the morality of public discussion," as Mill refers to it, is both theoretically and practically significant.

To support the claim that intellectual-vice concepts provide an illuminating (if partial) diagnosis of the breakdown of civility, I begin by noting several attitudes and actions often encountered in public-discourse venues like political debates and campaigns, newspapers, magazines, television news shows, blogs, and social media sites:

- Erecting and tearing down straw-man representations
- Engaging in "black and white" thinking
- Attributing vicious motives to an intellectual opponent
- Name-calling
- Listening poorly (if at all) to an opposing side
- Failing to fact-check
- Ignoring powerful objections or counter-evidence
- Willfully misinterpreting an opposing viewpoint
- Hiding, obscuring, or finessing the limitations or weaknesses of one's own point of view
- Gathering selective evidence
- Reporting in a biased manner
- Framing issues in terms of false dichotomies
- Making sweeping and hasty generalizations
- Failing to ask or answer tough questions
- Making claims without sufficient evidence
- Lacking awareness of one's cognitive fallibility
- Appealing to authority
- Relying on unreliable sources
- Dismissing an alternative point of view
- Failing to comprehend the possibility of reasonable disagreement[10]

I am going to assume—reasonably, I hope—that these features of public discourse go a significant way toward capturing the kind of incivility that is familiar in this domain.[11]

How do the attitudes and actions just noted stand with respect to the earlier characterization of intellectual vices? The fairly obvious answer: they are precisely characteristic of a wide range of such vices, including (but not limited to) intellectual dishonesty, narrow-mindedness, closed-mindedness, dogmatism, intellectual arrogance, intellectual carelessness, intellectual cowardice, and intellectual rigidity. Thus, intellectual-vice concepts put us in a position to describe, in personal or characterological terms, a good bit of the incivility characteristic of contemporary public discourse.

A reasonable question at this point might be: So what? Why is it significant that intellectual-vice concepts be applied to the relevant actions and attitudes? Is there anything particularly illuminating about this observation?[12]

I have two main replies to this question. The first is related to accuracy. Intellectual-vice concepts provide a fitting or accurate description of the relevant attitudes and behaviors. "Closed-mindedness" is an apt description of many of the listening behaviors that characterize public disagreement. "Intellectual arrogance" does a nice job of describing the kind of name-calling and lack of self-awareness that is also familiar in this context. "Dogmatism" is a fair characterization of familiar forms of selective evidence-gathering and biased reporting. And so on. Again, intellectual-vice concepts equip us with concepts and terms that have appropriate—and intellectually satisfying—application to the actions and attitudes in question.[13]

Intellectual-vice concepts differ in this regard from, say, moral-vice concepts or concepts of general intellectual aptitude or ability. Think, for example, about the kind of mishandling or ignoring of evidence, the seeming inability to conceive of alternative points of view, or the sloppy inferential reasoning common in public discourse. While failures of a sort, it isn't clear that these are moral failures. Moral-vice concepts don't have quite the right application in this context.[14] Presumably, this is because the failures in question are primarily cognitive or epistemic. For this reason, one might think that the relevant behavior can instead be understood in terms of low levels of raw intellectual ability or intelligence. But this doesn't seem quite right either. Many people who engage in the behaviors in question are extremely intelligent. Their shortcomings don't clearly reflect a deficiency of innate cognitive ability or talent. Instead, these shortcomings are more volitional, personal, or characterological.

Intellectual-vice concepts are useful and applicable precisely where moral-vice concepts and concepts of general cognitive ability leave off. Like moral vices and unlike deficiencies in general cognitive ability, intellectual vices are robustly personal and volitional. But like deficiencies in general cognitive ability and unlike moral vices, intellectual virtues are epistemically robust and manifest principally in intellectual activities. As such, intellectual-virtue concepts are uniquely well suited for characterizing the kinds of attitudes and actions that largely comprise the deficiency of civility in public discourse.

This leads to my second main reply, which is that conceiving of the relevant attitudes and actions as characteristic of intellectual vices also has notable explanatory payoffs. One such payoff is evaluative. The kind of incivility we are concerned with is objectionable, and it is objectionable in a way that is personally indicting. It reflects poorly on a person *qua* person when he routinely ignores evidence, gives straw-man characterizations of standpoints he rejects, and draws hasty inferences in his thinking about important topics. However, when described merely at this level (e.g., as a mishandling of or an insensitivity to evidence), it is not immediately clear why this behavior should elicit the rather strong and condemnatory assessment that it does. By contrast, if we view this activity as characteristic of intellectual vices, then an explanation is ready at hand. For, again, intellectual vices are character traits and thus reflect on their possessor qua person. To describe someone's intellectual conduct as consistently narrow-minded, rigid, or dogmatic is to suggest that there is something defective about the person in an intellectual-cum-personal respect.[15] In this regard, viewing the relevant features of public discourse from within an intellectual-vices conceptual framework helps explain their negative evaluative status.[16]

Another explanatory payoff of an intellectual-vices diagnosis is that it may shed important light on the psychological or motivational basis of the behavior and attitudes in question. Up to this point, I have taken pains (see, for example, note thirteen above) to avoid claiming that the kind of uncivil behavior we see in contemporary public discourse is indicative of actual intellectual vices—that is, of stable or ingrained habits to engage in this behavior. But suppose, plausibly enough, that at least some significant amount of the behavior in question is expressive of genuine vices—that it reflects standing dispositions to behave in the relevant, intellectually vicious ways. According to a fairly standard way of thinking about intellectual vices, they arise from an insufficient concern with or attachment to epistemic goods like truth, knowledge, and understanding.[17] The idea is that people who disregard evidence make little effort to characterize a position accurately before objecting to it, or they view the world in black-and-white terms that aren't sufficiently concerned with forming beliefs that are accurate or that might expand their understanding; instead, they tend to be more concerned with things like winning arguments, avoiding embarrassment, or achieving status, power, or the like. Given this account of the motivational basis of intellectual vices, an intellectual-vices diagnosis of the breakdown of civility has the potential to shed important light on the root of the problem.

This is valuable from a purely explanatory or epistemic standpoint because it yields a deeper understanding of the phenomenon at issue. But it is also significant from a practical standpoint. If we hope to do something to mitigate the problem of incivility—in ourselves or in society at large—it is important to understand something of its source. Accordingly, if we are right to think that the problem consists at least partly in the manifestation of intellectual vices, this may provide insight into the source of the problem and at least a preliminary idea of how the problem might be rectified (e.g., by addressing our own or others' motivational states with respect to epistemic goods).

Now that we have considered several reasons in favor of an intellectual-vices diagnosis of the deficiency of civility in public discourse, I turn to the second main claim of this section: namely, that intellectual-virtue concepts suggest a promising antidote to this deficiency. Given what we have just seen about intellectual-vice concepts and incivility, this claim is likely to appear fairly obvious and straightforward. Intellectual virtues are corrective of intellectual vices. For example, open-mindedness is corrective of closed-mindedness, intellectual honesty is corrective of intellectual dishonesty, attentiveness is corrective of dismissiveness, intellectual courage is corrective of intellectual cowardice, intellectual carefulness is corrective of intellectual hastiness, and intellectual humility is corrective of intellectual arrogance. Accordingly, if an important part of the problem of incivility in public discourse lies with actions and attitudes characteristic of intellectual vices, it is plausible to identify as an antidote the actions and attitudes characteristic of the corresponding intellectual virtues.[18]

Here again, we confront the "so what?" question. More specifically, someone might object, "To be sure, public discourse would be a lot more civil if people were more committed to interacting and disagreeing with each other in ways that are intellectually careful, thorough, fair, honest, open-minded, and humble. But why is this a substantive or illuminating claim?"

I will respond to this objection by explaining why an intellectual-virtues antidote to the problem of incivility is promising.[19] First, by thinking about intellectual virtues as an important corrective to the kind of incivility that is prevalent in public discourse, we immediately gain access to a wealth of resources concerning how the problem might be addressed. From ancient times up to the present, philosophers, theologians, psychologists, and others have devoted extensive and sustained attention to the mechanics of character formation, that is, to what individuals, rulers, and institutions can do to help people grow in character virtues and avoid character vices.[20] While talk of "intellectual character" and "intellectual virtues" is relatively new, the traits in question are structurally similar to moral virtues and civic virtues, such that it is very reasonable to think that the means effective for growing these other types of virtues will also be effective for growing intellectual virtues.[21] Thus, by thinking about the problem of incivility in public discourse at least partly through a conceptual framework of intellectual virtues and vices, we arrive at an idea of not only what a solution might look like in the abstract but also how the solution might be administered or implemented.

An intellectual virtues antidote is also promising on account of being implementable on a wide scale. As we have seen, intellectual virtues can be thought of as the character traits of a good thinker, learner, or inquirer; they have a distinctively epistemic orientation. As such, they also have important relevance to civic engagement and democratic participation. To be a responsible citizen in a deliberative democracy, one must seek out reliable information, weigh reasons, evaluate arguments, and so on; and one must do so well or excellently. In short, one must think and reason in an intellectually virtuous manner.[22] Harry Brighouse makes a similar point in his description of the threat of incivility—understood largely in terms of intellectually vicious activity—to a healthy democracy:

> Incivility, in other words, inhibits the search for solutions to common problems. Incivility makes it harder for people to listen to one another

> and thus acquire evidence about what one another's interests and needs are. It undermines mutual trust, and at the limit it appears to generate a considerable level of false belief among citizens, which makes it harder than it need be for them to scrutinize the effectiveness of law and the behavior of their politicians. . . . The idea that public debate about political matters can be conducted legitimately using ad hominem arguments, manipulation of—or complete disregard for—evidence, and demonization of opponents not only inhibits good policy formation, it may even spill over into other areas of life, making it more difficult for people to make evidence-based and reasonable decisions about key matters in their own lives or in common endeavors with others who live outside the purview of normal politics.[23]

Consider, as well, the proper aims of education. Among the most widely accepted of these aims are knowledge and citizenship. Schools, whether public or private, typically exist largely for the sake of providing their students with knowledge and helping them become good citizens. Assuming these aims are cogent, the features of intellectual virtues just noted (viz., their epistemic orientation and relevance to deliberative democracy) lead to the conclusion that schools should educate for growth in intellectual virtues.[24] That is, they suggest the need for a kind of "intellectual character education," the purpose of which is to foster growth in intellectual virtues like attentiveness, open-mindedness, intellectual carefulness, and intellectual courage in the context of traditional academic instruction.[25] In short, the promotion of intellectually virtuous conduct is very much at home in an educational context. If so, and if the practice of such conduct is an important antidote to the problem of incivility in public discourse, it follows that schools, whether public or private, can play a critical role in addressing this problem.

I have argued that the conceptual framework for intellectual virtues and vices, which lies at the center of virtue epistemology, (1) provides an illuminating (if partial) diagnosis of the deficiency of civility in contemporary public discourse and (2) contains important resources for addressing this deficiency. As we have already noted, at the heart of the proposed antidote to incivility is a call to the practice of virtues like intellectual humility, attentiveness, open-mindedness, intellectual honesty, intellectual carefulness, and more. In the section that follows, I turn to address several objections to such a call.

Objections and Replies

I will formulate and respond to five objections. The first four can be dealt with fairly quickly. The fifth will require greater attention.

The first objection is one that might arise in response to some of the specific intellectual virtues and is an exercise that I have argued is needed in the context of public discourse.

Rational Softness Objection

> Virtues like attentiveness, open-mindedness, and intellectual humility are rationally "soft." They demand listening instead of critically assessing, looking for the good in competing views instead of the mistakes, being slow to form negative judgments, and so on. As such, they threaten to make public discourse mealy-mouthed, uncritical, and wishy-washy, ultimately doing more epistemic harm than good.[26]

The first thing to be said in response to this objection is that it involves a mistaken view of the virtues in question. Open-mindedness and intellectual humility, for instance, do not prohibit critical assessment or the identification of flaws in competing views. One can be open-minded, intellectually humble, and intellectually rigorous and demanding. Therefore, it is an exaggeration (at best) to describe the intellectual activity characteristic of these and related virtues as wishy-washy or uncritical.[27]

Second, I have focused here on "softer" virtues like intellectual humility, open-mindedness, and attentiveness because they are corrective of several familiar forms of incivility, which, of course, has been our primary concern. However, these aren't the only intellectual virtues relevant to public discourse. Others include intellectual courage, tenacity, carefulness, thoroughness, and rigor. Accordingly, while this isn't my focus here, I wholeheartedly support a broader application of intellectual virtues to public discourse—one that goes beyond counteracting familiar manifestations of incivility. This includes thinking carefully about and thoroughly scrutinizing opposing (as well as like-minded) positions, holding fast or tenaciously to unpopular but well-supported beliefs or arguments, and courageously speaking truth to power. In sum, while intellectual virtues are likely to introduce a softer edge to acrimonious, bad-faith public disagreement and debate, they introduce other important rational constraints as well. Indeed, in other contexts (e.g., in intramural discussions in which the relevant parties are too quick to agree with one another), these "harder" or more demanding constraints may be most salient.

An argument against the notion of civility that has recently gained traction in the popular press and in some academic settings concerns a supposed tension between civility and the First Amendment right to freedom of speech.[28] Tailored to the present call to civility-cum-intellectual virtues, the objection might go as shown in the following section.

Freedom-of-Speech Objection

> The call to higher levels of intellectual virtue in public discourse is too restrictive. To the extent that it is heeded, individuals will feel reluctant to speak their views freely in a public context. As a result, this call is likely to have a dangerous "chilling effect" on the right to free speech.

By way of response, I will note, first, that I have not argued that intellectually virtuous conduct should be legally mandated in the context of public discourse or that intellectually vicious conduct should be legally forbidden. That would be wholly implausible. Instead, my claim is that we should non-coercively condemn and voluntarily refrain from the kind of uncivil speech and other behaviors characteristic of intellectual vices. As a general principle, this hardly seems controversial. We also should not be concerned that the call to engage in public disagreement in ways that are open, fair, and intellectually honest will have a problematic "chilling effect" on free speech more broadly. Rather, the call is akin to a (non-coercive) call for people to be less envious of one another or to be less greedy. It is a call to engage with one another according to a higher (non-compulsory) standard. We do not seriously or legitimately worry that public criticisms of envy or greed will have a problematic "chilling effect" on interpersonal competition or on the rights of the ambitious entrepreneur. Nor should we worry that aspiring to intellectually virtuous public discourse will threaten First Amendment rights.[29]

The next objection is similar to the first two.[30] However, here, the focus is on the way in which embracing the call to intellectually virtuous civil discourse might put certain controversial but critically important conversation topics off-limits.

Sensitive-Topics Objection

> The suggested practice of intellectual virtues will prevent certain important conversations from taking place in the public square (e.g., conversations about race, poverty, or climate change). For fear of offending others or being labeled intellectually arrogant or disrespectful, people will be reluctant to discuss certain sensitive, emotionally charged, but critically important social, political, and moral issues. This will prove especially harmful to the more vulnerable members of society, for it is often their well-being that is at stake in these conversations.[31]

Were we conceiving of civility as a kind of social propriety or politeness (e.g., one that upholds existing social norms and conventions), this objection might have considerable force.[32] For there is no question that politeness, propriety, or a desire to avoid offense have sometimes been invoked as a way of avoiding difficult conversations that are badly needed in a given community or society. However, the connection between intellectual virtues and politeness is tenuous at best. Recall that intellectual virtues are epistemically oriented: they're the character traits of a committed and reasonable truth-seeker. Therefore, as a general rule, the intellectually virtuous person will not (at least as such) be afraid to flout social conventions when the truth is at stake, including (perhaps especially) truth about important social or political issues.

Rather, the requirements of intellectual virtue, particularly in the context of public discourse, pertain primarily to how people interact with others and with others' views and arguments—not with the content of the views and arguments themselves.[33] These requirements demand that we give open and honest consideration to opposing views, do not distort or ignore evidence, remain mindful of and honest about the limitations of our own views and arguments, seek carefully and thoroughly to understand a position before arguing against it, and so on. There is, then, little concern that a call to higher levels of intellectual virtue in public discourse will stifle discussion of important social, political, or moral issues.

Therefore, while my intent has not been to offer a definition of civility—that is, an account that covers the full range of attitudes and actions identified with civility—adopting an intellectual-virtues-based conception of civility may turn out to be a good idea, at least from a functional or practical standpoint.[34] As the suggested way of thinking about civility is rooted in a concern with epistemic goods, this might make the notion of civility tolerable (maybe even attractive) to some who would otherwise be suspicious of a call to greater civility in public discourse. And, given that civility thus conceived still serves to counteract many familiar manifestations of incivility, civility enthusiasts may find reason to embrace it as well.

The objections considered thus far register general opposition to the claim that we should strive for higher levels of intellectual virtue in public discourse; however, the final two objections, which follow, are narrower in scope. While not discounting civility as an important norm of public discourse, they seek to identify important exceptions to this norm.

High-Stakes Objection

> While, in general, higher levels of intellectual virtue may be needed in the context of public discourse, this rule admits of exceptions that must not be neglected. In certain cases, a departure from intellectually virtuous conduct will be justified on account of the greater good of society. For instance, suppose the only way to get one's fellow citizens to vote for—or to get one's colleagues in Congress to pass—a particular measure that is truly just and extremely important is to argue for this measure in a dubious manner, which would include ignoring counter-evidence, oversimplifying the issue, building up and tearing down straw-man characterizations, drawing hasty inferences, etc. In at least some cases of this sort, the value of behaving in an intellectually virtuous manner is outweighed by a good that can be secured only by way of actions that are characteristic of intellectual vices.[35]

I will note, up front, my general agreement with this objection. I concur that there may be cases in which, all things considered, the best (or least bad) thing to do is to act in ways that are not characteristic of intellectual virtues—indeed, in ways that may be characteristic of intellectual vices. Thus, my argument is not that in every possible situation public discourse should satisfy the requirements of intellectual virtue. I will turn to this point below. First, however, a few qualifications are in order.

To begin with, it is important to note how rare cases of the sort just described are likely to be. *Ex hypothesi*, these are cases in which it would be *impossible* to secure an overriding good without caricaturing an opposing viewpoint, making hasty inferences, ignoring counter-evidence, or acting in other patently intellectually vicious ways. This kind of case is quite different from one in which, in order to secure a greater good, a person is forced to employ rhetorical strategies which, while not downright intellectually vicious, fail to instantiate the upper normative dimensions of intellectual virtue. We might think of this as activity that satisfies certain basic or minimal constraints proper to intellectual virtue but nothing more.[36]

As I get into more detail below, I suspect that the two sorts of cases just noted are frequently confused with each other. In particular, I suspect that people often (1) see themselves as needing to resort to intellectually vicious conduct in public discourse when, in fact, they could achieve the same (if not a better) outcome by adhering to certain minimal standards of intellectual virtue; or (2) mistakenly view a competing good (one that can be secured only by intellectually vicious means) as superior to any other goods that could be achieved via an intellectually virtuous course of action.[37] An important conclusion to be drawn from this is that, when it comes to judging whether we are in one of the truly exceptional situations in which the minimal requirements of intellectual virtue need not be satisfied, we must exercise considerable caution and imagination before making an affirmative judgment.[38]

All of this notwithstanding, just as I agree that there are rare cases in which lying is morally justified, I think it would be implausible to deny that there are any cases—even "real life" cases—in which intellectually vicious conduct in public discourse would be justified on account of some greater non-epistemic good that otherwise would be attainable. This is a consequence of the fact that other kinds of values and normative demands (e.g., certain moral, social, or political values) sometimes outweigh the value and demands of intellectual virtue.[39] This is not too surprising. And it does little to undermine the claim that, as a general rule, we should strive for considerably higher levels of intellectual virtue in public discussion and disagreement.[40]

With that, I turn now to a final objection, which is related to the previous one and which I suspect is most likely to motivate resistance to my thesis.

"Beyond the Pale" Objection

The call to higher levels of intellectual virtue in public discourse seems to imply that all viewpoints and arguments merit an open, attentive, and

> careful hearing. However, no small number of views and arguments defended in the public square (e.g., outlandish metaphysical or religious views and conspiracy theories) are extremely unreasonable; their epistemic credentials are veritably worthless. Accordingly, giving views like this an open and thoughtful hearing is intellectually foolish, not virtuous.[41]

Here, the idea is not that there is some distinct greater good that can be achieved only via a departure from intellectually virtuous conduct; it is, rather, that certain views or arguments are epistemically "beyond the pale," that they fail in their own right to merit an intellectually virtuous response.

I will begin by pointing out that being intellectually virtuous does not require giving any and every belief or argument an open and honest hearing. Suppose, for example, that I am approached by someone who requests that I read and give serious consideration to his arguments for thinking that the end of the world is at hand. And suppose I know enough about this person to be confident that he is an unreliable source. As I have argued elsewhere,[42] it would be no failure of open-mindedness or any other intellectual virtue if I were to pass on the opportunity to give an open and honest hearing to this person's arguments. Thus, the call to intellectual virtue in public discourse is consistent with the claim that some views are epistemically beyond the pale, failing to merit intellectually virtuous consideration.[43]

It is important, however, to say something about why certain views might not merit intellectually virtuous consideration. Taking cues from the example above, the fairly obvious reason is that, in cases of the relevant sort, honest and open consideration is likely to constitute a substantial waste of time and cognitive resources. This suggests the following "exception principle" (EP): intellectually virtuous consideration of a given viewpoint or argument is required only if such consideration might prove epistemically beneficial (e.g., only if it might help one gain a deeper or more accurate understanding of the matter in question).[44] EP explains the objection's (plausible) assertion that, under certain conditions, it might be justified (even wise) to refrain from engaging in honest and open dialogue with a particular person or standpoint.[45] However, it also introduces a significant problem that merits careful consideration.

I have been arguing, on the one hand, that we can and should do a much better job of practicing various intellectual virtues in the context of public discourse. On the other hand, I have conceded, as I believe one must, that this requirement holds only where its satisfaction might prove epistemically beneficial. The problem arises from the fact that a good deal of the kind of uncivil behavior we are concerned with arises from the conviction that the viewpoint being entertained, described, or criticized is epistemically hopeless (or worse). In short, people often do a poor job of listening to, are dismissive of, speak derisively about, or refrain from giving serious consideration to opposing views precisely because they think there is no chance that an intellectually virtuous treatment of these views would do any epistemic good.

The problem can be put in the form of a dilemma: Suppose, on the one hand, that the conviction in question is correct; that is, that the views that elicit (apparently) intellectually vicious treatment in public discourse really are epistemically worthless.[46] Given EP, the actions and attitudes in question are justified.[47] Therefore, my claim that higher levels of intellectual virtue are needed in the context of public discourse is unwarranted. Alternatively, suppose that the conviction is not correct in general, and that, specifically, people often underestimate the potential epistemic fruitfulness of engaging with an opposing position in an intellectually virtuous manner. This possibility threatens the call to intellectual virtue in a different way. If, as EP says, this call applies only when considering an opposing view might prove epistemically beneficial, and if, as suggested above, we tend to be unreliable at recognizing when this condition has been met, then the call is likely to have very little effect. It may very well leave the quality of public discourse largely unchanged.

The conviction at issue is suspect. From an experiential or common-sense standpoint, it isn't hard to believe, especially when it comes to public debate about important moral, political, and related matters, that we are often too quick to dismiss competing views or to fail to fully appreciate their epistemic credentials.[48] Mill sheds some light on why this might be the case:

> Unfortunately for the good sense of mankind, the fact of their fallibility is far from carrying the weight in their practical judgment which is always allowed to it in theory; for while everyone well knows himself to be fallible, few think it necessary to take any precautions against their own fallibility, or admit the supposition that any opinion of which they

feel very certain may be one of the examples of the error to which they acknowledge themselves to be liable.[49]

This impression is corroborated by empirical research, including research on phenomena such as the confirmation fallacy, bias blind spots, hindsight bias, and framing effects.[50] Put simply, this research suggests (among other things) that we tend to be insufficiently critical of our own beliefs and arguments and overly critical of the beliefs and arguments of others, especially those with whom we disagree. If this is right, then we should probably expect to regularly find ourselves in the position of thinking that an opposing viewpoint is epistemically beyond the pale, when, in fact, it is not.

It would seem, then, that we are left to reckon with the second horn of the dilemma. Here, the concern is a decidedly practical one. Again, the worry is that if the call to intellectual virtue in public discourse is relevant only to situations in which the consideration of an opposing viewpoint might prove epistemically beneficial, it will be uncompelling and ineffective. For we are overly quick to judge opposing positions as epistemically beyond the pale. As such, we will often think that the call to intellectual virtue doesn't apply to us when, in fact, it does. And, therefore, the quality of public discourse will remain poor.

Toward Greater Civility: Some Practical Suggestions

What can be done about this predicament? One response would be to reject EP at a practical level. That is, we might grant that, from a theoretical perspective, there are conditions under which we needn't give an opposing view an open and honest hearing. However, knowing how fallible we are at identifying when such conditions have obtained, we might adopt a policy of giving an open and honest hearing to any competing view that comes our way. While perhaps initially attractive, this solution faces a formidable practical challenge of its own. Virtually no one is in a position to give an open and honest hearing to every competing viewpoint that he or she encounters. If we are to proceed rationally, we must make judgments about which views to take seriously and which to ignore or disregard. Therefore, upon further reflection, the suggested solution turns out to be of little practical help.

The question we are grappling with is how to make reliable judgments about the epistemic credentials of an opposing viewpoint while knowing this is something that we tend to do quite poorly. Given that this is an eminently practical problem, I will offer a few practical suggestions concerning how it might be addressed. However, I concede up front that these suggestions, at best, make up but the beginning of a solution. Even when taken together, they are far from foolproof.

To get at these suggestions, it will be useful to consider a pair of excerpts from a 2014 essay on civility by Noah Smith, titled "Don't Be Rude, You Loser." The first excerpt begins with a reference to the point that certain views (e.g., that all red-haired people should be put into concentration camps) are unworthy of civil treatment:

> Putting red-haired people in concentration camps is obviously horrible, but most of our arguments are over things like Obamacare, or antipoverty programs, or financial regulation—issues on which reasonable people can and do disagree. If you're uncivil in this sort of situation—if you call your opponent an idiot, or a liar, or a nastier name simply because you think his or her argument is bad—you're basically being overconfident. You're assuming that there's essentially no chance that you're in the wrong, so it's in the public interest for you to rail against your opponent and score points with the crowd. If you do this, there's no chance that you yourself will learn anything from the encounter. People usually argue to win, but many times it's possible to argue to learn.
>
> It's a tough call to decide whether an idea is so awful that the only proper response is to denounce it (and its proponents) with full vitriol. In general, these cases are a lot rarer than we think. People rarely lie, and all but the worst arguments contain some grain of valuable truth. If you can't understand how your opponent could possibly believe what they believe, odds are that you could benefit from trying harder to understand. Not always, but usually.

Several practical suggestions can be drawn from these remarks. The first concerns Smith's point that the sorts of cases in which an intellectually virtuous consideration of a foreign or opposing viewpoint might be unwarranted (e.g., the view that all redheads should be incarcerated) are cases in which there isn't reasonable disagreement on the matter in question. This suggests a kind of litmus test that can be used to distinguish between cases in which we ought to consider giving an opposing view an intellectually virtuous hearing and cases in which this isn't necessary. Specifically, it suggests something like the following "principle of reasonable disagreement" (PRD): to the extent that reasonable disagreement on a given topic or issue is possible, intellectually virtuous engagement on this topic or issue is advisable. If I am abiding by PRD, then when I am confronted with an opposing viewpoint, I will ask myself questions such as the following: "Could reasonable people disagree about this issue?" or "Are there—or might there be—reasonable people who believe differently than I do about this?" or "Is it possible that my intellectual opponent has reasons which, at least by his lights, provide reasonable support for his view?" If I arrive at an affirmative answer to these questions, I will take this as a sufficient indication that I ought not dismiss the viewpoint out of hand.[51]

A second practical suggestion concerns the kind of stance or mindset that one adopts in the context of public disagreement or debate. As Smith's remarks suggest, it seems that the dominant aim in this context is often to win an argument, gain power or status, vent or rant, avoid being proven wrong, and so on. Less cynically, it is to speak or defend (what one sincerely believes is) the truth. Some of these motives are clearly better and more defensible than others. Nonetheless, Smith calls attention to a further stance—one that is lamentably rare in public disputes and arguments: namely, the stance of "arguing to learn."

What might this look like? And is it compatible with the (respectable) aim of communicating and defending (what one takes to be) the truth? If I am "arguing to learn," then when thinking about and evaluating an opposing viewpoint, I might ask myself questions like, "What grains of truth can be found in this perspective?" or "What is something I can learn from this view?" Of course, arguing to learn does not mean arguing merely to learn. I can ask myself, of a competing perspective, "What do I have to learn from this perspective?" while also probing its apparent flaws or weaknesses. Similarly, arguing to learn is entirely consistent with a commitment to communicating or defending (what one takes to be) the truth. I can look for what is promising or insightful in an opposing position and still proceed to clearly and forcefully defend my own point of view.[52]

There is a notable connection between arguing to learn and the virtue of open-mindedness. Open-mindedness is a willingness to take up foreign or opposing viewpoints and to give them an honest and fair hearing.[53] Part of this willingness is a matter of being quick to think about and identify what one can learn from an opposing standpoint. In other words, in the context of public disagreement or argumentation, open-mindedness involves arguing to learn. Therefore, if we are keen to avoid or to help others (e.g., our children or students) avoid prematurely concluding that an alternative position is unworthy of consideration, we ought to place a premium on the practice and cultivation of open-mindedness. Here again, we needn't worry that doing so will leave us unable to vigorously defend our own point of view. Taking up an alternative perspective on a particular issue is compatible with retaining and defending one's own position on the issue. It is even compatible with rigorous critique of the alternative position. In the latter kind of case, the point is that, before developing or launching into a critique of an alternative position, we should first do what we can to understand it—to enter into it and to see what (if anything) can be learned from it.[54]

A third practical suggestion concerns Smith's observation that a good deal of uncivil behavior in discussions of topics like Obamacare and antipoverty programs stem from a kind of epistemic overconfidence, or a sense that "there's essentially no chance that you're in the wrong." Put another way, they stem from an insufficient awareness of the limitations of one's own cognitive perspective or situation (e.g., of human cognitive fallibility in general or of one's evidence about a particular matter). This is a plausible observation and it underscores the importance of an additional intellectual virtue—namely, intellectual humility.

An intellectually humble person is alert to and disposed to "own" her cognitive limitations, which include gaps in her knowledge or evidence, natural intellectual weaknesses, intellectual character defects, and more. An intellectually humble person is "alert" to these limitations, in the sense that they appear "on her radar" in appropriate contexts, for example, in contexts when they might lead her away from the truth. She is not obsessively concerned with them; nor does she ascribe limitations to herself that she doesn't really have. Rather, she has an accurate and appropriate sense of her cognitive limitations. An intellectually humble person also "owns" these limitations in the sense that she accepts them and (where appropriate) takes steps to mitigate or overcome them. She is not in denial about her cognitive limitations. She doesn't seek to rationalize or hide them from others. When someone directly or indirectly calls attention to one of her cognitive mistakes or weaknesses, she doesn't get irritated, ashamed, or defensive.[55]

It should be clear enough that intellectual humility is an antidote to the kind of overconfidence that Smith associates with incivility in public discourse.[56] The overconfident person who thinks or acts as if there is no chance that he is wrong is out of touch with—or at least has failed to "own" or take responsibility for—his intellectual limitations. He is deficient in intellectual humility. Accordingly, we should also place a premium on the practice and cultivation of intellectual humility. Indeed, it is difficult to imagine how the quality of public discourse could significantly improve without a significant increase in the actions and attitudes characteristic of this virtue.

But what are some things we can do to practice intellectual humility in the context of public discourse? One suggestion might be that, when engaging or when considering whether to engage an opposing standpoint, we should do our best to attend to and "own" our cognitive limitations. However, as a standalone strategy, this is unlikely to be effective. For, as we saw earlier, there is strong empirical evidence that we are not, from an introspective or first-person point of view, very reliable at identifying our cognitive limitations, weakness, blind spots, or the like.[57] Therefore, for any such efforts to be successful, they must be supplemented with efforts of a more indirect and objective variety.

This might include reading up on some of the social science research that sheds light on the limitations and foibles of human reasoning (e.g., the literature on bias noted above). Deliberate and thoughtful engagement with this research can help us gain a more objective and honest perspective on our own cognitive limitations and vulnerabilities. If called upon in the context of assessing, or considering whether to assess, a competing view on some issue, the knowledge in question can have a positive calibrating—and, indeed, humbling—effect, making us less likely to underestimate the epistemic credentials of the opposing view.[58] A similar strategy would be to rely on others who know us well to help us develop a more informed view of our epistemic limitations. Thus, we might ask trusted friends or colleagues to speak candidly with us about what they perceive to be our biases, blind spots, and other intellectual character weaknesses. Finally, we can surround ourselves with friends and others who are recognizably intellectually humble. While we may have a difficult time gauging our own level of intellectual humility, it is less challenging to spot intellectual humility in others. Surrounding ourselves with others who value and practice this virtue can encourage us to the do the same.

The foregoing suggestions are far from foolproof. Indeed, they may be least effective for those who need them most. People in the grip of vices like intellectual arrogance, narrow-mindedness, and dogmatism may be the most unlikely to recognize instances of reasonable disagreement, find grains of truth in an opposing viewpoint, or acquaint themselves with research on the defects of human cognition. Such is our predicament.

Yet, as incomplete or imperfect as these suggestions may be, I submit that, if consistently implemented, they are capable of having enough of an impact to warrant a call to greater levels of intellectual virtue in the context of public discourse. If most contributors to public discourse were to put these suggestions into practice, it is difficult to imagine that, even given the truth of EP, the quality of public discourse would not significantly improve.[59]

Chapter 2

It's Good to Be Humble: An Empirical Account

Peter C. Hill
Biola University

Social psychologists have long documented the extent to which people view themselves positively. Such observations as the well-documented better-than-average effect suggest that we suffer from a "superiority complex," in that the desire to have an accurate self-perception only moderates the much weightier desire to have a positive self-perception. Thus, for example, even patients hospitalized from car accidents believe that they are better skilled than the average driver.[1] Other self-enhancing tendencies include the *overconfidence effect* (the tendency to be more confident than accurate in our judgments);[2] the *false-consensus effect* (the overestimation of how much others agree with our opinions or ideas);[3] and the *spotlight effect* (the overestimated belief that we are the center of others' attention).[4]

Furthermore, we create or find means by which we can justify such perceptions, either by attributing external causes for failure and internal causes for success,[5] or by self-selecting indicators of our above-average status (e.g., the extraordinary athlete who thinks that the only important attributes are those that involve physical skill; the gifted scholar who assumes that intellectual prowess is a premium to be valued above all other personal attributes). This may include creating criteria by which we justify our self-enhancing bias. For example, I once found an article on the web titled "A Psychologist Says a Disorganized Email Box Can be a Sign of Intelligence."[6] Since I so well qualified as having a disorganized email box—defined as the ratio between the number of inbox messages (mine recently read 7,054) to the number of messages filed as "starred" or "important"(mine read zero in both cases)—I was tempted to conclude that a disorganized email box is a sure sign of intelligence.

Of course, not everyone is equally prone to a self-enhancing bias. Some individuals maintain a non-defensive sense of self, in that they are willing to accept their own finitude, including personal limitations and mistake-making, with an increased respect for the strengths and wisdom of others from who they can learn. Such humility will be discussed here primarily as an intellectual virtue, in keeping with this volume's theme. As a psychologist, I also want to bring an empirical focus to this discussion, not to discount but rather to supplement other epistemologically varied approaches in our attempt to understand intellectual humility. That said, the empirical literature on intellectual humility is rather sparse, and there is not much to report. In the next few years, however, we should start to see the fruits of some empirical labor on this topic, as researchers, thanks largely to the interest and resources of the John Templeton Foundation, are beginning to explore humility as an intellectual virtue.

Empirical research on humility as a general dispositional characteristic, in contrast to humility that is specifically intellectual, is more established, so I first draw on this literature. But I do so with the realization that it is not clear to what extent intellectual humility is distinct from other forms of humility. Or, to state it another way, is intellectual humility just part of a general dispositional characteristic that displays itself in multiple forms? Of course, the problem is not unique to the study of humility and has long plagued psychologists. Should we treat cognitive functioning, including that which requires careful and high-level analytical ability, as a separate domain? Certainly, for analytical purposes, psychologists have focused on cognition as a specific object of study, and this has been valuable. But psychologists have repeatedly had to learn that whether talking about cognition, including high-level cognition, or any other domain (e.g., affect, motivation, behavior), it is quickly discovered that human functioning is a complex web. So, my inclination is to consider humility holistically, as a general construct, and to see intellectual humility as a subset of this broader characteristic; thus, intellectual humility is understood here as the study of humility applied to the intellectual domain. One important implication of a holistic position is that we can expect some humility overlap, not so much between domains (one may be humble about her own intellect but not her physical ability), but between a general characteristic and specific domains. Thus, one who is oriented toward humility in general may be more inclined toward intellectual humility, physical humility, interpersonal humility, and so forth. In empirical terms, we expect intellectual humility to correlate (perhaps even strongly) with a dispositional humility and, in fact, our own research shows this to be the case ($r = 0.61$). So, I will now turn to the more established research on humility as a broad dispositional construct and then follow it with an investigation of intellectual humility.

General Humility

Humility is, in the words of former CCT Center for Christian Thought fellow Stephen Pardue, a "forgotten virtue," in that it was once a "keystone for ordering the moral and intellectual life"[7] in the Christian tradition, but it seems to have lost, even more than other virtues, considerable stature in contemporary theology and philosophy. In psychology, the study of humility, even when viewed as a general disposition, has, until recently, been disregarded by psychologists, perhaps for several reasons, but two are noted here. First, psychologists may have avoided the construct because of its religious and moralistic overtones, which are perceived to run contrary to psychology's adherence to science—a distinction ill-founded, but one that may help explain the lack of interest. Second, humility has been a notoriously difficult concept to measure, especially given psychology's reliance on self-report measures (e.g., If humility is a desirable characteristic, how does the truly humble person report her humility?). Given that measurement is key to scientific progress, it is important that good measures be developed relatively early in a research program, though only after considerable work on initial conceptual development. In science, of course, empirical work is part of that conceptual development, and without good measures, advancement (both conceptually and empirically) is likely to be stymied. Psychologists are now convinced that the conceptual development of humility is advanced enough for systematic empirical research programs to be undertaken on the topic.

What Humility Is and Is Not

A folk understanding of humility is often misguided. Common misunderstandings include low self-esteem and a tendency to self-deprecate—a view summarily stated and frequently quoted from C. S. Lewis as "pretty people trying to believe they are ugly and clever men trying to believe they are fools."[8] This misguided notion may extend to more scholarly sources as well, in that, at the risk of oversimplification, it appears in the intellectual domain as a representation of Julia Driver's "ignorance" virtues.[9] Indeed, in conducting interviews with a largely low-socioeconomic sample in the greater Los Angeles area, we found that humility was easily confused with humiliation and that understanding humility in any other way was quite foreign to the way this population reported thinking about the concept.

Scholars, however, have questioned this "stoop-shouldered, self-deprecating, weak-willed soul only too willing to yield to the wishes of others" caricature.[10] Among psychologists, June Tangney was one of the first to provide an alternative conceptualization, by delineating six components: (1) a willingness to see the self accurately, (2) an accurate perspective of one's place in the world, (3) an ability to acknowledge personal mistakes and limitations, (4) openness, (5) low self-focus, and (6) an appreciation of the value of all things.[11] Subsequent work by psychologists, both at a conceptual and especially an empirical level, has suggested that at its conceptual core, humility as a psychological construct should minimally include (1) the willingness to see oneself accurately, which includes the identification of both one's limits and strengths; (2) an other-oriented, rather than self-focused, interpersonal stance, which appreciates others' strengths and contributions; and (3) a non-defensive willingness to learn from others.[12] Of course, humility can be induced by situational factors such as poor performance on an exam, a visit to the Grand Canyon, or immersion in another culture. However, our primary focus here will be on humility as a dispositional characteristic, including how it is displayed as an intellectual virtue.

Empirical Research

Below are key findings regarding humility that have thus far been established in the empirical literature. It should be noted that most of these findings are based on self-reports of humility as well as, in most cases, self-reports of the related behaviors (also described below). As the field progresses and as other forms of measuring humility are further developed (e.g., informant ratings, behavioral measures), we may need to fine-tune or even revise some of these conclusions.

- In general, religiousness and humility are positively correlated,[13] a finding that is not surprising, given that most religions promote humility as a virtue. However, certain aspects of religion, such as adherence to religious dogma, may moderate this relationship.[14] Humility has also been shown to negatively predict religious or spiritual struggle.[15]

- Humility has been linked with a number of other virtues or virtue-related behaviors, particularly in the social domain, including higher forgiveness,[16] helpfulness,[17] honesty,[18] gratitude,[19] generosity,[20] and a commitment to social justice.[21] Humble people also tend to be more cooperative[22] and more appreciative of the strengths of others,[23] and hence are viewed by others as being kinder and more likable.[24] Dispositional humility is also related to secure human attachment.[25] In addition, humble individuals report a greater sense of acceptance by others, a lower mistrust of others, and a more positive experience when they receive something (i.e., a gift, money) from others[26] than non-humble individuals.
- Humility has also been associated with success in a variety of areas, particularly in business management[27] and romantic relationships.[28] For example, Owens et al. found in their research on workplace leaders that leaders with good listening skills, transparency about their own limitations, and the ability to express appreciation for others' strengths and contributions—all characteristics of individuals who scored high on a humility measure—are more effective than their less humble counterparts in fostering employee work engagement.[29] Farrell et al. found that individuals in romantic relationships who perceive humility in their partners were more likely to be satisfied and more forgiving in their relationship.[30]
- Humble individuals experience fewer negative psychological symptoms[31] and report better mental health,[32] though these topics to date have received little empirical attention. The humility-health connection is a particularly provocative one, given that factors associated with humility, such as gratitude and forgiveness, have been linked with better mental health.[33] It appears that humility plays an important mediating role between health and the tendency to forgive.[34] Since humility includes an element of being open to others as well as having positive experiences when receiving something from others,[35] gratitude and humility may be reciprocally related.[36] It will be interesting to see if humility plays a similar role in unpacking the gratitude-health linkage as it does with forgiveness and health.

That said, there may be certain liabilities associated with being humble. For example, being open-minded may weaken the ability to maintain strong beliefs or convictions, owning limitations may lead to under-acknowledging one's own strengths, and being other-oriented may result in a loss of healthy self-differentiation.[37] Furthermore, the explicit pursuit of humility may result in a contrived and misguided understanding of what humility entails.[38] Nevertheless, it is safe to say that there is sufficient data to make the empirical case that humility promotes human flourishing. All things considered, it's good to be humble.

Intellectual Humility

Intellectual humility (IH) applies humility to epistemic issues and has drawn recent interest among philosophers as an intellectual virtue. In the context of virtue epistemology, which focuses on the processes by which beliefs are formed, the question has risen among philosophers regarding the extent to which intellectual virtues, such as IH, are necessary to the foundation and advancement of knowledge.

Conceptualizing Intellectual Humility

Whitcomb, Baehr, Battaly, and Howard-Snyder discuss several possible ways to conceptualize IH:[39] (1) as underestimating strengths, similar to that suggested by Driver;[40] (2) as accurately estimating strengths;[41] (3) as holding proper beliefs about the epistemic status of what one believes (i.e., an honest assessment of how much firmness the belief merits);[42] (4) as having a low concern for status or entitlement, especially in contrast to having an intrinsic concern for knowledge and associated attributes;[43] and (5) as owning one's intellectual limitations, the position favored by the authors themselves.[44] My purpose here is not to investigate all of the nuances of these various ways to conceptualize IH; rather, I wish to simply lay out the playing field as I understand it and to consider various psychological implications.

One psychological element common to each of these positions is that IH can be thought of in terms of motivation. This is perhaps most easily identified in the Roberts and Wood perspective, through its emphasis on a high concern for knowledge and its "various attributes"[45] and a low concern for status or self-importance. However, the other positions include a motivational component as well. A concern for accurate knowledge requires that a person be aware of and willing to acknowledge the limitations of his or her beliefs, knowledge, or system of thinking, from which three primary components of intellectual humility can be identified: (1) a willingness to hold beliefs tentatively, to the extent that one is willing to revise one's perspective, given a convincing reason to do so; (2) a willingness to undertake critical scrutiny of one's own perspective, which includes a balanced consideration of evidence that both supports and refutes one's perspective; and (3) a willingness to acknowledge that equally sincere, capable, and knowledgeable individuals may reasonably hold differing views.[46]

It seems that the underlying motivational component in each of the positions just mentioned is a lack of defensiveness that nourishes open-mindedness and cognitive flexibility, two important ingredients as one acknowledges and accepts the limits of her knowledge and perspective. Just as with humility in general, acceptance of intellectual limits can foster an attitude by which one is willing to seek new knowledge and accept feedback, including critical feedback, from others. The intellectually humble person is able to maintain her perspective while simultaneously respecting and valuing others' views, even when such views are opposed to her own.

Intellectual defensiveness can, from an Aristotelian perspective, take two forms. The first and more obvious form is akin to intellectual arrogance, in which the person believes he has very little to learn, ignores his knowledge limits, and does not seek knowledge for the sake of knowing or the common good. Endeavors strongly driven by affirmation of one's intellectual biases are likely more prone to distortions that impede epistemic progress, especially given the presence of self-enhancement tendencies such as those noted at the beginning of this chapter. Intellectual defensiveness can, however, also take the form of intellectual servility, whereby the individual, perhaps in a desire to promote social acceptance or avoid conflict, readily defers to others without adequate consideration and thus does not properly value her own views. IH involves a balance between intellectual arrogance and intellectual servility.[47]

Such a "balanced consideration" that respects one's own views while remaining open to revision from others requires a certain level of "ego stability."[48] Thus, the notion that humility, whether intellectual or otherwise, is "self-forgetting" applies more to egoistic attachment to one's epistemic beliefs than to self-focus. As Bauer and Wayment put it, humility's low self-focus is a detached awareness, where the "subjective interpretation of the present situation is not predicated on how that situation makes one feel about oneself;

that is, the person's awareness is detached from egoistic appraisals of the situation. . . ."[49] There is no reason to think that humble people should think about themselves—including their station in life, their meaning system, or their gifts and liabilities—less often or with less scrutiny than those who are less humble. Rather, a hallmark of humble people is that they do not fall prey to the idea that the world "revolves around them."

Before moving on to empirical considerations of IH, I wish to add an obvious but easily overlooked observation. Most of the historical discussion of IH has, quite understandably, been focused within communities where the intellectual domain is particularly salient, such as in academia. But, of course, it is also an important attribute in contexts where the intellectual domain is perhaps not thought to be quite so salient—and in contexts where leaders emerge, often on the basis of intellectual ability, and where discourse, both civil and uncivil, often occurs. One example might be found in the corporate structure of the workplace setting. Given that intellectually (and otherwise) gifted leaders have the potential to exert disproportionate influence over group ideas, which is sometimes necessary and justified, such individuals may also undermine group functioning, intentionally or unintentionally, by inhibiting other group members' intellectual contributions, especially when they themselves do not display IH. Thus, IH may help foster a communal fair exchange of ideas which, in turn, may improve group functioning.[50]

Empirical Research

In contrast to humility in general, empirical research on IH is sparse. As already noted, this should change in the near future, but drawing conclusions at this point is premature. Two of the empirical studies that do exist, however, focus specifically on IH and religious beliefs and, therefore, they will be discussed here. McElroy et al. found that IH was positively associated with trust, openness, and agreeableness, and it negatively correlated with neuroticism and the inability to forgive. They also tested for the importance of perceived IH in a religious leader following a betrayal by that leader, and they found that perceiving IH in the leader predicted the perceiver's ability to overcome feelings of unforgiveness toward that leader. The perception of IH in the religious leader was also associated with the perceiver having a more positive attitude toward God and less anger toward God.[51]

Hopkin, Hoyle, and Toner found that IH is associated with more favorable ratings of people (and positions) who hold views contrary to one's own regarding the importance of religious-service attendance.[52] Perhaps even more interesting were some ancillary findings that show a moderate curvilinear relationship between IH and strength of religious belief (both pro-religious and anti-religious). They found that people with stronger religious beliefs in both directions (pro- and anti-) showed less IH as defined by four dimensions: awareness of fallibility of beliefs, discretion in asserting beliefs, comfort in keeping beliefs private, and respect for others' beliefs. People with moderate religious beliefs showed the most IH. In comparing strongly pro-religious and strongly anti-religious groups, the strongly pro-religious demonstrated less IH than the strongly anti-religious with regard to awareness of fallibility of beliefs, discretion in asserting beliefs, and comfort in keeping beliefs private, while the anti-religious showed slightly less IH than the pro-religious in respect for others' beliefs.

The Unique Challenges of Intellectual Humility as It Pertains to Religious Beliefs

The operational definitions of IH used by Hopkin et al. (awareness of fallibility of beliefs, discretion in asserting beliefs, comfort in keeping beliefs private, and respect for others' beliefs) demonstrate some of the challenges facing individuals who value humility yet also maintain religious convictions that are sometimes strongly held. Researchers may also face such challenges in how to conceptualize IH in the context of religious belief. For example, does following the dictate of Christ's Great Commission negate IH if, indeed, IH is to be defined as comfort in keeping beliefs private? What might seem to some as a paradox of holding, with humility, one's religious convictions—especially when those convictions contain an exclusivist position such as what is found in Christian evangelical theology—require a rich, conceptually grounded understanding of intellectual humility, such as what I have tried to present here.

As Roberts and Wood have aptly pointed out, a worldview background lurks behind the specification of virtue.[53] Earlier, I mentioned the five accounts of IH as summarized by Whitcomb et al. Former CCT Center for Christian Thought fellow Kent Dunnington proposes yet another alternative account, one that he believes better captures a Christian understanding of humility, based on the theology of Augustine. He argues that there is an irreducibly theological dimension apprehended by Augustine that best frames IH for the theist. The full mark of IH for the theist is, quite simply, one's intellectual dependence upon and submission to God.[54] Such an understanding of humility is not, as Dunnington suggests, captured in any of the five accounts of IH reviewed by Whitcomb and colleagues; nor is it featured in any of the empirical research reported here.

By introducing this vertical account, is there the potential for tension with the horizontal conceptions of humility proposed in the literature and discussed here? Woodruff et al. suggest that it may be difficult to balance humility with a religious identity simply because the latter involves strongly held beliefs on important existential issues.[55] Yet the motivational account of IH taken here suggests that the underlying processes at work can just as easily apply to the religious domain as any other. That is, a proper understanding of IH does not require that it be reduced to some form of relativism whereby one does not take a position. In fact, where IH may matter the most is where a position is held but is tested by others. Perhaps there is no better domain than religion for testing one's ability to maintain a belief, yet to do so humbly. To the extent that one is open to learning from others, admitting to limitations of knowledge or perspective-taking, welcoming the possibility of revision, and not being driven to be right out of a preoccupation with status or winning an argument, one may continue to hold beliefs in an intellectually humble fashion, simply because those beliefs seem to be, given the best evidence available, the right beliefs to hold.

Conclusion

Several issues have not been addressed here. For example, I have not considered, except in passing, the difficult issue of measuring humility, which has been a major focus of my own work. I've also avoided the sticky topic of how to discern, even to oneself, genuine from artificial humility. Yet another issue not considered here is whether humility can, like some virtues, be taught. Or is it like other virtues, whereby the simple pursuit makes the virtue more elusive? The work ahead will be challenging. However, I am amazed at how quickly an empirical literature has emerged that suggests that, indeed, humility, whether intellectual or otherwise, is a virtuous trait that allows people to function as they optimally should. It's good to be humble.

Chapter 3

Civil Discourse at the Table of Reconciliation

Christena S. Cleveland
Center for Justice + Renewal

In 2014—in the immediate aftermath of black teenager Michael Brown's death at the hands of white, Ferguson, Missouri, police officer Darren Wilson—a predominantly white Midwestern Christian congregation that had long professed a theological commitment to reconciliation decided to act on it. Their community, like so many others in the United States, was smarting from the palpable racial tensions that had ruptured and exposed the misperception that we inhabit a post-racial America. The church decided to organize a one-time "reconciliation" event, to be held at the white church. The event was designed to "reconcile predominantly black and predominantly white churches in the city" by "creating space for friendship and conversation between blacks and whites."

With noble intentions, the white church prepared for the event with gusto. The pastor preached repeatedly to the white congregation about the biblical mandate for reconciliation. Meanwhile, the planning committee publicized the event as a racial-reconciliation-and-unity night, sent invitations to both black and white churches, hired a soul food restaurant to cater the event, and appointed a well-known black gospel choir to perform. The white leadership at the organizing church was confident that its efforts would stimulate opportunities for the kind of civil discourse that would result in real reconciliation.

Not one to miss an opportunity to observe an attempt at reconciliation, I decided to attend. When I walked into the room, I instantly noticed that all of the black people were on one side of the room and all of the white people were on the other. Based on the self-imposed racial segregation, it seemed as if an invisible wall divided the room. Later, the white pastor of the hosting church told me that he was perplexed and dismayed. Why hadn't interracial discourse taken place? he asked. Why hadn't racial reconciliation occurred? When I asked him what evidence of reconciliation he sought, he said, "I was expecting to witness lots of black people happily mingling with white people." When I asked him what such mingling would indicate, he responded, "Well, reconciliation, of course!"

The white pastor and congregation meant well—they noticed racial division and attempted to do something about it. However, their attempt at creating space for meaningful interracial discourse, much less true reconciliation, was woefully inept.

This story illustrates several ways in which reconciliation is often misunderstood in Western culture. First, reconciliation is often misunderstood as being simply a matter of theology. As long as we possess and profess a theology of reconciliation, we are reconcilers. It doesn't matter what we do—or, perhaps even more crucially, how we do it. In this case, the church acted—it did something—but its actions lacked strategy and an understanding of the complexity of race relations and civil discourse. It was as if the pastor and congregants believed that their good intentions were enough, that their Christian belief in reconciliation would suffice. In doing so, they failed to consider the sociological implications of their theological affirmations.

Second, reconciliation is often misunderstood as a passive unity, one that doesn't require much sacrifice on the part of the dominant group or any pursuit of justice. According to this pastor, reconciliation between blacks and whites involves individual black people joyfully conversing with individual white people—at the white church, on the white church's terms, and in the absence of any of the key markers of reconciliation, such as mutuality, solidarity, sociological imagination, or equality. Though the pastor had dutifully preached on the importance of reconciliation, emphasizing the truth that all people are created equal, he seemed unwilling or unable to grasp that not all people share equal power in our society and that true equality—justice—must precede a reconciliation that is based on the divine and inherent equality of all people.

Third, reconciliation is often seen as simply bringing groups together. As long as we can get people in the same room, meaningful discourse and relationship will naturally follow. This illustration illuminates the naiveté of such a belief. In our Midwestern church example, the two groups failed to comingle. However, if they had somehow been induced to interact, there was no guarantee that such interaction would have resulted in reconciliation. Social-psychological research shows that, under most circumstances, if two estranged groups are compelled to intermingle, the result is increased hostility, prejudice, and division—not less. Simply bringing groups together is not a strategic way to bring about reconciliation. Indeed, without addressing both the historical and current context and issues of power and equity, bringing groups together usually has disastrous consequences.

In the end, the well-intentioned pastor had unwittingly organized an event that not only failed to bring about reconciliation and discourse, but also perpetuated what twentieth-century French intellectual Aimé Césaire called the "thingification" of black people. Thingification occurs when a dominant group pieces apart the culture of a minority group and then engages only the parts of the culture that the dominant group values. Indeed, several black attendees at the event grumbled to me as they left, "I think they only want us for our food and music."

When I witness such conceptions of and attempts at reconciliation, I am reminded of the important critiques of common notions of reconciliation. Drawing from their analysis of the South African reconciliation process, Allan Boesak and Curtiss DeYoung write, "Reconciliation is often understood today as assimilation, appeasement, a passive peace, a unity without cost, and maintaining power with only cosmetic changes." [1] Palestinian practitioner Jean Zaru echoes Boesak and DeYoung's broad critique by specifying how theological concepts of reconciliation are misused in the Israeli-Palestinian conflict. She explains, "[Israelis] talk to us about reconciliation by suggesting a hasty peace. They speak of reconciliation instead of liberation or reconciliation as a managed process. These calls want us, the victims of violence, to let bygones be bygones and exercise a Christian forgiveness. In trivializing and ignoring the history of suffering, the victims are forgotten and the causes of suffering are never uncovered and confronted."[2] Indeed, the theological concept of reconciliation has become so corrupted that it is often used as a sociological tool to maintain the status quo.

The Table Model of Reconciliation

As evidenced in the illustration I just offered, these critiques are well taken, offering insight on what reconciliation is not and soliciting a positive definition of reconciliation. My understanding of reconciliation is based on an integration of theological and social-psychological perspectives, culminating in the following: reconciliation is a social, political, and spiritual process by which group relationships that were once characterized by enmity begin to move toward a common identity that is characterized by solidarity, sociological imagination, mutuality, and collaborative efforts toward equality.

As such, reconciliation can be described and understood as a round table with four legs. Common identity represents the tabletop and is supported by four legs: solidarity, sociological imagination, mutuality, and collaborative efforts toward equality.

Common Identity

In this model, common identity is the tabletop because common identity is the centerpiece of reconciliation. Indeed, social psychology and theology converge on this point. From a social-psychological perspective, the processes revolving around common identity fuel the transformation from enmity to reconciliation. Social psychologists Samuel Lowell Gaertner, John F. Dovidio, and colleagues have introduced the common ingroup identity model to describe the fundamental role that common identity plays in reconciliation. They write the following:

> If members of different groups are induced to conceive of themselves as a single group rather than as two completely separate groups, attitudes toward former outgroup members will become more positive through the cognitive and motivational forces that result from ingroup formation—a consequence that . . . increase[s] the sense of connectedness across group lines.[3]

In other words, the same explosive group forces that once served to create and sustain the two alienated group identities can now be harnessed and redirected to create and sustain a common group identity, one that can withstand the ongoing challenges of the reconciliation process.

Theological definitions of reconciliation also highlight common identity as a major pathway through which just relationship can be restored. For example, John de Gruchy states that reconciliation causes us to triumph over "alienation through identification and in solidarity with 'the other,' thus making peace and restoring relationships." Pastoral theologian James Earl Massey confirms that reconciliation results in "a rich togetherness where enmity and distance previously were the order." Jean Zaru also stresses the importance of common identity in the Palestinian and Arab concept of sulha reconciliation, a nonviolent approach to peacemaking. She writes that sulha reconciliation involves saying, "You are in our home. You are one of us and we take it upon ourselves to help and protect the person who has done us wrong."[4]

Solidarity

De Gruchy's solidarity, Massey's togetherness, and Zaru's unifying hospitality all describe a common identity that is significantly characterized by solidarity. Hence, solidarity is one of the four legs that supports the tabletop of common identity. In the newly reconciled relationship, physical and psychological distance decreases, and a willingness to engage the experience of the other increases. In effect, each group's participation in the common identity is rooted in the lived experience of the other. For whites or other majority members, it means reaching for a common identity that privileges and attaches itself to the lived experience of black people and/or other people of color. In the newly reconciled relationship, whites seek common identity with black people precisely by seeking to empathize with the perspective of black people.

Without solidarity, the common identity that reconcilers seek is shallow and fragmented; it lacks a true understanding and empathy for the other's perspective and lived experience. In the example of the church event, attendees were not invited to participate in interracial solidarity. Though the event was designed to address racial division, it did not create space for attendees to share their racial experiences and seek others' perspectives and lived experiences. It offered no opportunities to "walk a mile in the other's shoes," either figuratively or literally. There was no sharing of burdens or joys, and there was no mechanism through which one's story could possibly intersect with another's.

Sociological Imagination

Importantly, the common identity that is described here also implies an understanding of the social forces that impact the relationship between the two groups. Here, the table model uses the concept of sociological imagination, the second leg in the table model, to explain how social forces impact reconciliation. Sociological imagination, a term coined by sociologist C. Wright Mills, describes the way in which societal forces, such as systemic inequality, hinder or propel an individual's social mobility.[5] Within the context of group conflict and reconciliation, a sociological imagination involves recognizing and understanding how societal forces such as systemic inequality, previous wrongdoings, or the ongoing consequences of historical injustices affect the relationship between the two reconciling groups.

Specifically, when Zaru invites the former enemy into her home, she explicitly identifies the person as "one of us" and also as someone "who has done us wrong." Her recognition that both factors impact the newly forged common identity implies a sociological imagination. Within a sociological imagination, the new common identity is not an opportunistic pathway to a so-called clean slate or a license to ignore status differences. Rather, it is an opportunity for the groups to engage the status differences, the historical or ongoing inequalities, or the previous relational conflict. In other words, it does not seek to ignore or minimize the sociological forces that directly or indirectly impact the reconciliation process. Rather, it is aware of these forces, such as past wrongs, previous relational history, or ongoing inequality. For example, de Gruchy's solidarity, Massey's togetherness, and Zaru's unifying hospitality are all defined in contrast to the sociological forces of past wrongs, previous relational history, or ongoing inequality, and then the new relationship is defined and actualized in the context of such sociological forces. Again, in the example of the church event, there was a distinct absence of sociological imagination. Though much planning went into the event, there was no acknowledgment of historical or current systemic injustices that continue to impact the relationship between blacks and whites in this Midwestern city and beyond. In fact, as a standalone, one-time event, the event lacked meaningful connection to the past, future, or systemic present. The white church did not seek to ask: Historically and systemically, how did we get to this place of discord? How has the church participated in this ongoing division and inequity? What are the roots of the anger and grievances that we are finally hearing? How long have black people been expressing such anger and grievances? Why weren't we able to hear it before? What are the current racial realities? Where are whites and blacks located in the social stratosphere? How does this affect our attempt at reconciliation?

At the table, sociological imagination and solidarity interact to shape a new common identity, one that reckons with and is even defined by sociological forces. In this way, the dominant group, by choosing to stand in solidarity and form a common identity with the marginalized group, recognizes that sociological factors do not solely impact the marginalized group; rather, they impact the emerging relationship between both groups and must be engaged by both groups.

However, solidarity and sociological imagination alone are not enough, because we are still left wondering how the groups will interact with each other in their newly forged relationship. While solidarity and sociological imagination acknowledge previous estrangement and identify solidarity as a viable antidote to that estrangement, they do not offer a relational map that will effectively guide the groups' interactions. Social-psychological research has demonstrated that engaging in solidarity practices such as perspective-taking can significantly diminish prejudice and hostility toward a target group. However, to date, solidarity practices alone have not been found to be a sufficiently powerful force for common identity. A more powerful, psychologically engaging relational schema is needed.

Further, it is important to recognize that although sociological factors, such as past wrongs, continue to impact the reconciliation process, they do not offer a restorative process that will presumably help the groups address these mitigating factors as they develop their growing relationship. For these reasons, I offer that the tabletop of common identity must also be supported by the third and fourth legs: mutuality and collaborative efforts toward justice. For theological insights, I turn to Miroslav Volf and his Trinitarian model of reconciliation.

Mutuality

In *Exclusion and Embrace*, Miroslav Volf uses the patristic notion of perichoresis as a cognitive map by which we can begin to understand the relationship between the three persons of the Trinity. Perichoresis, the "reciprocal interiority" of the persons of the Trinity, seeks to describe both what God is like and how the various persons of the Trinity relate to one another. The conclusion is that they remain wholly distinct while also wholly overlapping one another, so much so that that one can say that the Son only is in the sense that the Father and the Spirit indwell the Son. Volf's discussion of perichoresis highlights the mutual but differentiated identity of the members of the Trinity, noting that their mutual identity, which is powered by self-giving, makes space for and facilitates differentiated identity:

> For perichoresis suggests a dynamic identity in which "non-identity" indwells the "identity" and constitutes it by this indwelling. The Father is the Father not only because he is distinct from the Son and the Spirit but also because through the power of self-giving the Son and the Spirit dwell in him. The same is true of the Son and of the Spirit.[6]

Reciprocal overlap, then, defines not only the relations between the three persons of the Trinity but also the identity of the persons themselves. From the mutual indwelling that flows out of their mutual identity, each divine person differentiates and fully actualizes.

But perichoresis does not merely define who God is by describing God's essential mutual overlap. Perichoresis also declares a foundational truth about human relationships, establishing what really is. Indeed, Volf argues that the mutual overlap of the divine persons provides the relational model for what he calls "nonself-enclosed identities"; that is, identities in which each makes space for the other, resulting in mutuality. Practically speaking, pastoral theologian and psychologist Chanequa Walker-Barnes argues that "an individual with a nonself-enclosed identity" is "one who has permeable boundaries—that is, a person who has a clearly differentiated sense of self and who is also open to the risk of being changed through meaningful interaction with others."[7]

In this model, Walker-Barnes offers a much-needed relational map to guide the two reconciling groups. This relational map is marked by mutuality, in which each group not only embraces the other group's identity but also remains open to being embraced by the other group. Not only is the group's sociological imagination now informed by the other group, as de Gruchy, Massey, and Zaru suggest, but so is their identity. Much like the Son is because of his relationship to the Father, the reconciling group is because of its relationship with its former enemy. This mutuality binds the common group together by intertwining the identities of the two separate groups.

This theological concept is consistent with social-psychological perspectives on reconciliation. Indeed, noted social psychologist and reconciliation scholar Herbert Kelman asserts that mutually influential identity is one key factor that distinguishes reconciliation from mere conflict resolution. He writes, "The primary feature of the identity change constituting reconciliation is the removal of the negation of the other as a central component of one's own identity . . . and that each party revise its own identity . . . enough to accommodate the identity of the other."[8] Through the process of reconciliation, group identities that were once defined by the negation of the estranged group become permeable and open to the influence of the other group.

Research on mutual relationships can be applied to theologies of reconciliation to illuminate the sociological processes by which perichoresis between conflicting groups is achieved.[9] Research shows that, over the course of a mutual relationship, the self-schema literally transforms, expanding to include the other. As such, the other is perceived as part of the self, and his or her resources, desires, needs, perspectives, identity, values, self-evaluations, and characteristics are included in the self. Consequently, the self, while remaining distinct, becomes significantly defined by not only its close relationship with the other but also by the characteristics and identity of the other with whom the self closely relates. Restated in theological terms, when engaged in interpersonal relationship, the self and other begin to approximate the mutuality of perichoresis. The two identities become essentially related, and the specific wholeness of each becomes actualized through the relationship to the other. This relationship does not neutralize or synthesize the two identities. Rather, it transforms each identity by readapting it to the identity of the other. For our purposes, it is crucial to note that group researchers add that these processes of self-other overlap extend to important group memberships, creating what might be called nongroup-enclosed identities that mutually influence each other.[10]

While Volf's perichoresis model advances our understanding of reconciliation, it is not without limitations. One, it fails to discuss common identity or its impact on reconciliation and, as a result, fails to account for the complex conflicts that can arise in group situations. Even though Volf discusses the relationships within the Trinity, a group construct, it is not clear that he is actually examining group processes. For example, while he articulates how individual members of the Trinity engage in one-on-one relationships that impact the others' identities (e.g., Father and Son), he does not make mention of the Trinity's common group identity or address how the said identity impacts the members or their relationship to one another. Though common group identity is implied vis-à-vis his usage of the Trinity, a group, as his model, what he explicitly describes is essentially an interconnected web of dyadic relationships. The Father relates to the Son, the Son relates to the Spirit, etc. But it is unclear if or how those dyadic relationships interact with one another to create collective group processes such as a common identity.

This dyadic rather than group approach to examining the relational processes in the Trinity is further cemented by his application of the model to the question of gender-identity reconciliation. He focuses on a one-on-one relationship between male and female with little mention of the ways in which a common identity might influence male and female identity or reconciliation between males and females. While Volf acknowledges that both male and female bear the *Imago Dei*, he does not use their common identity as image bearers to influence his discussion of male and female identities. Instead, as he does with the members of the Trinity, Volf focuses exclusively on the dyadic relationship between male and female. He writes, "Gender identities are essentially related and therefore the specific wholeness of each other can be achieved only through the relation to the other."[11]

It is possible that Volf's focus on dyadic relationships in the context of the group of the Trinity reflects an individualistic bias that is common in Western thought. Even though the self is influenced by both one-on-one and group interactions, social psychologists Hazel Markus and Shinobu Kitayama note that in individualistic cultures, people are most aware of the ways in which the self is formed in one-on-one relationships with other individual selves.[12] However, in collectivistic cultures, which are more prominent in the East, people are most aware of the ways in which the self is formed in group relationships with groups of selves. This is due to the fact that, in individualistic cultures, the self is the basic social unit; therefore, one-on-one relationships are most impactful. Conversely, in collectivistic cultures, the group is the basic social unit; therefore, group relationships are most impactful. In fact, some Asian perspectives on perichoresis go beyond the one-on-one relationship on which Volf focuses, to include common group processes. First-generation Chinese American immigrant Patrick Cheng's understanding of perichoresis invokes the notion of a common humanity as he discusses not only dyadic mutuality but also a commonality with all. He argues that the mutuality of perichoresis reflects his relationship not only with other Asian Americans but also with all of humanity.[13]

The limitations of Volf's model inhibit its ability to address complex group-identity processes, such as dual identities, in reconciliation. When two groups forge a common identity, each group results in two identities—a common superordinate identity that is shared with the other group and a subordinate identity that is not shared with the other group. Gaertner and Dovidio are quick to point out that adopting a superordinate identity does not mean that one must completely forsake one's less inclusive identity. They use the example of offensive and defensive squads on the same football team to demonstrate that one can and should conceive of two distinct groups within the context of a superordinate group. Further, they suggest that to reject important subordinate group distinctions (i.e., race) is to lose important information about individuals and run the risk of being color- or culture-blind. They suggest that individuals maintain dual identities, rather than rejecting the less-inclusive identity, identifying with a subordinate group within the context of a superordinate group. This dual-identity model applies not only to groups but also to individuals, making space for the complexities of intersectionality in which one person or group can possess multiple identities at the same time.[14]

The accommodation of dual identities is crucial, because reconciliation is concerned with multiple intersecting dimensions of identity—not just one. Perichoresis, which brings together multiple identities in one entity, cannot retain its authenticity while ignoring one of the identities of its members. The concept of perichoresis, in which the identities of Father, Son, and Spirit, are held in unity and tension is able to robustly accommodate multiple layers of identity. It is precisely the intersectional identity of the Trinity that theologically compels us to engage the intersectional reality of identity in which our understanding of race cannot be extracted from our understandings of class, gender/sexuality, and other social identities. Further, the concepts of common identity and mutual interiority require that we care not only about the reconciliation and justice issues that most affect us or interest us. Rather, we are compelled to care about the issues that affect those with whom we are in perichoretic relationship.

In our church event example, no attention was given to the concept of mutuality. In other words, the white Christians did not create opportunities for black Christians to impact them in significant and lasting ways. But even on a surface level, the fact that the event took place at the white church—on the white church's turf, so to speak—suggests a lack of thoughtfulness around the values of mutuality and equality.

Collaborative Efforts toward Justice

In addition to mutuality, a collaborative effort for equality is needed to sustain the common identity needed for reconciliation. On this point, Volf's model of perichoresis, which is sensitive to, rather than dismissive of, social inequality, makes the case that equality is necessary for perichoresis. He builds upon Elizabeth Johnson's analysis of perichoresis, in which she rejects classic, hierarchical understandings of the Trinity, such as perspectives that characterize the Father as being first and/or the source of the Trinity and thus presiding at the top of the hierarchy. Rather, she speaks of radical egalitarianism in the Trinity, asserting that "In God there is no sooner or later, no before or after, no intervals of time or place. Jointly, inseparably, mutually the three persons dwell within each other and exercise powerful activity. Sequence, then, does not necessitate subordination."[15] Volf makes this egalitarian understanding of the Trinity his starting point, recognizing that it is only in the context of equality that mutual overlap can exist. He rightly points out that overlap in a hierarchical relationship is simply colonization of the other.[16] In this model of reconciliation, equality is a prerequisite for the mutual overlap that marks perichoresis. As a result, ongoing collaborative efforts toward equality must play a central role in the common group's relationship.

Social-psychological research on intergroup contact converges on this point. Before groups can begin to engage in the intergroup contact that potentially leads to a common identity, they must address existing status differences. Once addressed (at the very least, in the context of the reconciliation process), groups must continue to exert effort to ensure that equal status is maintained. Since status differences in the larger society likely remain intact, these differences can easily "spill over" into the reconciliation situation.

The white pastor in our example intended to stimulate civil discourse among blacks and whites, but he failed to recognize that civility can only potentially emerge between groups that share equal status. Said differently, if one group has more power than the other, they cannot truly share space at the table of reconciliation. For example, research shows that even among well-intentioned groups, the dominant cultural group in a particular society can easily dominate the reconciliation process. Social psychologist Ifat Maoz found that in structured, intergroup encounters between Jewish and Palestinian teachers, members of the dominant group tended to control the cooperative task. Even though all involved were interested in maintaining equal status, the high-status group members fell into old patterns of domination and oppression.

Further, if issues of status, privilege, and power are not effectively addressed prior to reconciliation, existing divisions deepen, and the image of God in diverse people is dishonored. Research on teams demonstrates that cross-cultural situations have negative consequences, particularly when social inequities remain, when minority group members do not have equal status with other group members, and when minority group members do not feel that they are valued members of the group. Consider this troubling finding: while cultural diversity might be uncomfortable for all group members, low-status minorities often bear the brunt of the discomfort; they are less satisfied with the group, experience less psychological closeness to the organization, perceive less supervisor support, and experience less procedural justice within the organization than other group members.

Taken together, both the theological understandings of perichoresis as well as social-psychological understandings of the negative correlation between reconciliation and inequality make it clear that reconciliation and justice must be construed as two sides of the same coin. Justice is a necessary prerequisite to reconciliation, as it creates space for equal relationships. Meanwhile, reconciliation consummates an equal relationship, forging a mutual interdependence.

Steps toward Civil Discourse at the Table of Reconciliation

Returning to the case study that I described at the start of this chapter, I can now use the table model of reconciliation to briefly share the steps I would recommend should the pastor and congregants decide to pursue true reconciliation. The model suggests that reconciliation cannot be conceived of as a one-time event. Rather, it is an ongoing and costly process, one that requires careful but bold steps and should span years. As such, I would recommend that the pastor and church leaders lead constant efforts to form their community toward reconciliation. This could involve sermon series, small-group Bible studies, Sunday school curricula, guest speakers, pilgrimages, immersive/interactive learning, and more.

Beyond this, I would recommend that the pastor begin by leading himself and others in acquiring a sociological imagination. Before they even begin to interact with a different racial group, they need to not only understand where they are located in the social structure relative to other racial groups but also to recognize the societal forces that create and maintain social inequities. Next, I would recommend that the pastor and the congregants begin to practice mutuality by first seeking to be influenced by the local black churches and leadership rather than seeking to influence. Questions I would pose might include the following: What can you learn from black approaches to biblical interpretation? How can you benefit from black leadership? How does blackness inform your understanding of what it means to be white? To be human? Then, I would recommend that they begin to practice solidarity with the local black churches. This could involve attending events at black churches. It could also involve playing a supporting role in the efforts that black churches are making in the community. Finally, after an extended period of time, in which they have demonstrated their ongoing commitment to reconciliation, I would suggest that they carefully begin to engage in collaborative efforts toward interracial discourse and racial equality with local black churches and community members, reminding them that the steps they are taking are just the beginning of a lifelong commitment to justice and reconciliation.

Chapter 4

Rationality and Rightly Ordered Affections: C. S. Lewis on Intellectual Virtue and Civil Discourse

George M. Marsden
University of Notre Dame

When I first thought about writing about C. S. Lewis and civil discourse, I had some doubts as to whether he would be an especially helpful model. In mid-twentieth century England, he was often a polarizing figure. That was especially true within the community in which he spent most of his career: Oxford University. "You don't know how much I am hated," he once remarked with great feeling to a younger friend.[1] His Oxford colleagues denigrated him sufficiently enough to prevent him from receiving a chair there, despite his academic merits, which Cambridge eventually recognized. His experience reflected the peculiar culture of English academics who relished witty arguments and put-downs. Lewis himself partook of that very culture, and he gave as much as he got. He loved debate and, for years, headed The Socratic Club, which cultivated clever arguments.

One example of his ability to give put-downs is found in his rejoinder to Norman Pittenger, a liberal Episcopal theologian at General Theological Seminary in New York City. In 1958, Pittenger published, in the *Christian Century*, a condescending critique of Lewis, asserting that Lewis was a theological amateur of the sort who would "substitute smart superficiality for careful thought." Lewis, who earlier had said that published replies are almost always a mistake, nonetheless took Pittenger on in a scathing critique. After answering some particular objections, Lewis pointed out that Pittenger had entirely missed that if one is to communicate to popular audiences, one has to translate into their terms. "For this purpose," wrote Lewis, "a style more guarded, more nuance′, finelier shaded, more rich in fruitful ambiguities—in fact, a style more like Dr. Pittenger's own—would have been worse than useless." The reader, Lewis went on, "would have thought, poor soul, that I was facing both ways, sitting on the fence, offering at one moment what I withdrew the next, and generally trying to trick him." If the "real theologians" had been doing their jobs for the past one hundred years, Lewis explained, there would have been no place for someone like himself.[2]

Lewis's reply to Pittenger is devastatingly clever and great fun to read, but it does not exactly cultivate civility and further constructive dialogue.

Another negative tendency was that when Lewis got into his debate mode, he had a tendency to overstate the implications of the position that he opposed. That was the case, for instance, when in 1948 he entered into the discussion of whether women should be allowed to be priests in the Anglican church. Having women be our representatives before God in worship, he argued, would inexorably lead to an entire overturning of gendered images in Scripture, as regarding God as Father, Jesus as Son, and the entire church as the bride of Christ. So, he argued, "Now it is surely the case that if ever all these supposals were ever carried into effect we should be embarked on a different religion."[3] The point here is not whether Lewis was right or wrong to defend the traditional practice of not ordaining women; rather, it is that his manner of argument can sometimes be polarizing. He is not content to say that women's ordination would be merely inconsistent with Scripture and tradition; rather, he opts to say that its logic must lead to an entirely different religion.

Even so, recognizing Lewis's occasional polarizing tendencies, I think we can learn much from him as a model for cultivating intellectual virtues—and for promoting civil discourse.

First, it is clear that Lewis often thought about the Christian life as a matter of cultivating virtues. In *Mere Christianity* he talks about the four "cardinal virtues" of prudence, temperance, justice, and fortitude, and of the three "theological virtues" of faith, hope, and charity. He sees the proper cultivation of human character as a matter of developing virtuous habits and practices. "And, taking your life as a whole," he says, "with your innumerable choices, all life long, you are slowly turning this central thing [your self] either into a heavenly creature or into a hellish creature: either into a creature that is in harmony with God, and with other creatures, and with itself, or else into one that is in a state of war and hatred with God, and with its fellow-creatures, and with itself."[4]

In *The Abolition of Man* we can find what amounts to Lewis's view of intellectual virtues. He cites St. Augustine as defining virtue as *ordo amoris*, or the right-ordered affections. Intellectual virtues have to be understood in that context. Lewis's complaint in *The Abolition of Man* was that recent school textbooks, reflecting the vogue of logical positivism, were teaching that all statements about value, such as "that waterfall is sublime," reflected merely the subjective state of the observer and did not pass the modern scientific test of rational objectivity. Lewis's response was to cite Augustine, and Plato before him, who said, as Lewis puts it, "the head rules the body though the chest." So "[r]eason . . . must rule over the mere appetites by means of 'the spirited element.'" And by the "spirited element," he means the properly cultivated sentiments, affections, or loves. These higher sentiments, affections, or loves are to be distinguished from the "mere appetites," or the passions. These sentiments or affections or higher loves need to be cultivated as virtues. The guiding principles cultivating these virtues, or rightly ordering these affections, he argues, can be found in what he calls the Tao, or natural law principles endorsed by all sorts of cultures, such as duties to family and nation, or principles of justice, honesty, mercy, and magnanimity. So even while reason retains a primacy in ruling over our mere appetites, it does not do so purely dispassionately or as an independent, objective agent. Rather, it operates through, or in the context of, our sentiments, affections, or higher loves, and these may be formed well or poorly.[5]

Lewis provides an example of how he thought about such matters in a paper titled "On Obstinacy of Belief," published in 1955. There, he criticized the positivist scientific ideal that people should tailor the strength of a belief to the strength of the evidence supporting that belief. Lewis pointed out that in ordinary experience, it is often laudable to commit to a belief that goes beyond the immediate evidence that we have for the belief. For instance, we often need simply to trust the authority of others for all sorts of firmly held beliefs. Furthermore, we sometimes need to trust a person on a crucial matter when we have almost no other evidence for the belief. Lewis illustrates the legitimacy of such trust as sometimes an intellectual virtue by pointing out that there are situations in life when we can help others only if they simply trust us. "In getting a dog out of a trap, in extracting a thorn from a child's finger, in teaching a boy to swim or rescuing one who can't, in getting a frightened beginner over a nasty place on a mountain, the one fatal obstacle may be their distrust. We are asking them to trust us in the teeth of their senses, their imagination, and their intelligence." So Christians who say that they should continue to trust in the personal God whom they have once encountered, even when they face doubts and trials that test that faith, are not, on that account, acting irrationally. Of course, trust in a person can sometimes be misplaced. Yet continuing to trust in a person even in the face of some contrary evidence is often a legitimate basis for a belief or commitment.[6]

So the larger point is that, even though Lewis has a high view of the value of rational argument, he sees our rationality as operating at its best only in the context of rightly ordered affections. These affections, or higher loves and sentiments, are properly shaped by, among other things, our personal relationships involving trust or love, which go beyond what strictly scientific standards can deal with.

* * *

If I may make what I think might be an illuminating digression, I think that Lewis's view that we can obtain true intellectual virtues only in the context of properly ordered affections has similarities to that of another Christian thinker who, in recent decades, has gained a lot of resonance—and that is my friend Jonathan Edwards. For Edwards, right belief cannot be separated from the affections. "True religion," he says, "in great part consists in holy affections." It involves what he calls "sensible knowledge." So he writes, "that sort of knowledge, by which a man has a sensible perception of amiableness and loathsomeness, or of sweetness and nauseousness, is not just the same sort of knowledge with that, by which he knows what a triangle is, and what a square is. The one is mere speculative knowledge; the other sensible knowledge, in which more than the mere intellect is concerned; the heart is the proper subject of it."[7] Typically, Edwards describes faith as like being given a sixth sense, being given eyes to see the overwhelming beauty of divine things—ultimately, God's perfect love in Jesus Christ—and that this experience of supreme beauty draws us to God. That experience of beauty, like meeting a person whom we immediately recognize to be perfectly beautiful and good, reorders our affections, shapes our love and trust in the person, and convinces us of truths about that person.[8]

Alvin Plantinga discusses how Edwards's approach speaks to current discussions of warrant and of intellectual virtues in the epistemological sense. Plantinga argues that on such models (which he finds variations of in Augustine, Calvin, Edwards, and his own view), it is not really possible to say whether intellect or will is first in initially coming to Christian belief.[9] Yet once one's heart is changed, rationality properly operates as a personal reality, in the context of one's new affections toward God. So one who has encountered the beauty of God in person is rationally warranted in believing some things in that framework that others who lack the affections connected to such an encounter find unwarranted. Lewis does not explore the interrelationships between affections and intellect as fully as Edwards or Plantinga do, but I think the model is similar. Lewis's complaint against modern rationalistic positivist trends is that they are creating "men without chests," or, in effect, people without hearts or affections.[10] More broadly, the theological point is, as Edwards puts it, that when it comes to knowing God, unbelievers have hardened their hearts. Following Scripture, a hard heart, he explains, "is like a stone, insensible, stupid, unmoved and hard to be impressed. Hence the hard heart is called a stony heart, and is opposed to an heart of flesh, that has feeling, and is sensibly touched and moved."[11]

Lewis's effectiveness as a winsome apologist has a great deal to do with his similar recognition that, in matters of religion, the intellect does not operate independently of the affections. So, even though Lewis is a skilled logician who uses many effective arguments, he surrounds his arguments with a host of images and analogies to make the meaning of what he is saying come alive. That approach fits his view that reason must rule through the chest or the affections. As Lewis explains it, he sees imagination as "the organ of meaning" and reason as "the natural organ of truth."[12] The best way we have for understanding the meaning of something we are not entirely familiar with is to see it by way of analogy to something we do know about. So Lewis, a poet at heart, constantly uses images, analogies, and metaphors to explain things. Such explanations help his audiences relate to what he is saying affectively, as it connects with something that is already part of their experience. His quotes above about the dog in the trap, or the child with a thorn, etc., which illustrate why trust is often a proper condition for reason, are typically vivid instances of how he elicits an affective understanding of an argument.[13]

How might these understandings of intellectual virtues relate to more civil discourse? The first and most important point is that Lewis's approach of putting intellectual virtues in the context of cultivating other virtues is an essential step in the right direction. Being a person of prudence and integrity who is concerned with proper duties, beneficence, justice, mercy, veracity, and magnanimity—cultivating the basic virtue that Lewis calls the Tao—would go a long way toward helping to get a hearing in the public arena for our more particular or peculiar Christian views. Lewis's writings, especially his fictional works, have wide resonance because he makes it clear that he is dedicated to those ideals. And respect for Lewis continues in part because we can see how he worked on cultivating such virtues in his personal life.

That is the central lesson that we can learn from Lewis: that the intellectual virtues must operate in the framework of moral virtues.

But going beyond that, I also want to identify more specifically intellectual virtues or habits of mind found in Lewis's work that might contribute to greater civility.[14]

One of those intellectual traits is that Lewis is always looking for timeless or perennial truths as opposed to the "latest insights" or the culturally bound. He is rightly famous for his critique of the "chronological snobbery" that characterized twentieth-century thought. Chronological snobbery was the attitude that outlooks of the past could be dismissed without serious consideration simply on the grounds that they were, for instance, "romantic" or "medieval."[15] By way of contrast, Lewis saw that historical perspectives provide a critical place to stand in evaluating modern intellectual fashions. He articulated that well in a lay sermon preached in Oxford in September of 1939, just after the outbreak of World War II. Why continue to study the past, he asked, when the world is in such immediate crisis? His answer was that especially in times of crisis, people need to know the past in order to recognize that "much which seems certain to the uneducated is merely temporary fashion." One "who has lived in many places is not likely to be deceived by the local errors of his native village; the scholar has lived in many times and is therefore in some degree immune from the great cataract of nonsense that pours from the press and the microphone of his own age."[16]

Perspectives from the past helped Lewis avoid political temptation, one of the greatest threats to civility. Having cultivated the virtue of looking for perennial truths, Lewis was disinclined to invest primary energy in promoting causes that were "merely temporary fashion." Lewis did not absolutely avoid political expression, but he was careful not to endorse any current political agenda as being "Christian."[17] When he addressed the topic of "social morality" in his BBC broadcasts, which came to be called *Mere Christianity,* he emphasized that beyond "love your neighbor as yourself," Christianity had no specific political program. A truly Christian society, he supposed, would seem progressive and, in a way, socialistic in economics, but conservative in family values and conventional morality. However, there would never be a Christian society in which people loved their neighbors until they first learned to love God. He also warned specifically against identifying Christianity with a political program. Screwtape, the master devil, recommends to his protégé Wormwood that he suggest to his "patient" (who is in danger of becoming a true Christian) that his political views are part of his religion. "Then let him, under the influence of partisan spirit, come to regard it as the most important part." Then the final step is to have "the patient see his Christianity as valuable chiefly for the excellent arguments it provides for his party's positions."[18] Lewis recognized that the politics of each era provides only partial and largely illusory solutions that could never be fully Christian. He thereby avoided the danger of closing off debate by approaching a current political cause as though it were a Christian crusade.

At the same time that he avoided politics, Lewis was relentless in attacking the underlying "temporary fashion" of the mid-twentieth century: especially its overblown trust that naturalistic scientific models would provide definitive new understandings of the human condition. In Lewis's interplanetary novels, the villain, Weston, wants to exploit the other planets for economic profit. In the title of the first chapter of *The Abolition of Man,* Lewis calls characters like Weston "men without chests" who lack proper sentiments and understand nothing about the true human condition.

Critiquing popular contemporary assumptions in the light of broad historical perspectives and traditions seems to qualify as an intellectual virtue in the sense that it improves the chances of getting things right, but it is not so clear that such dismissal of our contemporaries' assumptions is conducive to promoting civil discourse. Furthermore, we might ask whether using satire and fiction for such dismissals is the most civil way to make our case. Satire does not invite further conversation. Nonetheless, flat-out argument has a similar problem. One rule in life is that our best arguments almost never convince our opponents; they only drive them to be more resourceful in finding counterarguments. So we end up further apart than when we began. Perhaps, then, there is a case for fiction and even sometimes satire as ways to make our points without confrontation—especially if we do so with good humor, as in the case of *The*

Screwtape Letters. Even better is the approach in Narnia. Lewis works his critiques of modern thought into those stories, but he does so in a whimsical way that wins assent by indirection.

In almost all of his fiction, Lewis depicts something like a distinctly Christian cosmos but also finds a point of contact with broader audiences in common human moral realities that any reader can recognize. In the interplanetary trilogy, he suggests how people use modern scientific outlooks to help blind themselves not only from spiritual dimensions of reality but from their own self-centeredness. In *The Great Divorce*, he sharpens that theme, depicting the inborn human trait that combines self-centeredness with free will to the point that many people would freely choose to be left to themselves even at the cost of foregoing eternal bliss. In *The Screwtape Letters*, he depicts subtle ways that we all rationalize our failures and guilt. In the Narnia tales, in addition to connecting with readers through an engaging imaginative reality that appeals to common human longings, Lewis connects to the moral sensibilities of readers of all sorts. In each of the Narnia books, one or more of the characters is confronted with his or her own guilt. In *The Voyage of the Dawn Treader*, for instance, Eustace, who is an insufferable know-it-all, is acting so beastly that he gets turned into a literal dragon. But then,

> [h]e realized that he was a monster cut off from the whole human race. An appalling loneliness came over him. He began to see the others had not really been fiends at all. He began to wonder if he himself had been such a nice person as he always supposed.[19]

From his own experience and his studies of human nature, Lewis knew that one of the great barriers that prevents many modern people from sympathizing with Christian outlooks is that they think they are good just as they are. Christianity, he emphasizes, is most essentially God's remedy for human moral failures. So a first step in gaining some appreciation for Christian viewpoints is to help people recognize, even when they may profess moral relativism, that they intuitively believe that there, indeed, are some universal moral standards. The next step is to bring them to recognize that, if they are honest, they themselves do not live up to those standards.[20]

By studying various cultures throughout history, Lewis cultivates the intellectual virtue of looking for traits of perennial moral standards that provide him points of contact with those whom he might differ ideologically. The most important of these common traits are, once again, the moral standards that he calls the Tao. So even though Lewis recognizes the vast gap between Christians and people whose combination of selfish affections and modern learning make them deaf to what Christians are saying, Lewis still sees a point of contact in what eighteenth-century moral philosophers called "the common sense of mankind." Lewis was an admirer of such thinkers, especially of Samuel Johnson. In Lewis's case, faith in common sense is not naïve, since he clearly recognizes the prior dispositional, affective, and intellectual obstacles to common understanding. Nonetheless, all humans still hold many beliefs in common, and one can build on such commonalities as Lewis does with great skill.

Lewis's study of the past also made him acutely aware that another barrier to modernized people's appreciation of perennial Christianity is modern disenchantment. Even many churchgoers are so shaped by naturalistic assumptions that they fail to appreciate the momentous implications of Christianity. Lewis addresses this factor directly in his famous sermon "The Weight of Glory." After invoking our deepest desires and longing for beauty, he then asks,

> Do you think I am trying to weave a spell? Perhaps I am; but remember your fairy tales. Spells are used for breaking enchantments as well as for inducing them. And you and I have need of the strongest spell that can be found to wake us from the evil enchantment of worldliness that has been laid upon us for nearly a hundred years. Almost our whole education has been directed to silencing this shy, persistent, inner voice; almost all our modem philosophies have been devised to convince us that the good of man is to be found on this earth.[21]

Once again, fiction and storytelling are one of the most effective ways to help break that spell of modern disenchantment. By creating alternative imaginative worlds, as in the interplanetary novels and in Narnia, Lewis provides contemporary people with ways of viewing the most basic underlying assumptions or mythologies of their own culture. It helps people see, for instance, that even though modernized scientific outlooks have their usefulness, if they are turned into the basis for one's view of all reality, they can cut us off from the possibility of recognizing other parts of the universe that we should be perceiving.

The comically pathetic character of Uncle Andrew in *The Magician's Nephew*, the story of the origins of Narnia, provides one of the most memorable illustrations of the limited outlook of the disenchanted. Uncle Andrew believes he is a magician, but he is actually a hopelessly modern person who is both self-centered and severely limited by his modern scientific assumptions. So when Aslan begins to sing the beautiful song that creates Narnia, Uncle Andrew convinces himself that he is hearing only a roar, because, "Who ever heard of a lion singing?" Unlike the other characters, Uncle Andrew cannot hear Aslan or the other animals speak, because he knows that it is impossible for them to do so.[22]

Opening people up to recognizing there is more to reality than is allowed by modern, disenchanted conventions is an important step toward bridging what, otherwise, is often an unbridgeable barrier to communicating with our secularized contemporaries. However, such reenchanting, and hence connecting, with the perennial and cross-cultural dimensions of historic human experience will, of course, win only some people—and it will seldom touch the Uncle Andrews of the world who do not have the ears to hear.

Another virtue that contributes to Lewis's civility as a Christian apologist, scholar, and novelist is that he was careful to present himself as a representative of "mere Christianity." By that, he meant an unembellished common core of "belief that has been common to nearly all Christians at all times." That, he said, was not a "vague and bloodless" lowest-common-denominator Christianity; rather, it was "something not only positive but pungent."[23] Lewis was eager to avoid sectarianism, identification with a party or movement, and doctrines that were commonly disputed among Christians. He did insist that every Christian needed to find a particular church with its own particular emphases; nevertheless, he believed it to be unhelpful for Christians to debate these differences, except among themselves and when nonbelievers are not present.

Such an approach has two easily recognizable advantages in contributing to civil discourse and helps explain Lewis's degree of success as a communicator to diverse audiences. The first advantage is that we can speak with more weight if we are representing the essential Christian truths of the ages, rather than speaking as partisans for a recent sect, movement, or party that can be more easily dismissed. The second advantage is more strictly an intellectual virtue: one can speak as a peacemaker. That is an especially important virtue in promoting civil discourse among all sorts of more-or-less traditional Christians.

Mere Christianity is less helpful, however, in fostering dialogue between more traditional and liberal Christians. As his encounter with Professor

Pittenger illustrated, Lewis himself was quite dismissive of the liberal Christianity of his own day. In *Mere Christianity*, he disparaged it as "Christianity and water," a real insult coming from an Irishman who appreciated a fine malt.[24] But among most of the Christian communities of the world, Lewis's approach of cultivating the virtue of distinguishing between the essential and the peripheral is a helpful guide for promoting civil and truly ecumenical dialogue.

One final intellectual virtue that Lewis displays, which I think is especially important both for being an effective evangelist and for communicating civilly with diverse audiences, is that even when he is talking about himself and his own intellectual and spiritual journey, he is not primarily drawing attention to himself. In an essay of literary criticism, "The Personal Heresy," Lewis argues that when we interpret a poem, we should not just try to understand the poet's state of mind. "The poet is not a man," he wrote, "who asks me to look at *him;* he is a man who says 'look at that' and points; the more I follow the pointing of his finger the less I can possibly see of *him.*"[25]

Lewis would have said the same for his work as an advocate of Christianity. Even though his personality is very much present in his apologetic writings, he acts, as many commentators have observed, like a friendly companion on a journey. Much of Lewis's writing has the tone of one who has made a wonderful discovery and wants to share that discovery with others. As a young man, he longed for success as an author and could not help but take pleasure when he did become a very successful author in his middle years. At the same time, he was acutely aware of what he often preached: that pride was "The Great Sin." Competitiveness and pride are deeply engrained in the human condition. "It is pride which has been the chief cause of misery in every nation and every family since the world began," he declared. Pride is especially dangerous since this "worst of all vices can smuggle itself into the very centre of our religious life." Lewis's account of "The Great Sin" in *Mere Christianity* has been one of the most illuminating parts of that book for many readers.[26] It is especially effective because Lewis combined his study of pride as the primal source of human sinfulness in the Christian heritage with recognition of the dangers of pride in himself.[27] Not incidentally, just at the time when Lewis was emerging as a prominent spokesperson for Christianity, he began the regular practice of weekly confession to an Anglican confessor.[28] Such explicit cultivation of disciplined virtues was an important precondition for Lewis to be able to so often point beyond himself in his writings. On the one hand, his references to his own experience are essential to creating a sense of personal authenticity. Yet, on the other hand, the essence of that experience to which he points is something beyond himself. Rather than presenting himself as an authority, he points people to the beauty of what he has seen, always with the hope that they too will see its compelling beauty and be drawn, as he was, by its illuminating power.

Nonetheless, for all Lewis's moral and intellectual virtues, and for all his winsomeness, he still could be a very divisive person. During his last series of broadcasts of what became *Mere Christianity*, the BBC surveyed listeners and reported to him, "They obviously either regard you as 'the cat's whiskers' or as 'beneath contempt.'"[29] Lewis responded, characteristically, "The two views you report (Cat's Whiskers and Beneath Contempt), aren't very illuminating about *me* perhaps: about my subject matter, it is an old story, isn't it. They love, or hate."[30]

That sums up one dimension of the problem that we, as Christians, have in trying to promote both intellectual virtues and civility. The primary intellectual virtues are those that aid us in discovering the truth. Yet, for Christians, that truth leads to the offense of the cross (Gal. 5:11) and to viewpoints our fellow citizens will either love or hate. So if we, following Lewis's example, are frank in pointing out how radically Christianity separates us from most contemporary views of things, then inevitably we will, like him, experience the disdain of some of our contemporaries.

Nonetheless, the counter to the inevitable tensions involved in the offense of the gospel is to surround our truth-seeking intellectual virtues with all of the moral virtues that promote civility. Here, Lewis turns out to be a very helpful guide, in that he recognizes that the intellectual life takes place within the framework of the moral life. Hence, if we are to be effective intellectually and as communicators, beyond the circles of our fellow believers, we need to start by cultivating moral virtues such as humility, self-criticism, winsomeness, self-deprecating humor, compassion, concern for justice, concern for mercy, and love for our enemies. We need, as Lewis did, to look for common humanity and for what we share with those who differ from us. Such moral virtues shaping our intellectual life will still not keep us from the offense of the cross and, therefore, some conflict. But if we consciously practice and cultivate such virtues, it may help us counter our tendency to think that we can win the day by mere argument.

Chapter 5

Respect as an Intellectual Virtue

Adam C. Pelser
United States Air Force Academy
Ryan West
Grove City College

It is commonly observed that one key ingredient of civility missing from much public discourse is respect. The term "respect" can refer to an attitude, a judgment, a manner of behavior, or a feeling—a family of concepts in which the unifying theme is "the appreciation of excellence or worthiness." But there is also a moral virtue of respect and an intellectual variant of that virtue.[1] Arguably, no intellectual virtue is more important for advancing civil discourse than respect. Yet, while philosophers and psychologists have paid a good deal of recent attention to traits like intellectual humility, open-mindedness, and intellectual courage, little of their work has focused on respect as an intellectual virtue. Here, we take a step toward filling this lacuna by sketching an analysis of the intellectual virtue of respect.

Our analysis begins with a distinction between two species of broadly moral respect: egalitarian respect for human dignity, and special esteem for distinctive excellence.[2] Whereas all people deserve basic respect in virtue of their equal moral worth (or dignity), one's worthiness of special esteem depends on the comparative value of one's excellences and achievements. Insofar as the inherent, non-comparative worth of all humans and the comparative excellences of some humans are both broadly human excellences, each properly inspires respect. As Robert Roberts puts the point, "If we are rational, we feel greater respect for persons of integrity and high moral achievement than for moral slackers and the vicious. But the moral life, in some traditions, requires a respect for people that is blind to such differences (while still being an attribution of a broadly moral property)."[3] In keeping with Roberts's insight, we distinguish two kinds of intellectual respect: equal basic respect for all epistemic agents and special respect that is properly reserved for subject-matter experts, the intellectually virtuous, and the otherwise intellectually excellent. Both varieties of intellectual respect can be differentiated from their broadly moral counterparts in at least two ways. First, the basis of intellectual respect—the reason such respect is due—is itself an intellectual matter: namely, the intellectual excellence of the respected person. And second, intellectual respect applies directly to, and/or is fittingly expressed in, an intellectual context. (We are using the term "intellectual" broadly here, as having to do with the life of the mind, the exchange of ideas, and so on—and not necessarily as that pertaining to formal settings of teaching and learning). The person with the intellectual virtue of respect is intelligently disposed to both egalitarian and comparative intellectual respect.

In what follows, we consider the two kinds of respect in turn, exploring how each is relevant to the intellectual virtue of respect. Along the way, we consider the connections and differences between intellectual respect and related traits. We then conclude with reflections regarding the cultivation of this underappreciated virtue.

Egalitarian Respect for Intellectual Dignity

The intellectually respectful person appropriately respects all epistemic agents as rational persons. Minimally, this involves believing that others might have ideas worth considering and, therefore, listening to them or reading what they've written carefully and charitably. Rather than dismissing another's views at the first sign of a flaw in her reasoning, the intellectually respectful person listens patiently, with the assumption that the speaker might arrive at a valuable insight—simply because the listener takes the other to be worthy of such treatment. Robert Roberts and Jay Wood suggest that respect is an important aspect of other intellectual virtues, such as intellectual charity. They observe that "if one reads a text charitably, one is reading the text as coming from an author who would like to be treated with respect and goodwill."[4] Such respectful reception of ideas tends to come easily when our interlocutors wear their intellectual greatness on their sleeves, or even better, share our views. But when interacting with one's ideological opponents, or those whom society casts as intellectually substandard, it requires a special sort of character.

In her book *Team of Rivals*, Doris Kearns Goodwin highlights the ways Abraham Lincoln exemplified virtuous habits of respectful asking and listening, even—indeed, especially—with his most virulent critics. Frederick Douglass, for instance, publicly denounced Lincoln for failing to address discriminatory military policies that inhibited the recruitment of black soldiers, such as unequal pay and no opportunity for black soldiers to be commissioned as officers. Still, as the following account of their first meeting suggests, Lincoln's respect for Douglass was palpable:

> Finding a large crowd in the hallway, Douglass expected to wait hours before gaining an audience with the president. Minutes after presenting his card, however, he was called into the office. "I was never more quickly or more completely put at ease in the presence of a great man than in that of Abraham Lincoln," he later recalled. . . .
>
> Douglass laid before the president the discriminatory measures that were frustrating his recruiting efforts. "Mr. Lincoln listened with earnest attention and with very apparent sympathy," he recalled. "Upon my ceasing to speak [he] proceeded with an earnestness and fluency of which I had not suspected him." Lincoln first recognized the indisputable justice of the demand for equal pay. When Congress passed the bill for black soldiers, he explained, it "seemed a necessary concession to smooth the way to their employment at all as soldiers," but he promised that "in the end they shall have the same pay as white soldiers." As for the absence of black officers, Lincoln assured Douglass that "he would sign any commission to colored soldiers whom his Secretary of War should commend to him."[5]

Given Lincoln's greater political power, and the intimidation that naturally accompanies meeting the president (in the White House, no less!), a less respectful Lincoln might have sought the intellectual upper hand by belittling Douglass, say, by letting him sweat it out in the waiting area or by putting on airs to keep him from feeling at ease. And, given the desire for (eventual) justice that secretly motivated the indisputably unjust (but intentionally temporary) remuneration policy, a less respectful Lincoln might have contemptuously disregarded a complaint so insensitive to the ways of incremental justice. And, given the racial sensibilities of the day, a less respectful Lincoln might have allowed the culture's systemic devaluation of African Americans to taint his reception of Douglass.[6] But the real Lincoln was alive to Douglass's dignity and demonstrated it through remarkably respectful conduct. This was not lost on Douglass.

> In subsequent speeches, Douglass frequently commented on his gracious reception at the White House. "Perhaps you may like to know how the President of the United States received a black man at the White House," he would say. "I will tell you how he received me—just as you have seen one gentleman receive another." As the crowd erupted into "great applause," he continued, "I tell you I felt big there!"[7]

Thus, Lincoln's respectful behavior fostered at least three intellectual goods: the fruitful exchange of ideas, reciprocal respect from Douglass, and self-respect in Douglass. This result should not surprise us. As Tom Morris observes, "One of the most ennobling gestures any of us can make toward another human being is to ask her, sincerely, what she thinks about what we are doing together. What is her take on the truth? When we ask, wanting to hear, we treat the other person with a fundamental respect, and this behavior is then much more likely to be mirrored back to us."[8]

Despite the potential impediments to respectful treatment noted above, respecting Douglass was no doubt eased by the fact that he was an intellectual giant. The egalitarian form of respect we're considering in this section, though, also befits the intellectually unimpressive. Consider Jenny, a second-grade teacher at the local elementary school. Jenny's seven- and eight-year-old pupils aren't among society's best and brightest. In addition to the intellectual limitations that inherently come with youth (lack of education, dearth of experience, and so on), many of these children aren't particularly "intellectually respectable" (in the comparative sense) even for their own reference class (say, lower-elementary school students in suburban Los Angeles). What would it mean for Jenny to treat these students with intellectual respect? For starters, she'd field their questions and comments with a default seriousness. Roberts and Wood note that one virtue that "supports comprehensional openness is a basic respect for others—the assumption that, until proven stupid, the interlocutor from another discipline or another historical period or culture"—and we might add, another age group or level of intelligence—"is likely to have something intelligent to contribute."[9] As a respectful teacher, Jenny operates under this kind of assumption: "Every one of these kiddos is a *thinker*; as such, their ideas—even their wildest ones that seem to have traveled from the farthest reaches of left field—deserve a fair and charitable hearing. There's even a decent chance that their classmates and I will learn something from them." This mindset might motivate Jenny to put her imagination and intellectual energy to work in teasing out the kernels of truth and interesting implications that are latent in her students' inchoate ideas. In this way, Jenny's virtuous respect will be aided and expressed by certain intellectual skills or powers (such as creativity and perceptiveness) and will tend to cluster with other intellectual virtues (such as intellectual generosity, which disposes her to give credit to her students for the insights she draws from their comments, rather than using such opportunities to show off—to her students or to herself—just how smart *she* is).

On a Christian worldview, intellectual respect is properly due to all people as creatures made in God's image. Our cognitive capacities were all made by the same hand, and all of us—even the least mentally "capable"—bear the imprint of God's rationality in our nature as rational persons. Moreover, biblical teachings such as God's use of the ineloquent Moses to bring his message to Pharaoh (Exod. 4:1–16) and Paul's teaching that God uses the weak and foolish things of the world to shame the strong and wise (1 Cor. 1:18–31) provide the Christian with additional motivation for giving a respectful hearing to everyone, including the simple and uneducated. Jesus himself indicated that spiritual truths are not always best grasped by the putatively sagacious when he prayed, "I thank you Father, Lord of heaven and earth, that you have hidden these things from the wise and understanding and revealed them to little children" (Matt. 11:25, ESV). Therefore, in addition to the common observation that profound insights sometimes come from unexpected sources, Christians have theological reasons not to be dismissive of the ideas of others on account of their age or lack of education, not to mention their race or contrary point of view.

In a sense, we have, so far, been filling out Roberts's and Wood's suggestive remark that intellectual respect "supports comprehensional openness." But respect and openness (or open-mindedness) are distinct virtues. According to Jason Baehr's influential account, "an open-minded person is characteristically (a) willing and (within limits) able (b) to transcend a default cognitive standpoint (c) in order to take up or take seriously the merits of (d) a distinct cognitive standpoint."[10] But one's mind can be open for various reasons, and virtuously open minds can vary in texture. For instance, Lincoln might count as virtuously open-minded if he were disposed to take Douglass's point of view seriously, perhaps out of a virtuous desire for the truth, even if he did not respect Douglass. The respectfully open-minded, though, do not so neatly separate ideas from their sources; rather, they give ideas a fair hearing (in part) because the people who offer those ideas are worthy of such treatment. In this way, respect can both motivate and color open-mindedness (even if it need not) and open-minded actions can express respect (or not). Perhaps the support relation can go the other way as well; it may be, for instance, that Lincoln's disposition to respect Douglass developmentally depended (in part) on his open-mindedness, given his culture's default cognitive standpoint vis-à-vis African Americans.

Another way intellectual respect may differ from open-mindedness is that the latter virtue arguably pertains to a narrower range of intellectual endeavors: namely, receiving or entertaining ideas. But the intellectual virtue of respect also impacts the manner in which its bearers disseminate knowledge.[11] When Jenny plans tomorrow's lesson, she is not prepping a mere time-killer or a dressed-up babysitting session. Rather, she is preparing to help budding thinkers—little chips off the divine block, with all the (potential) rationality that entails—to understand the world in which they live and move and have their being. These little tikes might not be geniuses, but like all humans—if Aristotle is right—they desire to know, and they are capable of doing so. (As Charlotte Mason puts it, "Children no more come into the world without provision for dealing with knowledge than without provision for dealing with food."[12]) So Jenny prepares with care, under the assumption that these students are worthy of such preparation. One element of her respectful preparation and teaching will be acting as though her students, as divine image-bearers, are not mere receptacles for receiving and piling up data. Respecting the image of God in them includes treating them not as droids preparing for standardized tests but as humans: real people with histories, families, dreams, and emotions; people who need not just information but also understanding and wisdom; and people who will learn well only if approached humanely—with opportunities for rest and play (after all, we are bodily creatures), a workload that befits their age, abilities, and needs (after all, we are developmental creatures), a physical and attitudinal atmosphere that encourages learning (after all, we don't thrive in just any environment), and so on. One way teachers (often unintentionally) intellectually disrespect their students is by treating them like computers and the teaching-learning context like an upload-download transaction.[13]

Now, intellectual respect for agents does essentially involve a willingness to listen carefully to their ideas, to interpret them charitably, and to present ideas to them in a way that befits their dignity. But it also involves an affective component. On this score, Jenny's colleague, Matt, is deficient in intellectual respect. Matt has observed Jenny's treatment of her students and covets the positive results she appears to be getting. After all, as we saw with Lincoln and Douglass, respect tends to produce certain intellectual and social rewards, such as a more open atmosphere in which to discuss ideas, and thereby a greater ability to discover truth—not to mention a more generally respectful and self-respecting community, perhaps via a kind of responsive or mimetic trickle-down effect. (Jenny's classroom, like Lincoln's Oval Office, is likely a place where one feels one's "bigness" and the "bigness" of one's fellows.) So Matt has started imitating many of Jenny's outwardly respectful practices, to some good effect. Inwardly, though, Matt does not intellectually respect his students. This is not to say that he does not care for his students; he does and wants them to succeed. But Matt has a bit of a Nietzschean streak, and really only has moral/emotional categories for respecting distinctive excellence. Since his students, like Jenny's, are rather intellectually substandard, he doesn't see them (with the eyes of his heart) as being worthy of his respect. So, when one of Matt's students reveals her ineptitude by asking a truly off-the-wall question, he feels annoyed and perhaps even mildly offended by her ignorance and lack of sophistication and is inclined to roll his eyes and correct her in a somewhat condescending tone. But he checks himself—not because he's cut to the heart and is working on his respectfulness, but because he's observed that contemptuous responses seem not to work very well. In the teacher's lounge, we might find out how he really feels about little Sally, who obviously wasn't paying much attention during Matt's riveting lesson about iguanas.

What is different about Jenny? For one thing, to borrow Robert Adams's language, she is "for" her students' dignity and intellectual interests. Adams has pointed out that a person can be for a good, such as intellectual dignity, in a variety of ways, including "loving it, liking it, respecting it, wanting it, wishing for it, appreciating it, thinking highly of it, speaking in favor of it and otherwise intentionally standing for it symbolically, acting to promote or protect it, and being disposed to do such things."[14] As we've seen, Jenny's being for her students' intellectual dignity and interests has a number of behavioral implications. But it also has emotional implications, insofar as it underwrites her affective awareness of her students' worthiness.

Following Roberts, we take emotions to be "concern-based construals":[15] perceptual states wherein the subject's loves (what they are "for") take up residence in the subject's way of seeing her situation. Generally speaking, when we construe an object (whether emotionally or not) in one way rather than another, we are mentally organizing its complex features so as to make sense of it. For example, we might construe Jastrow's famous duck-rabbit either as a duck or as a rabbit, depending on whether we see the hump-like protrusions as a beak or as ears. Emotions constitute a subset of construals: the concern-based ones. That is, via our emotions, we construe our situation as valuable or disvaluable in some particular way (e.g., as a loss, as offensive, as disgusting, as satisfying, etc.), insofar as it impinges upon our concerns. Fear, for example, is a construal of some object as a threat (as dangerous) to our own well-being or to the well-being of someone about whom (or something about which) we are concerned. The concerns in which emotions are based include desires, loves, attachments, and other ways of "being for."

The concern fundamental to the intellectual virtue of respect is a deep appreciation and valuing of the intellectual worthiness of others. Because Jenny cares about the intellectual dignity of others, she is disposed not merely to believe that they have worth, but to see them in terms of their worth. Sometimes, this will be by way of the emotion of respect, when the other's dignity is focal in her emotional vision. But the intellectual dignity of others can enter her emotional vision in other ways as well. For instance, we can imagine that when Jenny overhears Matt's condescending rant about little Sally, she'll get angry, seeing Matt as a blameworthy offender against Sally's dignity (and his own). In fact, her students' inherent dignity will tend to color all of Jenny's emotional perceptions of them, even when she isn't attending to their dignity as such. Jenny thus will tend to be patient with struggling students, often feeling compassion, rather than frustration, when they fail to grasp a concept or master a new intellectual skill. When they lazily refuse to exert intellectual effort, though, Jenny might feel disappointed (construing them as failing to live up to her hopes for their intellectual growth), sad (construing them as having missed a valuable intellectual opportunity), or even angry (construing them as offending against their own dignity).

Different moral outlooks will diverge in their prescriptions regarding emotions of respect. The Kantian or Christian will think that such emotions can fit more targets than will, say, the Nietzschean, who is anything but egalitarian. Moreover, the internal structure of the prescribed emotions will vary. The perceptual view of emotions, according to which emotions are conceptually structured, nicely illuminates this point. Since concepts and narratives from particular moral outlooks can enter into one's emotional life, there can be such a thing as an explicitly Christian emotion (and virtue) of respect (where the subject views the other as a creature made in God's image) as well as a distinctively Kantian emotion (and virtue) of respect (where the subject sees the other being as a rational end in herself).[16] This isn't to say that all putative "virtues" really are virtues; that'll depend on the nature of reality.[17] But by Christian lights, a key aspect of growth in the intellectual virtue of respect is learning to care about and see the dignity of others in explicitly Christian terms. (More on this below.) Articulacy about such theological matters, though, seems not to be a necessary condition for having the virtue in a less-than-ideal form. That is, one might possess and exhibit the virtue to a rather impressive degree without being able to articulate with much sophistication the doctrine of the *imago Dei*. If asked why she listens to people so indiscriminately and with such interest, such a person might simply say something to the effect that all people are God's children and that wisdom can come "out of the mouth of babies" (cf., Matt. 21:16, Ps. 8:2 , ESV).

In sum, then, respect for human dignity has bearing on the intellectual virtue of respect in that the intellectually respectful person cares about—is "for"—the intellectual dignity of all persons, has eyes to see each person's worthiness, and acts accordingly, both in giving and receiving ideas.

Special Esteem for the Intellectual Distinction

The foregoing does not imply that the intellectually respectful person is blind to differences in people's epistemic excellence. No, she is also intelligently disposed to feel and give special esteem on a sliding scale, so to speak, in cases where epistemic authorities, the intellectually virtuous, and the otherwise intellectually excellent are "more worthy" of such respect than are the uninformed, the intellectually vicious, and the unintelligent.

Consider Sam, a first-year graduate student in philosophy, who has read one book and a handful of articles on the Israeli-Palestinian conflict. He knows the general contours of the issues at stake but is surely no expert. That debate comes up in conversation with one of his fellow graduate students, Joy, who voices a decidedly pro-Palestinian position. Sam isn't convinced. He somewhat forcefully objects to Joy's view, repeating an argument he remembers reading last week, with the intention of not only correcting Joy but also revealing to her that she is less informed than she realizes. Sam's response expresses basic respect for Joy dignity as a thinker, for he doesn't belittle her, and he takes her seriously as someone who can consider counterarguments. Sam also feels and shows some measure of special esteem for Joy's intellectual distinction. She is, after all, a fellow grad student, and she has even shown herself to be Sam's intellectual superior during their time together. But he isn't obsequious or excessively timid—Joy is uninformed on this issue and may be overly dogmatic given her lack of careful study, and Sam responds accordingly.

Now imagine that Sam attends a lecture by Nicholas Wolterstorff, a prominent Christian philosopher who, through his research and role as a public intellectual, serves as an outspoken advocate for the rights of Palestinians. Say Wolterstorff voices the same position that Joy did, perhaps using the very same words. During the Q&A, Sam saunters to the microphone and marshals the same argument against Wolterstorff that he used to put Joy in her place, insinuating by his manner that Wolterstorff is in the learner's seat. By acting as though Wolterstorff is as ignorant of the issues as Joy was (even if he "recognizes," in a thin, merely cognitive sense, that Wolterstorff is an expert), Sam evinces a lack of appraisal respect: he fails to treat Wolterstorff with the special esteem that such a distinguished scholar deserves. This is not to say that Sam shouldn't raise his objection; there is nothing inherently disrespectful about disagreeing with an expert, even one who is well known for his intellectual accomplishments. Indeed, as with Joy, so with Wolterstorff: voicing objections can express respect. But in disagreeing with a thinker of Wolterstorff's caliber, the intellectually respectful will feel proper emotions of respect and will demonstrate, in both the manner and matter of his disagreement, that he appreciates the expert's special worthiness. For instance, Wolterstorff's epistemic excellence will loom large in the respectful subject's emotional vision by way of emotions like admiration or even a kind of reverent fear. Moreover, the respectful graduate student's posture, both attitudinally and physically, will show that he stands ready to take the place of the pupil: there will be no sauntering; his language will express openness to, and may even explicitly invite, correction; if he sees fit to refer to the relevant literature, he won't preface his verbal footnote with condescending caveats about how, "*of course* you're aware of the argument found in the latest issue of *Ethics*"—a common and disrespectful way of feigning respect—but will simply give the argument, cite the source, and politely ask for and then listen carefully to Wolterstorff's response.

In his interaction with Wolterstorff, Sam not only lacks respect he also lacks humility. But the respective "lacks" are doing different work in his psychology. Humility, on our understanding, is itself a lack: an intelligent lack of the various forms of vicious pride.[18] So, when we say Sam "lacks humility," we really mean that he fails to lack something he should lack: namely, vicious concerns for his own intellectual status, glory, etc. Sam's lack of respect, by contrast, is more straightforward: he simply fails to appreciate Wolterstorff's intellectual status and thus fails to treat him appropriately (i.e., respectfully). As Roberts points out in Chapter Seven, vicious pride tends to function like an astigmatism, wherein our illicit self-focus distorts our perception.[19] This is just how Sam's pride works here: his attention to his own intellectual status blinds him to Wolterstorff's. If Sam could lose some of his intellectual arrogance and vanity, then he might have eyes to see Wolterstorff for the great scholar he is; and if, in spite of his prideful state, Sam could somehow catch a glimpse of Wolterstorff's comparative eminence, he might be duly humbled. In this way, humility and respect are distinct and mutually reinforcing intellectual virtues.

The intellectual virtue of respect disposes its bearers to give special esteem not only to scholars like Wolterstorff but also to those who may not have much by way of formal education, but who exhibit uncommon expertise in a particular domain or display general wisdom about how to live well. It is in this vein that Aristotle encourages a kind of default intellectual esteem for the elderly and those with a great deal of life experience, even if they cannot give persuasive arguments for their views: "the unproved assertions and opinions of experienced and elderly people, or of prudent men, are as much deserving of attention as those which they support by proof; for experience has given them an eye for things, and so they see correctly."[20] Thus, unless she has some overriding reason not to, the person with the intellectual virtue of respect will give special weight to the experienced mechanic's car maintenance advice, to the seasoned doctor's medical assessment, to the established colleague's professional guidance, and to the counsel of those who demonstrate, through their own well-lived lives, a significant amount of practical wisdom.

So, the intellectually respectful appreciate intellectual excellences that warrant special esteem. But they are also sensitive to intellectual deficiencies, even in those they otherwise greatly respect. Reflecting on his longstanding disagreement with fellow philosopher Robert Nozick over an issue that both thinkers considered basic and beyond contention (despite their diametrically opposed convictions!), Hilary Putnam goes so far as to suggest that when someone whose intellectual virtue we highly respect appears to be exhibiting a fundamental error in her thinking or emotional vision (a kind of irrationality), the appropriate responsive attitude (emotional perception) is a kind of contempt:

> I say I respect Bob Nozick's mind, and I certainly do. I say I respect his character, and I certainly do. But, if I feel contempt (or something in that ballpark) for a certain complex of emotions and judgments in him, is that not contempt (or something like it) for *him*?
>
> This is a painful thing to explore, and politeness normally keeps us from examining with any justice what exactly our attitudes are towards those whom we love and disagree with. The fact is that none of us who is at all grown up likes and respects *everything* about *anyone* (least of all one's own self). There is no contradiction between having a fundamental liking and respect for someone and still regarding something in him as an intellectual and moral weakness, just as there is no contradiction between having a fundamental liking and respect for oneself and regarding something in oneself as an intellectual and moral (or emotional, etc.) weakness.
>
> I want to urge that there is all the difference in the world between an opponent who has the fundamental intellectual virtues of open-mindedness, respect for reason, and self-criticism, and one who does not;

> between an opponent who has an impressive and pertinent store of factual knowledge, and one who does not; between an opponent who merely gives vent to his feelings and fantasies (which is what all people commonly do in what passes for political discussion), and one who reasons carefully. And the ambivalent attitude of respectful contempt is an honest one: respect for the intellectual virtues in the other; contempt for the intellectual or emotional weaknesses (according to one's own lights, of course, for one always starts with them). "Respectful contempt" may sound almost *nasty* (especially if one confuses it with contemptuous respect, which is something quite different). And it *would* be nasty if the "contempt" were for the other as a person, and not just for one complex of feelings and judgments in him. But it is a far more honest attitude than *false relativism*; that is, the pretense that there is no giving reasons, or such a thing as better or worse reasons on a subject, when one really does feel that one view is reasonable and the other is irrational.[21]

At first glance, Putnam's categories of respectful contempt and contemptuous respect appear paradoxical—the emotional equivalents of square circles. For, in their basic forms, respect and contempt are as opposed to each other as two emotions can be. Whereas respect presents its object to the subject as dignified or comparatively excellent, contempt's object looks low, deserving of scorn, or even worthless to the subject. Macalester Bell offers an insightful analysis of one particularly foul form of contempt, which we call "global contempt."[22] Global contempt takes a whole person as its target (rather than an individual trait or action), insultingly and dismissively presenting her (full stop) to the subject as being inferior to the subject—the kind of person the subject "would not stoop to be"[23]—on account of some failure of character. Putnam calls global contempt "nasty," and it isn't hard to see why. In virtue of its totalizing negativity and reflexively comparative evaluation, such contempt utterly blinds the subject, at least temporarily, to the other's excellences (including her dignity as a divine image-bearer) by presenting her solely in terms of her worst qualities—qualities that are taken to indicate that she not only fails to measure up to some objective standard of goodness but also is beneath me (the subject). Nasty indeed.

But even if global contempt looks incompatible with respect, as Putnam suggests, one might feel a more circumscribed contempt for some aspect of another person, such as her morally detestable or irrational behavior or character (including her judgments and perceptions), without defining that person (unqualifiedly) in terms of that aspect. This is why Putnam's *prima facie* paradoxical phrase "respectful contempt" is apt. It is contempt insofar as it presents its object ("a certain complex of [Nozick's] emotions and judgments," not Nozick simpliciter) as grossly falling short of respectability. It is respectful insofar as the contempt is filtered through a lens of general recognition respect for the other's basic dignity and perhaps even a great deal of special esteem for the other's distinctive excellences (such as Putnam expressed for Nozick). By contrast, we might think of contemptuous respect as a limited (perhaps even begrudging) respect for some excellence of another, filtered through a lens of global contempt.[24] A racist, for example, might find it difficult not to respect an intellectual opponent's painfully obvious intelligence, even while globally contemning her for her race. With Putnam, we take contemptuous respect to be vicious in a way that respectful contempt is not (which is not to say that we endorse the latter).

Let's press a bit further. What about instances when one's interlocutor shows no signs of "the fundamental intellectual virtues of open-mindedness, respect for reason, and self-criticism," signally lacks "a pertinent store of factual knowledge," and unwaveringly "gives vent to his feelings and fantasies"? Might not global intellectual contempt fit its object then?

Consider the following case. Sam meets Rick when they are seated next to each other on a flight. Rick casually mentions his support of the Palestinians when prompted by a news story about the conflict, and, in response, Sam voices the same objection he raised to Joy and Wolterstorff. Over the course of their conversation, Sam discerns from Rick's heated, illogical, and factually misinformed replies that Rick is no model interlocutor (to put it kindly). Whatever good reasons there are for policies advancing the Palestinian cause, they don't seem to enter into Rick's dogmatic and sloppy thinking. Out of respect for Rick's dignity as a thinker, we think Sam should not respond in a demeaning or condescending way. At the same time, though, Rick does not deserve to be taken seriously on this issue (at least for now; but see below). Realizing that Rick is willfully deaf to arguments against his view, Sam might gently (or, if the situation calls for it, firmly) suggest that Rick's reasons for his view are not good; or he might just decide to end the conversation by politely changing the subject. Either way, he would be following the wisdom of Proverbs 26: "Answer not a fool according to his folly, lest you be like him yourself. Answer a fool according to his folly, lest he be wise in his own eyes" (vv. 4–5, ESV). If Sam feels any emotions toward Rick—as he surely will if he cares deeply about the issue at hand—they won't be emotions of respect or admiration, but rather negative ones like disappointment (that might shade into anger), or even some form of contempt (which might be the best emotion-term we have for what we feel when another impresses us with his foolishness). In seeing Rick in this unfavorable light and choosing not to consider his bad arguments, Sam is not necessarily being disrespectful. Indeed, like the grateful person whose virtue of gratitude can be expressed in a lack of gratitude upon receiving a thoughtless or manipulative gift, Sam might actually be manifesting the intellectual virtue of respect in his discriminating recognition that Rick is (in some ways) an intellectual lowlife, but a precious lowlife made in God's image.

In our view, the respectful caveat just mentioned will be ever-present in the fully virtuous agent's moral perception, thus keeping his contempt from being genuinely global.[25] Still, in the heat of the moment, Rick's badness might become so pungent that Sam's contempt for him takes on something approaching global scope—say, if Rick shows himself to be not merely illogical but also unrepentantly anti-Semitic. (It may be that totalizing contempt in response to radical evil is a recalcitrant feature of human psychology, at least for those with a passion for the good.) But, just as informed people aren't inclined to believe that the sun literally rises, despite ineliminable appearances to the contrary, so also Sam will know better than to assent to his heart's global assessment of Rick. Moreover, if Sam does feel something like global contempt, that mental state will be inherently unstable. For, if Sam is really "for" Rick's dignity (and thus emotionally sensitive to it), Rick's inherent worth will have a way of shining through to Sam over time. And if Sam's respect is buttressed by other virtues (such as contrition and compassion), situational factors that don't relate intrinsically to respect will tend to enter his emotional vision as well, thereby defusing his contempt and coloring it while it remains. Were this to occur, his contempt would become not only respectful (i.e., filtered through a lens of respect for Rick's dignity) but also contrite (i.e., imbued with the heartfelt sense that Rick is Sam's fellow lowlife, at least in some respects) and compassionate (i.e., suffused with the appreciative understanding that Rick's lowness is a source of suffering for him that ought to be alleviated).

It might be objected at this point that while Rick deserves basic moral respect, he is not a proper object of intellectual respect.[26] For, while it might have been appropriate to treat him and his ideas seriously at first, he has shown himself to be so intellectually careless, irresponsible, and, indeed, disrespectful, that it no longer makes sense to feel or show any respect for his intellect. We agree that Rick no longer deserves much, if any, esteem for intellectual distinction. Nevertheless, a baseline of distinctively intellectual recognition respect still befits him, for he is a rational creature made in God's image (however irrational his current intellectual behavior may be). Thus, even if Sam need not presently give Rick a hearing on the Israeli-Palestinian issue, it would be intellectually disrespectful of him to write off Rick as someone with nothing of value to say on anything. Moreover, Sam arguably ought to remain open to the possibility that he could learn something from Rick, even about the Middle East conflict, if only Rick could behave (intellectually) a bit less viciously. Suppose, for example, that Rick falls asleep for an hour and, upon awakening, expresses a desire to reengage Sam on the issue; but this time, he does so with quite a bit more gentleness and openness to Sam's arguments. Perhaps he even apologizes for his previous stubbornness or simply displays a willingness to listen by sincerely asking Sam to explain his arguments again. In this scenario, Sam's finely tuned disposition to give due esteem will be reactivated, awakened by the first signs of intellectual worthiness in Rick. The circumstances might be such that Sam will choose not to reengage; but he might. In this way, intellectual respect is supported by, and supports, yet another related and underappreciated intellectual virtue: intellectual forgivingness.

In carving out conceptual space for the virtuously respectful to respond to certain egregious failures of character with (non-global) contempt, we are not thereby commending contempt.[27] Rather, we are attempting to discern the outer limits of what intellectual respect permits; and, for the reasons given, we think it permits a nuanced form of contempt. In the end, it may be that, for reasons external to considerations of respect, the intellectually respectful should nevertheless refrain from all forms of contempt, perhaps favoring emotional takes on foolishness that are less nasty and more loving (like disappointment, compassion, and humor). One way or another, though, they'll be disposed to recognize fools for what they are and withhold from them the relevant forms of special esteem.

The Intellectual Virtue of Respect: A Synopsis

Let's sum up. The intellectual virtue of respect, in its ideal form, involves (at least) the following:

1. An abiding concern for the intellectual dignity of all persons;
2. An abiding concern for intellectual goods (such as knowledge, understanding, virtue, and intelligence) and excellence with regard to which render one worthy of esteem;
3. A discriminating emotional-perceptual sensitivity to both kinds of worthiness (expressed not only in emotions of respect but in a whole range of emotions);
4. A range of skills and action dispositions relevant to the respectful giving and receiving of ideas; and
5. The practical wisdom to integrate all of the above into a morally and intellectually good life.

The first three aspects together form what we might call the emotion disposition that characterizes this virtue: the intellectually respectful person is "for" others' intellectual dignity, virtue, etc. (see 1 and 2), and so is emotionally attuned to their presence and absence (see 3). The concern summarized in (2) is shared by multiple intellectual virtues but plays a special role here, inasmuch as it underwrites the agent's emotional responses vis-à-vis comparative worthiness. Of course, as summarized in (4), the intellectual virtue of respect involves dispositions not only to feel proper respect for others but to show or express it across the various contexts of intellectual discourse (formal education, reading, writing, informal conversation, etc.). Both sets of dispositions will be informed and supported by other moral and intellectual virtues, such as intellectual humility (which removes prideful impediments to respect), open-mindedness (which disposes one to consider others' ideas respectfully), intellectual generosity (which disposes one to promote the intellectual well-being of others, including their enjoyment of intellectual self-respect), and even intellectual forgivingness (which disposes one to overcome the anger and contempt that might otherwise impede respectful dialogue).

Grounded as it is in a concern for an aspect of the good (viz., intellectual dignity and worth), the virtue of respect belongs to the category of substantive or motivational virtues.[28] As with all substantive virtues, the action and emotion dispositions constitutive of intellectual respect are predicated on an appreciative understanding of the goods the virtue is "for." The person with this virtue not only grasps and appreciates the intellectual dignity and excellences of others and of herself, she also understands how best to promote those goods in ways that foster (or at least do not unduly hinder the achievement of) other moral and intellectual goods. Such understanding involves a keen perceptual sensitivity to the ways that the various goods of human life intersect as well as the ability to deliberate well about how to act in a variety of moral and intellectual contexts. As suggested by (5), the understanding central to the intellectual virtue of respect is thus a kind of wisdom—and an aspect of the virtue of practical wisdom.[29]

The foregoing summary is but a sketch. No doubt, the features of the virtue we've identified could be refined. Perhaps further features could be distinguished. Even so, we think these five elements provide the outlines of the emotional and behavior signature of the intellectually respectful person.

To this point, we have merely gestured at what failures of respect might look like. Given the many ways one could go wrong here—from condescension, to aloofness, to sycophancy, and beyond—we doubt that the intellectual virtue of respect lies in a simple Aristotelian mean. Although we cannot provide an analytical taxonomy of this virtue's sundry relative vices, in the next section we offer some practical suggestions for overcoming just a few of the most common obstacles to respect.

Cultivating Intellectual Respect

How might we non-ideal thinkers come to approximate the ideal of respect more closely and encourage others to do likewise? Our advice falls into three categories: behavioral, contemplative, and social. As we'll see, these categories are ultimately separable only in thought; in real life, they inevitably intermingle.

To begin, recall Matt, the Nietzschean elementary school teacher who feigns respect for the sake of its benefits. Few educators (parents, employers) share

Matt's principled resistance to respecting their less-than-excellent students (children, employees). But many of us sometimes share his emotional blindness and end up failing to treat those "below us" in a way that befits the dignity we (should) know they have. In a culture that prizes overt "excellence" (note the scare quotes), often encouraging respect for putative dignitaries over respect for dignity, it is all too easy to allow the evaluative category of comparative esteem to overwhelm its egalitarian counterpart.[30] And even when we retain some capacity for basic respect, for intellectual dignity, that capacity can be desensitized over time. After all, even if it doesn't always breed contempt, familiarity has a way of blinding us to the infinite worth embodied in the precious ones who call us Mrs. So-and-So, or Daddy, or Boss. When this (hopefully occasional) shortcoming grows into a vice, it goes by the name "aloofness." It isn't that the aloof think badly of others; they're just emotionally numb to others' inherent value and (mis)treat them accordingly.

As an initial remedial step, the aloof might (partially) follow Matt's lead and simply pretend to be respectful, regardless of their feelings. In a well-known passage, C. S. Lewis nicely captures the sense in which our emulation of Matt must be only partial.

> [T]here are two kinds of pretending. There is a bad kind, where the pretence is there instead of the real thing; as when a man pretends he is going to help you instead of really helping you. But there is also a good kind, where the pretence leads up to the real thing. When you are not feeling particularly friendly but know you ought to be, the best thing you can do, very often, is to put on a friendly manner and behave as if you were a nicer person than you actually are. And in a few minutes, as we have all noticed, you will be really feeling friendlier than you were. Very often the only way to get a quality in reality is to start behaving as if you had it already.[31]

Matt's pretending is bad, for he has no interest in becoming genuinely respectful. Good pretending, by contrast, is undertaken in an effort to "put on" (in the rich Pauline sense) the real thing. Of course, we cannot stop at mere behavior change. But outward changes have a way of shaping the heart, and the perceptual view of emotions provides a plausible explanation of how this works. When we act as if our seven-year-old student struggling with her math has inherent dignity—say, by listening attentively and patiently to her explanation of how she got the answer she did, in the hopes of really understanding what isn't clicking for her, rather than simply trying to get her to say the right answer so we can get on with the rest of the lesson—the educational exchange takes on a respectful appearance to both teacher and student. In a way that parallels Douglass's Oval Office experience, by behaving as if the student were "big," both she and we find it more natural to see her bigness emotionally. In other words, treating others with dignity increases our sense of their dignity by making it salient to us.

While the cultivation of respectful manners can be an important first step in the cultivation of more robustly virtuous dispositions, communities that emphasize the importance of behavioral propriety and politeness run the risk of treating good manners as a substitute for more robustly virtuous character traits, which essentially include internal aspects of thought, emotion, and motivation. Thus, we would do well to supplement behavioral practices with contemplative ones.

Recall that appreciative understanding of the intellectual dignity and excellences of others, together with wisdom about how best to honor such worthiness, is central to the intellectual virtue of respect. It follows that deepening such understanding (wisdom) by contemplating the psychological structure of the virtue itself, together with the goods it is for and the vices opposed to it, can be an especially fruitful way to cultivate respect. This can be done by conducting a careful philosophical analysis (as we have tried to model and motivate in this chapter) or by fixing one's imaginative gaze upon virtuous exemplars and their vicious counterparts, whether real or fictional (say, by openheartedly reading an intellectual biography of someone like Abraham Lincoln). The underlying thought here is that, in some measure, we become what we behold. That is, by setting our minds (hearts) upon what is truly excellent, the object of our contemplation will tend to shape us in its image. (Two correlated warnings follow: we likely will not become what we do not behold; and less-than-excellent objects have heart-shaping power, too.)

The Christian will want to seek progress here by ruminating on relevant biblical material (for example, see the passages discussed above). By "meditating day and night" (Ps. 1) on both the intellectual features of God's image in all people and on God's use of the weak and foolish things of the world to shame the strong and the wise, we allow God's word to form in us a heartfelt appreciation for forms of intellectual dignity to which worldly eyes are often blind. And by repeatedly pondering Proverbs' guidance for intellectually respectful action and the Gospels' depictions of Christ's interactions with others, we invite Solomon's and Jesus's habits of mind to become our own.

The foregoing might be thought of as off-the-spot contemplative practices, since we engage in them independent of opportunities to practice intellectual respect directly (though one could, of course, demonstrate intellectual respect, or not, in the way one reads the Bible, or a biography, or this chapter). For those of us habituated to less-than-respectful patterns of action and perception, though, it will often be necessary to take the conceptual lenses we've endeavored to form via contemplative study and prayer (but which have not yet been fully integrated into our heart's default perceptual apparatus) and actively peer through them, seeking to correct our thoughts, emotions, and actions in situ by contemplating ourselves and our interlocutors on the spot, as it were. Some contexts of discourse call for special vigilance in this regard.

For better or worse, social media sites such as Facebook and Twitter have become primary avenues for public discourse on topics ranging from the trivial and inane to the timely and important. Unfortunately, these modern modes of communication are breeding grounds for disrespect. As we've seen, disseminating our ideas and listening to criticisms and opposing viewpoints in ways that befit our interlocutors' dignity are key aspects of intellectual respect. These are lost arts—and certain aspects of social media discourage us from reclaiming them. Such outlets are essentially platforms for self-publication, with no filter or editorial standards: we can write whatever we want, in whatever tone we want. And, because our audience is hidden behind a digital web, we can avoid the kind of interpersonal and social sanctions on disrespectful engagement that arise more naturally in face-to-face interactions. When we are in the physical presence of others, their apparent dignity naturally confronts us in a way that it does not when we view them through the lens of their profile pictures on our smart phone. For those with any sensitivity at all to others' intellectual dignity, this feature of face-to-face interactions serves as a built-in sanction against blatantly disrespectful behavior. The digital medium weakens this sanction. Additionally, in flesh-and-blood interactions, our interlocutors have the ability to correct us or offer opposing arguments. But in the virtual world of disembodied digital discourse, we can simply choose not to read their responses (a kind of willful anti-listening) or even forcefully silence them by "blocking" their posts from view.

In light of these temptations to disrespectfulness, social media can provide us with opportunities for on-the-spot contemplation aimed at cultivating intellectual respect. For starters, we can engage in a practice of watchfulness, in which we attend to our own patterns of thought, emotion, and action. We might ask ourselves questions like, "Are there certain people, or groups of people, whose intellectual worth I am inclined not to respect?" If the answer is yes, we must learn to repent—literally, to think again—in the moment of temptation. For instance, when we catch ourselves illicitly contemning another, or find our fingers furiously formulating an unnecessarily nasty reply before we've really had a chance to think, we pause. We breathe. And we look again with fresh eyes, this time actively seeking whatever intellectual goods might characterize the other.[32] Toward this end, we might form a habit of asking ourselves respect-driven questions like, "What can I learn from her?," "What intellectual virtues or skills does he have?," "Am I treating them as fellow divine image-bearers?," "How can I communicate my ideas in a way that better befits the intellectual worth of my audience?," and so on. It might also prove helpful to seek out opportunities to read books or articles (and, yes, even social media posts) by these people, or to talk with them (face to face, if possible!), being explicitly on the watch for insights to admire rather than mistakes to demolish. In this way, we actively resist the natural current of digital discourse (and of our own malformed hearts) by deliberately attending to the intellectual worthiness of others. Of course, such on-the-spot contemplation can be useful in other moral and intellectual settings as well. But for many people today (especially young people), social media platforms provide a particularly fecund context for contemplating and cultivating their character.

We've been treating the foregoing practices as activities for individuals. But they can also take on a social dimension as we seek to build communities of respect in direct defiance of the vice-conducive social trends noted above. For instance, institutions like the Bear Creek School in Redmond, WA, the Intellectual Virtues Academy in Long Beach, CA, and the Rosslyn Academy in Kenya have pioneered work in re-imagining curricula, classroom practices, syllabi, and institutional awards in ways that support and communicate intellectual respect (and other virtues).[33] Short of such large-scale institutional changes, small groups of teachers (or parents, or even Facebook friends) might take the time to think together about ways their discourse is insufficiently respectful, to brainstorm solutions, to encourage one another to act respectfully against the grain, and to hold one another accountable.

The church might have a special role to play here, living as a counterculture of respect in the midst of a society rife with disrespect (including disrespect for Jesus and his way). Together, as we endeavor to prize each person's dignity, honor each person's excellences, and humbly acknowledge, bear with, and address each person's shortcomings, we can serve as a city on a hill to a watching world—and to each other. That is, by living respectfully together, we can demonstrate for one another what it means to live respectfully and thereby mutually enhance one another's understanding of and capacity for respect. This is one reason Aristotle argued that friendships based on mutual admiration of character are schools of virtue.[34] As Talbot Brewer explains, even if it were possible for people to achieve something approaching the deep understanding and practical wisdom necessary for living virtuously on their own—that is, without witnessing the virtues lived out by others—such "Lone Ranger" understandings of the good life would be sorely lacking:

> They would be in the position of the accomplished ballet dancer who has never actually watched a ballet: they would lack full appreciation of the nature and point of the activity at which they excelled. (Though of course it strains credulity to imagine that there could be an accomplished dancer who had never seen others dance well, just as it strains credulity to imagine that anyone could become a consistently praiseworthy agent without having attended to, and developed an appreciation for, the way in which other praiseworthy persons navigate their changing circumstances.)[35]

In our day, it strains credulity to imagine a thoroughly respectful community. Nevertheless, even as we acknowledge the inevitability of faltering, with God's help, the church can—indeed, must—endeavor to be such.

Acknowledgments

We are grateful to Bob Roberts, as well as to audiences at Biola University, Grove City College, and l'Univeristé Catholique de l'Ouest, for their helpful feedback on previous drafts. Support for this work was funded in part by a grant from the Templeton Religion Trust. The opinions expressed in this article are the authors' own and do not necessarily reflect the views of the Templeton Religion Trust. Neither do the views expressed in this article necessarily reflect the official policy or position of the US Air Force, the US Department of Defense, or the US government.

Chapter 6

Humanity as Common Ground: Tolerance and Respect as Ideals in Communicative Discourse

Robert Audi
University of Notre Dame

The serious discourse needed for politics, education, and much of personal life is often marred by a failure to find common ground—which is a basis from which to reach agreement, or at least clarity, about where disagreement lies. This chapter takes our humanity itself to provide elements that constitute an important common ground. These elements include birth, growth, and success and failure in fulfilling one's aims, but there is much more. Common ground does not erase differences, but it provides a place from which mutual understanding and tolerance can grow. This chapter argues that certain ethical standards should be more widely recognized than they are in order to help us find our common ground, support tolerance and humility as virtues important for both public and private discourse, and enable us to deal civilly and rationally with much of the disagreement that is inevitable in a pluralistic democracy. It offers a partial account of both tolerance and humility, considers their bearing on disagreement, and offers some ethical principles that can contribute to achieving civic virtue.

Being human is no mere classification as it applies to you and me. The great monotheistic religions have taken our humanity to signify our being children of God; Kant's humanity formulation of the categorical imperative places humanity at the center of moral obligation; and any plausible set of ethics treats humanity as an important moral status. Humanity is a common ground among all the peoples of the world. That this commonality is morally important cannot be seriously denied. But just how is humanity morally important? And how should that affect our tolerance for disagreement and our conduct in civic discourse?

The Concept of Humanity

The concept of humanity is vague and likely does not admit of rigorous definition. Typical readers of this book are paradigms of human beings. They were such paradigms, I believe, even at birth; but there are borderline cases, such as anencephaly. It may also help to say that normal human beings are people, though this is not even an equivalence, much less a definition. Personhood may belong to very different kinds of beings and is widely taken to be instantiated by God. (Alvin Plantinga is among contemporary philosophers of religion who stress God's being a person.) We do not need a definition, since our concern will be met if the uncontroversially paradigmatic cases are the focus and our discussion is adequate to those.

Among the uncontroversial facts about human beings are that we experience birth, growth, development, language use, sociality, sickness, and death. This phenomenon is significant for ethics, law, public policy, and, of course, civic discourse. Consider Shylock's poignant speech:

> Hath not a Jew eyes? Hath not a Jew hands, organs, dimensions, senses, affections, passions; fed with the same food, hurt with the same weapons, subject to the same diseases, heal'd by the same means, warm'd and cool'd by the same winter and summer, as a Christian is? If you prick us, do we not bleed? If you tickle us, do we not laugh? If you poison us, do we not die? And if you wrong us, do we not revenge? If we are like you in the rest, we will resemble you in that.[1]

From the good and the bad we can see the right and the wrong. There is no doubt that value—or disvalue—is realized in the cases Shylock describes. We see in his words the human, the humane, and the inhumane. That it is a short step from the good and the bad to the right and the wrong does not, however, imply consequentialism in ethics. To say that bringing about the bad is prima facie wrong and bringing about the good is prima facie obligatory is not to commit oneself to the view that the only right actions are those optimizing the proportion of the good to the bad in the world—or even of some part of it that we can hope to know how to affect. Nonetheless, it is important for ethics—and is an aim of this chapter—to see how we human beings share in our capacity for both the good and the bad. This presupposes their bearing—and I think a necessary and major bearing—on what counts as right or wrong; but we can grant that without taking moral obligation to depend, as does consequentialism (as the term is usually understood) on maximizing intrinsic value; for instance the proportion of the non-morally good to the non-morally bad. (Consequentialist views in ethics usually derive obligation from considerations of non-moral value, since they seek to "measure" obligation without presupposing moral notions.)

Some Foundations of Ethics: Values, Principles, and Virtues

Civic discourse should be governed by sound ethical standards, but in daily life it cannot be achieved at a high level without civic virtue, which I take to be the virtue appropriate to citizens as such. This is not to say that only virtue ethics can guide civic discourse. Indeed, I propose to speak of values and principles with the idea that both intellectual and moral virtue are guided by them, and that, in the moral case, virtue may be taken to be, at least in good part, equivalent to an internalization of sound rules and a commitment to sound values. I begin with the hedonic values, which are important both normatively and, as central elements in human motivation, psychologically. It will be essential, however, to consider other values, including moral values not reducible to matters of pleasure and pain.

Pain and pleasure play highly prominent roles in the narrative of human development. Think of the guileless smile of a child. And who can forget the wailing of the bereaved mother in wartime? The good Samaritan must have had a deep sensitivity to such things:

> A priest happened to be going down the same road, and when he saw the man, he passed by on the other side. So too, a Levite, when he came to the place and saw him, passed by on the other side. But a Samaritan, as he traveled, came where the man was; and when he saw him, he took pity on him. He went to him and bandaged his wounds, pouring on oil and wine. Then he put the man on his own donkey, brought him to an inn and took care of him. The next day he took out two denarii and gave them to the innkeeper. "Look after him," he said, "and when I return, I will reimburse you for any extra expense you may have." (Luke 10:31–35)

Taking pleasure and pain as seriously as I am doing does not imply any commitment to hedonism. There are other rewards besides pleasure, and pain does not exhaust the negative in our experience. But both are elemental and important.

A natural path from the kinds of facts of human life I have sketched to an ethics strong enough to guide not only everyday interactions, but also civic discourse might be found by beginning with the common-sense intuitionist position of W. D. Ross. He certainly drew on Aristotle and other major philosophers, but he was doubtless also sensitive to the point, so vividly put by Hobbes, that outside human society, life would be "solitary, poor, nasty, brutish and short." Here is a summary of Ross's widely known list of "prima facie duties"—roughly, obligations that represent, overall, what one should do unless the relevant obligation is outweighed by one or more contrary obligations:

1. Justice: including the positive obligation to prevent and rectify injustice and the negative obligation to avoid the commission of injustice
2. Non-injury: roughly, the obligation to avoid harming others
3. Fidelity: promise-keeping
4. Veracity: an avoidance of lying—this obligation, like that of fidelity (under which Ross subsumed it), is a kind of fidelity to our word
5. Reparation: the obligation to make amends for wrongdoing
6. Beneficence: the obligation to contribute to virtue, knowledge, or pleasure in others
7. Self-improvement: the obligation to better oneself
8. Gratitude: the obligation to respond in an appropriately appreciative way to those who do good deeds toward us[2]

Only one comment is needed here.[3] We should surely take justice to entail treating people not only in accord with their merit (as Ross put it) but also equally, in some proportionate sense. Equal treatment is something to which people are sensitive even early in life. Take small children of the same age who are given visibly different portions of ice cream or a child who is not allowed to ride a tricycle that her peer is enjoying. The sense of unpleasantly unequal treatment begins in just such cases.

There are also, in my view, other Rossian elements—roughly, principles that are of the same a priori status and are apparently basic in guiding intuition and inference:

9. Preservation and enhancement of liberty
10. Obligations of manner (roughly, of respectfulness): these concern the way we do what is obligatory as opposed to what we must do (they are introduced and discussed in *The Good in the Right*)[4]

Moral virtues—at least most of them—may be viewed as an internalization of at least one of these ten principles, together with sufficient practical wisdom to apply the relevant principle(s) in complex situations. Here, "internalization" is not a historical term, and "internal realization" might be preferable, since the structural condition (rather than how the person acquires it) is what is crucial. As likely as it is that such principles figure in some way in the moral education of people who become virtuous, there is the abstract possibility that role modeling alone (or something like brain manipulation) can yield the relevant internal state, which then might issue in crucial and inferential behavior of a sort that indicates a kind of guidance by the principles or at least a disposition to believe them. Practical wisdom, however, is not possible without a degree of intellectual maturity; it requires a measure of insightfulness, good judgment, and human understanding. This alone indicates one dimension of intellectual virtue. Each of these is clearly an intellectual virtue in its own right.

A more specific element in people with intellectual virtue also bears directly on the Rossian principles, which are good candidates for self-evidence: I refer to intuition, a rational capacity that is present, in varying degrees, in all normal adult human beings.[5] Intuition is in part a receptivity to the self-evident. In normal human lives, the basic moral principles listed above are in some way taught, or at least formulated, and a person of intellectual virtue will tend to apprehend their truth. This is most easily seen if we substitute, for the semi-technical notion of a prima facie obligation, the notion of a moral reason for action. Who would deny—at least outside contexts of skepticism or a commitment to a controversial philosophical theory—that the principles identify some kind of moral reason for action? Suppose someone breaks a promise to us for a selfish reason—say mere convenience. Is there any doubt that there was some reason to keep the promise? The person's denying there was would normally be flatly rejected.

Here, I find it instructive to call attention to a perspective—call it the victim's point of view—not commonly brought into ethical discussions of this epistemological sort. Consider someone treated unequally relative to another person in a comparable situation, as with prison sentencing. Here I can speak from experience in talking with prisoners in a penitentiary. They resented inequality in terms served for the same crime, when the difference was due simply to skill in convincing the parole board of a prisoner's readiness to go free. A different case of unequal treatment is being given less opportunity than your peers to speak, a point that is crucial in conducting meetings in which civic discourse is needed.

Seeing a principle, however, is one thing; internalization is another, and motivation still another. We cannot simply assume that seeing moral truths yields assent or, especially, motivation to act accordingly, much less their integration into the fabric of character. But this integration is not uncommon, and it is not a hope unrealizable under favorable social conditions.

A Moral Framework for Tolerance and Respect for People

Rossian principles have an important kind of theoretical neutrality. They can be integrated with Kantian, utilitarian, or virtue-ethical positions. They also comport with major ethical standards in at least most of the world's major religions (including eastern religions).[6] Taking them to indicate moral reasons for action that is crucial for civic life begs no major questions.

It should be obvious how the principles I have been discussing are such that their internalization implies some measure of respect for people. That, in turn, tends to lead to tolerance, but this is not entailed, even though respect for people limits the kind and degree of intolerance possible for the person in question. Tolerance is, in any case, crucial for civic discourse in a democracy, and we should consider it in some detail. Its dimensions are both behavioral and intellectual.

To tolerate a person or action or thing implies disapproval, or at least dislike, and is, in part, to abstain from preventive actions, or certain kinds of discouragement, toward them. The tolerance may be behavioral. It is not just abstaining from interference; a casually interested but intolerant person could do that. It is at least abstaining from certain kinds of interferences despite a negative attitude toward, or at least a kind of dislike regarding, the person or other thing in question. Here, in relation to tolerance, "behavioral" applies to the intellectual domain and certainly to that of discourse: citizens in general must avoid dismissing unfamiliar or unconventional views out of hand. Civil opposition to what seems wrong is consistent with attitudinal tolerance toward it and behavioral toleration of it; but such manifestations of disapproval do not rise to suppression or other kinds of interferences.

Tolerance, then, has considerable moral complexity. It may be attitudinal as well as behavioral. It may be criticizable as an unduly negative attitude even where it is behaviorally justified. Suppose a student uses the expletive "like" excessively in a presentation. On some such occasions, an instructor should not interfere, thereby exhibiting behavioral tolerance. One might still have an unduly hostile attitude toward the student's using the expletive, however. This in itself might be an unreasonably negative response and could lead to criticizing the tendency more harshly than one should in speaking with colleagues about standards for presentations. The possibility of such unjustifiable expressions of a negative attitude does not imply that tolerance requires attitudinal neutrality or that it undermines efforts to dissuade; but, in some cases, forbearance may be best. Even apart from that, there is a kind of intellectual error in harboring a more negative attitude than what is tolerated deserves, whether one acts on it or not.

In framing standards for civic discourse, it is important to see that tolerance, either behavioral or attitudinal, may be justified or unjustified, and that even when it is justified in both dimensions, it may be expressed in ways inappropriate to civic (or other) discourse—say, in a manner that is condescending or too personal. It must achieve a mean between an excess constituted by unjustified interference or unwarranted criticism and a deficiency constituted by apathy regarding what should be changed. Here, religious practices, such as prohibiting women from playing certain clerical roles, may illustrate the point that there are good and bad ways to tolerate. First, consider toleration by religious authorities of protests against such prohibitions; toleration here may have the assuredness that can come from assuming divine intention. Consider also the opposing view of those who disapprove of the prohibitions. Here, we might find tolerance marked by disciplined forbearance from intervention, where the people in reference await hoped-for changes in attitudes. The former kind of tolerance may be regretful but condescending; the latter kind, especially on the part of third parties who seek to change policy by persuasion rather than force, might be felt by these protesters to be supportive.

If tolerance can achieve a mean between excess and deficiency in the suggested ways, that is reason to think that, when it is a trait of character and not a behavioral response, it is a virtue. It does not follow that every manifestation of a tolerant nature is virtuous. A good case can be made, however, for a kind of tolerance being a virtue, but not a moral virtue. Given the role of mere dislike in providing occasions for tolerance, an amoral person could be tolerant by transcending dislike. Tolerance is filtered through preferences in a way moral virtues are not. To be sure, a moral person can also be tolerant for non-moral reasons. Tolerance, then, need not imply virtue, and even toleration by someone having the virtue of tolerance need not be morally motivated.

There are other morally important traits that, because they do not essentially contain within themselves a commitment to moral standards, are not moral virtues. Consider courage and conscientiousness, which are in themselves good traits but (in a way not possible for, say, justice and veracity) can effectively serve immoral ends. I suggest that courage and conscientiousness and other traits be put in a distinct category. They are adjunctive virtues—adjunctive from the point of view of moral virtue, in the sense that they assist the person in realizing moral virtue but are not themselves moral virtues—in the way that virtues such as justice, fidelity, and veracity are. Without courage, for instance, one will not stand up well for one's moral standards under threat; and without conscientiousness, one may misapply or even forget those standards.

The Normativity of Tolerance as a Virtue

I want to begin this section with a contrast between aretaic and behavioral tolerance. If tolerance is like courage in being a virtue at all, then even if it is not moral, it is normative. Consider courage first. Being courageous requires making sound judgments in situations where different values conflict; say, self-protection on the one side (which is typically operative where courage is manifested) and, on the other side, the furtherance of a valued cause (such as with victory in battle). Such a tradeoff judgment can be normative even if it concerns balancing non-normative values. Courage is not, however, manifested merely by exhibiting bravery in habitually putting at risk, for the sake of something we care about, something else we care about. To risk one's life to save a toy sailboat that has fallen into rapids would be foolish. Plunging in might show "guts," but that is too close to a passional willingness to take risks to count as exhibiting either courage or, perhaps, any other kind of virtue. In situations calling for its exercise, tolerance as a virtue, as opposed to mere tolerance, is similarly governed by rough standards concerning the range of values in question.

It should be apparent, then, that tolerance conceived as a psychological disposition constituted by a suitably strong tendency to resist aversive impulses is very different from tolerance conceived as a trait of character governed by values of a certain kind. Moral values are crucial for understanding the virtue of tolerance, and in the political and civic realms, the freedom and the autonomy of people are central values to be preserved and honored. Valuing these—having positive valuations toward them—is particularly important in political and religious matters. Civic virtue would seem to have a measure of tolerance—even, perhaps, a measure of the virtue of tolerance—as a necessary element. Tolerance is most needed when people exercise rights of liberty and self-government in ways that evoke disapproval or dislike among others. These cases are among the most characteristic of those calling for civic virtue.

With these points in mind, suppose that a citizen is not only tolerant by disposition but has the virtue of tolerance. Suppose further that a person with this virtue has a principled tolerance, where the guiding principles are the set of self-evident Rossian common-sense ones described above. Self-evidence runs out when prima facie principles conflict, as they often do, and in this case, the issue is final judgment. From the point of view of the police, for instance, it may be self-evident that there is some obligation not to interfere with a noisy protest (since one would harm people), but it may not be self-evident that this obligation outweighs the promissory obligation to protect neighborhood homes. This point about conflicting prima facie obligations applies to intellectual as well as practical matters, such as how to determine final duty in individual matters and in law and public policy.

In cases like this, another adjunctive virtue may lead to both greater social harmony and better moral decisions: humility. Humility finds a mean between such excesses as boastfulness and inflated self-appraisal and, on the other hand, the deficiency indicated by timid lack of conviction or unreasonable self-deprecation. It does not carry any specific moral standard, but it assists its possessors morally by, for one thing, increasing the disposition to review one's decisions for error and to interact open-mindedly with those who bring a different perspective to a situation calling for action. In the case just cited, police who have due humility might consult with civic leaders both before and during a protest, and they might avoid being self-righteous in dealing with a protest or its aftermath.

Aretaic tolerance, which is strengthened by humility and arguably requires some measure of it, is not only a moral virtue governing behavior but also counts toward intellectual virtue and, when well-developed, may perhaps constitute one. This is in part because judgment is required to determine what to oppose and what to tolerate. That, in turn, will require both normative appraisal as well as assessing evidence and weighing probable consequences. One occasion for tolerance is judging that the evidence of a wrongdoing is insufficient; another is the humble judgment that a problem is beyond one's capacity. Here, humility supports tolerance whether or not the tolerance in question embodies the kind of reflective humility that contributes to its candidacy for intellectual virtue.

Disagreement and Intellectual Humility

Tolerance is important in both intellectual matters, where no moral issue is in question, and in political life. Tolerance has an intellectual side that bears on how one views disagreements, such as those inevitable in political matters. One way to focus this is to consider what has come to be called peer disagreement, the kind that occurs regarding some proposition, p, when the disputants (a) have the same relevant evidence regarding p, (b) are equally rational in the ability to assess the relevant evidence in relation to p, and (c) do so equally conscientiously (and this may not be conscientiously at all—the degree is what matters here).

Could there be rational peer disagreement on even a self-evident proposition? And if there is such disagreement, should the party who is in the right still be humble regarding the proposition? One might wonder here whether humility and a full responsiveness to self-evident moral principles are incompatible aspirations. In fact, however, there have been rational disagreements that might be argued to exhibit epistemic parity over the Rossian principles.[7] In the light of those, I take it that humility is possible and sometimes needed, even in proposing or defending something self-evident.

As required in the intellectual domain, humility has many dimensions. One is cognitive: one should not have an inflated (i.e., an unreasonably positive) view of one's own justification or credibility. Another is behavioral: one should not be boastful. A third concerns dispositions to believe and to behave: a normal human being with the virtue of humility should be strongly disposed to believe propositions to the effect that (1) one is not perfect and is, indeed, fallible in some important matters; (2) one has not achieved his or her accomplishments entirely on one's own (as Aquinas emphasized); and (3) others may have or may develop some of the merits that one attributes to oneself.[8] Similarly, such a person should be strongly disposed to (a) hear others out in matters of (civilized) disagreement, (b) discuss with others the merits of a proposition on which they disagree, and (c) respectfully offer reasons for one's views on which others disagree. These are rough necessary conditions and are not sufficient without qualifications.

Toleration and Rational Disagreement

The question of what to tolerate and how best to do so commonly arises when those facing it are considering people they do not regard as equally reasonable on the matters about which they differ. But suppose all the parties are fully rational. Surely the ethics of citizenship in a pluralistic democracy must take account not only of actual disagreement between citizens who may or may not be equally rational, but also of the possibility of fully rational disagreement between epistemic peers relative to the matter in question. Rational disagreement between epistemic peers can occur not just inter-religiously—among people who differ in religion (or among those who are and are not religious)—but also intra-religiously, as with people in different Christian denominations. If we think that a disagreement is with an epistemic peer and we wish to retain our position, we should try to find new evidence for it or at least to discover a basis for thinking the disputant is not as rational or as conscientious as we are in appraising the issue. But there may be times when the most reasonable conclusion is that there is epistemic parity between us and, for that reason, the disagreement cannot be readily resolved in one's favor—if it can be resolved at all. This may seem to many conscientious citizens to be how things stand on the permissibility of assisted suicide, capital punishment, or abortion.

We can gain understanding here if we ask what the appropriate response is to a persisting disagreement with an apparent epistemic peer. One response is skepticism, concluding that neither party has knowledge or even justification. There could, however, be a difference in the disputants' purported justifications, which neither can discover. This is a common phenomenon. But should we always suppose both that this is so and that our own view is rationally preferable to that of an apparent epistemic peer? I suggest not.

A quite different response to persisting disagreement is the kind of humility that goes with respectful disagreement. Minimally, we might conclude that we might be mistaken, or at least less justified than our peer, for holding a contrary position. Humility is a response with major implications for law, public policy, and even civic discourse. It tends to prevent (though it need not always prevent) taking one's view as a basis for establishing coercive laws or public policies. In that way, it gives some support to the idea that in sound democracies, liberty is the default position: the preferred position when there is not a cogent reason for coercion. With all this in mind, I propose the following principle of toleration: if it is not reasonable for proponents of coercion in a given matter to consider themselves epistemically superior in that matter to supporters of the corresponding liberty, then in that matter, the former have a prima facie obligation to tolerate rather than coerce.[9]

The idea underlying this principle applies to institutional as well as individual acts. Imagine two academic departments arguing over their proper role in the curriculum. To simplify, imagine just two departments, *A* and *B*, where *A* has power over *B* and is considering forcing *B* to do something. The principle implies, on plausible assumptions, that *A*'s justification for coercing *B* to do it for reason(s) *R* decreases with any increase in the strength of the evidence for the parity of *A* and *B* regarding their disagreement on whether *R* constitutes adequate reason to require *B* to do the thing in question.

A number of clarifications are needed here. First, it should be clear that this principle is supported, as are other elements in my view, by considerations of reciprocity. The proposed principle of rational disagreement is certainly in the spirit of "do unto others." Suppose we are averse to doing something that we are urged by our employer to do, such as serve as a caterer for a political gathering organized by the American gun lobby. It is personally objectionable to us, but we are given a plausible argument for compliance, though not one so convincing that it eliminates our hesitation. In cases like this, we can acquiesce in having to do it if we see that we would approve of coercion of someone else in the same manner were the political meeting organized by a group we approve of. A second consideration is whether the argument comes from someone we consider epistemically on a par with us in the matter. Humility may incline us to view someone in this way. In such cases, we would often realize that we would expect the same response as the one we gave, whereas we would tend to resent being pressured or forced to do the required things given the same kind of argument from someone we consider unreasonable or significantly less informed than we are in the matter. But where a requirement comes from someone we consider an epistemic peer in the matter, tolerance of what we dislike comes more easily and may have little effect on our conduct. Humility is especially relevant here: intellectual humility tends to lower the threshold for considering someone we disagree with to be an epistemic peer.

A third point is that abiding by the rational disagreement principle may require some sophistication. It does not, I think, require more than is possessed by a competent high school graduate in many educationally "advanced" countries. I assume, to be sure, that it can be taught with concrete examples and not just as an abstract standard. The principle also helps nourish a kind of humility and respect for others' views that is a desirable element in democratic societies of any kind.

Fourth, I have not specified how weak the justification for coercion becomes as the case for parity becomes stronger. If the case is conclusive—though that would be, at best, rare—I suggest that the obligation to tolerate becomes overriding. This is in good part because the justification for coercion in a given instance approaches zero as the strength of the case for epistemic parity among disputants—over whether the relevant coercion in that instance is warranted—approaches conclusiveness. This point seems to hold in interpersonal relations generally, but I also take it to apply to governmental matters arising in democratic societies. The principle thus clarifies the sense in which liberty is the default position in a sound democracy.

It must be granted that, in practice, the principle of toleration can easily be abused. The value of the principle in the life of a democracy depends on the conscientiousness of those with the power and inclination to coerce. The kind of conscientiousness in question is related to humility: the less of it, the less likely conscientiousness is about the principle of toleration. If unconscientious, those with power would readily think it reasonable to take defenders of the liberty in question to be less than epistemic peers in the relevant matter. If conscientious, they would tend to resist this view if there was any serious question at all about who is right. Indeed, highly conscientious government officials—or virtually any conscientious, rational, and tolerant person with coercive power over others—will, if unopposed by actual disputants, try to think of the best hypothetical defense they can construct in favor of the liberty they would restrict or eliminate. The appeal to hypotheticals is particularly appropriate for judges. Given how unpredictable the future is, judges are often quite right to extend the principle to such cases. A conscientious search for the kind of justification needed for coercion does not necessarily conclude when the best counterarguments actually given are decisive. We should not coerce—and are generally averse to being coerced—even when there is a discernible prospect of finding decisive counterarguments. Good ethics requires exploring not just the evidence presented but also relevant hypothetical cases.

Some Pathways to Common Ground

There are both top-down and bottom-up approaches to seeking common ground. These are just metaphors, of course, but they can be quite useful given adequate clarification. Both are important for civic discourse, but they are also important in moral education beginning in childhood. It may suffice here to say just this: a top-down approach is dominated by central, and usually initial, stress on principles or rules. We have to state rules in bringing up children, and we have to teach principles in many academic fields and in guiding those we are responsible for. A top-down approach need not be dogmatic, but heavy reliance on it tends to produce pronouncements easily felt to be dogmatic. By contrast, a bottom-up approach begins with examples or narratives and guides behavior by saying or implying something like "go and do likewise." Such an approach may leave generalizations implicit, but insofar as it takes the mind "upward," it is often accompanied by formulations of a general character.

To see the bearing here of intuitionism and the associated common-sense morality, take Rossian generalizations as a case in point. They can be stated in simple terms—say, in telling children that lying is wrong and that one should share toys with other children (something that can be illustrative of both beneficence and of equal treatment of others and oneself, as justice requires). But they can also be taught by role-modeling that is accompanied by positive comments, such as when one offers to share food with a dinner companion. Ross rightly thought that in normal human development, we do not even understand the general principles until we experience instances, but he, of course, thought that the moral philosopher may, in representing the standards of ethics, proceed in good part from the top down.

In contrast with Ross, Kant (viewed in a way he invites) is a top-down theorist.[10] One way to see that neither a starkly top-down nor an anti-theoretical bottom-up approach is sufficient in either education of civic discourse is to note that even the self-evident is disbelievable. There is, at the "top," nothing, or virtually nothing, substantive (as opposed to formal) that is both an adequate guide to human life and is not subject to some objection that has some plausibility of is at least not irrational objection. Top-down approaches are inadvisable where there is not antecedent agreement on the relevant principles. Here, virtues, as well as examples, may be easier to appeal to. Virtues may perhaps be conceived of as mid-level standards: if you urge me to be tolerant, you are neither stating a principle nor giving an example; rather, you are pointing both to general patterns I should approximate and evoking the sense of representative cases. If I ask you to explain, your response may go up or down or in both directions.

In the light of the possibility of an approach that allows recognition of the merits of both top-down and bottom-up strategies in ethics, it will help cite one mid-level principle of civic virtue that I have long defended:

* * *

The principle of secular rationale (PSR) or, alternatively, the principle of natural reason: citizens in a democracy have a *prima facie* obligation not to advocate or support any law or public policy that restricts human conduct, unless they have, and are willing to offer, adequate secular reason for this advocacy or support (e.g., for a vote).[11]

Note two important points about this principle. First, it provides for religious reasons to be considered relevant and does not even imply that they are epistemically inferior to secular reasons. Second, the focus is on prima facie obligations rather than on rights. This principle, despite its requirement of secular reasons—which might equally well be called natural reasons—is strongly accommodationist regarding religion. This is not the place to defend it. I mention it as a stimulus to exercising intellectual virtue: good judgment is required both to determine when a reason is or is not epistemically dependent on theology or religion and to ascertain when a reason is adequate. The felt need to do this also provides an occasion for humility and tolerance. The principle is not, to be sure, directed toward discourse as such, and it does not restrict freedom of speech; but most contexts of advocacy or support of coercive laws or public policies interpersonal and require discourse—and often public discourse marked by disagreement.

Anyone internalizing the set of principles I have presented as guides to civic virtue can see that they support respect for rational disputants and even concessiveness—at least of the higher-order kind that goes with intellectual humility. One can admit both fallibility and a need for further evidence even if one does not abandon or qualify one's position. There is also the possibility of seeking common ground by finding shared assumptions or agreement in practice on what should be done, even if one's reasons are different or incompatible. Where disagreement is extensive or heated but held in check by the kinds of virtues I have described, humility and tolerance will encourage expressions of gratitude wherever they are appropriate to acknowledge effort on the other side.

There is a strategy that can be used fruitfully in civic discourse, provided it is used with great discretion. It is leveraging by reasons, as distinct from arguing from them, which presupposes believing the propositions that express them (in a sense, implying that one represents oneself as believing them). Here, one seeks common ground by providing a path to agreement from reasons that are not one's own (where the reason-expressing propositions in question are either withheld or disbelieved) but that belong to the opposition's perspective. With a combination of intellectual acuity and respect for others, one can determine what a disputant is committed to that supports or might support what one is trying to convince the other to accept. I might say, for example, that I believe you hold that p, q, and r, and that these can be seen to support my view. To be sure, it is manipulative to twist a person's view in a way that yields a similar result by evoking assent to premises where the other should not give it. It is also deceitful to assert the relevant premises as if one endorsed them when one does not. But leveraging does not imply these things.

Leveraging may also occur in a weaker form: one takes a reason to be good, holding both the proposition expressing the reason and the view for which one offers it as support, but is motivated to hold or act on the view only by some other reason. This is probably not uncommon where one is citing reasons drawn from someone else's point of view in an effort to get the other party to join them in a position or action they support. We can attribute evidential adequacy to considerations without taking them into our perspective as motivators along with our own reasons. This, like non-concurring leveraging, can be, but need not be, manipulative. Used by a person of civic virtue, it will normally not be manipulative but be a way of finding common ground by getting inside the perspective of the other person and reasoning from there. Properly used, it is a good adjunct to the kind of civilized attempts to change belief or behavior that go with democratic discussion.[12]

Civic Voice as an Element in Discourse and Ethical Character

Before concluding, I should emphasize that I have been considering civic discourse in the context of democracies that are not only constitutional (rather than merely procedural) but also morally constituted. Pure proceduralism, by contrast, is strongly majoritarian and takes a law to be legitimate if a majority of citizens freely votes for it. Constitutionality is a constraint on proceduralism: a democratic constitutional society permits amendment, but I take it to require a vote by a super majority or some other procedure that goes beyond mere majority vote. Moral constitution is different: it requires that elusive status of legitimacy and presupposes sound notions of liberty and basic political equality as default standards. It does not require that these be embodied in a constitution, but they must have a certain active role in the political life of the society in question. Some of what is needed may be specified in a bill of rights, but the moral constitution of a democracy does not require a written list of these. Detailed explication of such notions would require a treatise in political philosophy, but the rough ideas suggested here suffice for this chapter.

An element in civic virtue that is important for a morally sound democracy is what I call civic voice. Let me explain the idea in the context of the kinds of ideals of toleration that I have proposed. The desirability of having adequate natural (secular) reasons and motivation—motivation expressible in terms of natural reasons—for coercion of others is related to the desirability of having a way to voice one's political aims. To understand voicing, we should make a distinction that conscientious citizens (among others) should observe: a distinction between what we say to others and what we communicate to them. What we communicate often goes beyond what we say and is heavily dependent on our voice. We speak with different voices on different occasions, to different audiences, and for different purposes. A soft voice may be soothing, but it may also conceal suppression of anger; uttering someone's full name—all forenames and last name in a row—can express delight at their arriving after a long trip, surprise at their apparent perversity, or indignation at their proposal. Even when quite different voices carry the same content, they can express mere repetition of someone else's view, a conviction of one's own, a suggestion delicately floated, or a detachment that leaves the hearer wondering where the speaker stands. It is largely the causal basis of our affirmations, including (and especially) our motivation, and not the content of what we say, that yields our voice. Our voice is determined far more by why and how we say what we do than by the content of what we say.

In my view, cultivation of a civic voice is not only an element in well-developed civic virtue; it is also an aspect of following the commandment to love our neighbors in our lives as citizens. One element in civic virtue consists in having and using an appropriate civic voice. It may be called for in a small discussion or in public discourse. It conduces to civic harmony in pluralistic democracies. It is a natural expression of a degree of humility and a support of tolerance. If enough citizens use a civic voice in debating issues of importance, especially fundamental issues such as abortion, assisted suicide, and vouchers for private education, then civic harmony will gain important support. Being genuinely motivated by the reasons we offer, religious or secular, conduces to sincerity. The perception of such motivation—which careful listeners and readers will often have—conduces to the expectation that one's deeds will accord with one's words. Sincerity is an important element in a civic voice; without it, there is unlikely to be the expectation that people's deeds will adequately conform with their words—which is something democracy depends on.

The kind of ethics and political philosophy proposed here is an integration of principles, virtues, and intuitions. In a way, I have proceeded from common grounds to common ground; in another way, which is more nearly top-down, I have proceeded from potentially common grounds—as self-evident truths are for those who can understand them—to actually common grounds. But I have emphasized that the recognition of self-evident moral truths does not invite dogmatism in affirming them. Indeed, I have argued for humility and tolerance and even for steadfastly maintaining a commitment to the liberty and equality that is central to the flourishing of democracy. Neither notion is without vagueness, and practical wisdom is needed for determining their proper limits in daily life. It is also needed for a judicious observance of the principle of secular rationale and other such principles aimed at anchoring law-making in reasons that are, or readily can be, rooted in common ground. Pluralism and disagreement are inevitable in the contemporary world, and both strain the tolerance of some for the liberty of others. The principles of toleration and justification of public policy that I have proposed, and the civic voicing I have emphasized, are intended to contribute to the strength of democracy where it exists now and to its growth where it is yet to come.

Chapter 7

The Virtues of Pride and Humility: A Survey

Robert C. Roberts
Baylor University (Emeritus)

On questions about the ethics and epistemology of humility and pride, philosophers have often divided into pro-pride and pro-humility factions, both sides regarding pride and humility as mutually exclusive.[1] For example, Tara Smith of the pride faction comments,

> If humility were a virtue, it would instruct a person to root out any stirrings of pride. Thus, to the extent that a person was proud, he would not be humble. The two traits cannot peacefully coexist *as virtues*.[2]

Or take this quote from David Hume:

> It is impossible a man can at the same time be both proud and humble.[3]

Or this from Richard Taylor:

> Pride is quite correctly perceived to be incompatible with . . . the supposed virtue of humility that is so congenial to the devout mind and so foreign to the pagan temperament.[4]

And here is the devout Gregory the Great, of the humility faction:

> Pride is the commander of the army of the devil . . . , the queen of the vices . . . , the root of all evil.[5]

And Jonathan Edwards:

> There will be no pride in heaven. . . . Though all are perfectly free from pride yet, as some will have greater degrees of divine knowledge than others, and larger capacities to see more of the divine perfections, so

> they will see more of their own comparative littleness and nothingness, and therefore will be lowest and most abased in humility.[6]

The result of this dividing attitude is that the opposing partisans tend to talk past one another, and members of each faction prevent themselves from appreciating an important aspect of the life of virtue. They also forfeit the opportunity to enrich and refine the account of their favored virtue by attempting to understand it alongside its virtue counterpart.

Note that in Jesus's teaching about humility, the language of paradox works both ways: whoever exalts himself is humbled, and whoever humbles himself is exalted. Thus Jesus seems to endorse both humility and a certain kind of exaltation. Happy awareness of being exalted would seem to be in the neighborhood of pride. Disciples should aspire both to humility and to the corresponding kind of exaltation (see Matt. 18:4, 23:12, Luke 9:46–48, 14:11, Mark 9:33–35, and John 5:44). This chapter will attempt to delineate such a pride, as well as the virtuous humility that coexists with it and supports it. Søren Kierkegaard perhaps reflects this teaching of Jesus when he says,

> Never has a human being lifted his head as proudly in elevation over the world as did the first Christians in humility before God! . . . No, proud as they were in their humility before God, they said, "It is not for us to hang back and dawdle along the way; we do not stop—until eternity."[7]

Their humility enables them to worship, obey, rejoice in their creatureliness, and be authentically thankful, while their pride makes them eager and confident and secure in their agency to take on the tasks God has assigned them.

I think we can make some headway in reconciling the factions by letting a more specific vocabulary guide our investigations. In English, we have a rich vocabulary for the vicious traits and attitudes that are plausibly lumped together as pride and a less developed vocabulary for the virtues that may be called pride. We also have a somewhat less rich vocabulary for the vicious or dysfunctional traits and attitudes that might fall under humility (and, in fact, are lumped together by members of the pro-pride faction). Thus we might speak of both the vices and virtues of pride and the vices and virtues of humility. Here, I explore such a strategy of conceptual reconciliation. I doubt such conceptual finesse will resolve all differences; the metaphysical differences between

Aristotle and the New Testament, for example, prevent total reconciliation. But I do think we can greatly broaden the amount of agreement. A detailed exploration of all the virtues and vices shown in table on the next page would require book-length treatment, so this chapter can go into only some detail and with only a small selection.

I offer a rough introduction to relevant vocabulary in the accompanying Table of Vices and Virtues of Pride and Humility.

My thesis is that, to each of the distinct vices of pride, a distinct virtue of humility corresponds, which consists in the absence of the vice of pride; and that to each of the distinct virtues of pride corresponds a distinct vice of humility that is *not* just the absence of the corresponding virtue, but a positive dysfunctional emotional conception of oneself. In the most mature cases, each virtue of pride is a *submerged interested dispositional self-construal.*[8] I have tried, probably with incomplete success, to give the rows modal consistency; for example, domination and the corresponding kind of humility, timidity, and the corresponding virtue of personal authority all seem to be traits related to one another as belonging to the subject's interpersonal style of dominance-submission interaction. My lexical division of the conceptual territory here is, no doubt, disputable in its details, and refining it may take nothing less than working out the analysis of each of the displayed virtues and vices, along with others that I may have neglected here. In English, we use the language covering pride and humility, virtuous and vicious, with some elasticity, and individuals may differ in their semantic intuitions. I don't mean to insist on the details of this particular table, but I do think something like this one is needed for elucidating pride and humility. The table is only a rough indication of the geography of humility-pride, and as such, it leaves unindicated many of the conceptual relations.

Some may want to construe the table in terms of Aristotelian means. On such a construal, vicious pride might be too much self-exaltation and vicious humility too little of the same, and both the virtue of pride and the virtue of humility would be just the right amount of self-exaltation, neither too much nor too little. One possible objection to doing this might be that virtuous pride and virtuous humility end up being the same trait, which goes against our feeling that they are different, even if they're both virtues and both about an issue in the neighborhood of self-exaltation. I think the objection is right, but it is true that some of the kinds of pride are very closely related to the corresponding virtuous

Table 1: The Virtues and Vices of Humility and Pride

	Vices of Pride	Virtues of Humility	Vices of Humility	Virtues of Pride
Value of Self	Conceit	Humility	Deep shame	Self-respect
Beheld Importance of Self	Vanity	Unvanity	Social insecurity	Self-confidence
Social Self-Assertion	Pretentiousness	Unpretentiousness	Glory intolerance	Independence
Entitlement-Claiming	Arrogance	Unarrogance	Servility	Entitlement serenity
Social Dimension of Self-Making	Hyper-autonomy	Humility	Defeatist lethargy	Secure agency
Control of Others, Leadership	Domination	Humility	Timidity	Personal authority
Moral Rectitude	Self-righteousness	Un-self-righteousness	Self-flagellation	Being in Christ
Comparative Excellence	Invidious pride	Humility	Envy	Sense of dignity
Value of Associates	Snobbery	Unsnobbishness	Shame of associates	Pride in associates
Standards of Work	Conceit	Humility	Slovenliness	Pride in one's work
Others' Control, Leadership	Refractoriness	Agreeableness	Obsequiousness	Independence
Ambition	Grandiosity	Humility	Pusillanimity	Aspiration

humilities. My general strategy is to construe them as supporting one another rather than as being identical. Another objection to using the concept of the mean is that its quantitative conception of what makes a modality virtuous or vicious is inadequate to the realities, which require a qualitative treatment. A chief example is the relation between self-importance and importance as a person, which cannot be explained as places on a continuum.[9]

The Vices of Pride and the Virtues of Humility

In his *Nicomachean Ethics*, Aristotle describes a character type that he designates "great-souled" or "large-minded." Some translations render *megalopsychos* (Latinized "magnanimous") as "proud." Aristotle's description of this person is, for those of us who are heirs to the Christian tradition, one of the most counterintuitive in his great book. The megalopsychos exemplifies all the virtues to the highest extent and fully appreciates that his personal excellence entitles him to be highly honored by others. Aristotle tells us that

> He will feel (*hēsthēsetai*) he is receiving only what belongs to him, or even less, for no honor can be adequate to the merits of perfect virtue, yet all the same he will deign to accept [his admirers'] honors, because they have no greater tribute to offer him. Honor rendered by common people and on trivial grounds he will utterly despise (*oligōrēsei*), for this is not what he merits.[10]

Conceit

The megalopsychos appears here to measure carefully the honor that others bestow on him, by reference to the standard of his own excellence and merit, and to find it generally inadequate; he will, however, accept honor that comes from people he deems good judges of his excellence, since they have nothing more fitting to offer him. But he has only contempt for the accolades of "common people."

Imagine common people who have a vague sense of being in the presence of something great, but whose understanding is dim and whose praises are awkward and naïve. I think we feel that the megalopsychos is colossally ungenerous in treating them with contempt and that his ungenerosity comes from his preoccupation with his own merit and associated sense of entitlement. Instead of focusing with appreciation on the good (if underqualified) hearts of his admirers and ignoring the awkwardness of their praises as much as possible, he focuses sharply on his own desert and judges those hearts abysmally insufficient to the purpose.[11]

We want to say to him, "Look, Big Soul, you are awesomely virtuous all right, but it's not all about you! Can't you turn a bit of appreciation on others?" The great-minded man's preoccupation with himself and his merit seem to blind him to the glories of others, and so to betoken small-mindedness, a constriction of his attention and appreciation that sullies and diminishes his real virtues. We think he misses a lot in life because of his self-preoccupation. His glory blinds him to the excellence and humanity of others.

We want to encourage him to look away from himself, to look up and out so that he can see others more clearly and sympathetically. The self-inattention or self-unconcern that we have in mind can be called humility, and it stands in contrast with the vice of pride that we call conceit (for insofar as he takes himself to be entitled to hold others in contempt because of his greatness, he is also arrogant). The great-minded person who is humble may know as well as anybody that he's more virtuous than others, but he isn't preoccupied with this knowledge (and doesn't illicitly infer entitlements from it). He finds other things more interesting, more worthy of his attention. This case illustrates that the vice of conceit doesn't require that the conceited one err in evaluating himself. His vice consists in his preoccupation with his excellence—his interest in his excellence making him important to the exclusion of proper attention to others or causing what attention he does give to be contempt of others.[12] (It is true, though, that by our lights, in his preoccupation with his excellences, he fails to appreciate the defect that that very preoccupation constitutes.)

Aristotle also tells us that the megalopsychos is a man "for whom nothing is great."[13] This is because his own glory is, to him, so overpowering that the greatness of all else fades to insignificance. If anything in the world is wonderful, then his preoccupation with his own glory will hamper him intellectually, because it will disable him for appreciating that wonderfulness. Despite Aristotle's approving presentation of the great-souled man, apparently he is not Aristotle, because in his treatise on *The Generation of Animals*, Aristotle warns young scientists not to underestimate the glory of even the humblest of animals:

> We must . . . not let ourselves succumb to childish repugnance for the investigation of the less noble animals, for there is something wonderful in all the works of Nature. We must recall the words they say were spoken by Heraclitus to some foreign visitors who, on the point of entering, stopped when they saw him warming himself in front of his stove: he urged them to enter without fear, saying that there were gods there as well.[14] Likewise, we must approach the inquiry concerning each animal with the belief that there is something natural and beautiful in each one.[15]

This passage seems to express the wonder that Aristotle is well known to have said is the beginning of philosophy. The "openness" to see the wonderfulness of insects and worms requires a kind of transparency of vision—a vision of the heart—that is astigmatized by preoccupation with one's own importance or glory. Think of the scientist who, in observing the wonders of her specimens, is always preoccupied with her scientific reputation, with being the first to discover this or that, with the concern that such-and-such animal or animal part will be named after her or that she will receive some prestigious prize for her discovery.[16]

In addition to its other demerits, conceit is a kind of intellectual astigmatism. Astigmatism is an irregularity in the curvature of the cornea or lens of the eye such that rays of light striking it from a luminous object don't converge neatly at any one point on the retina, but scatter somewhat, producing a confused image. The *Oxford English Dictionary* cites a figurative use, a "mental astigmatism [that] was not noticed while the fires of great genius flamed high."[17] We can well imagine that the distortion of insight brought on by conceit might go unnoticed when the powers of intellect are great, and that they might become evident only later, perhaps in the midst of anomalies and objections to the genius's claims—claims motivated perhaps by overconfidence or self-serving bias. The metaphorical application of this phenomenon in virtue epistemology is that the preoccupation with self-importance that characterizes the vices of pride creates a blurring or dispersion of the cognition of the object under examination. For example, confronted with the wonders of the physiology of some worm species, my preoccupation with the credit that I got or will or won't get for my discovery might cause the vagrant light of my own imagined glory falling on the retina of my soul to confuse my appreciation of the worm's glory.

Domination and Hyper-Autonomy

The great-souled preoccupation with self also shows itself in matters of helping and being helped.

> [The great souled one] is fond of conferring benefits, but ashamed to receive them, because the former is a mark of superiority and the latter of inferiority. He returns a service done to him with interest, since this will put the original benefactor into his debt in turn, and make him the party benefited. The great-souled are thought to have a good memory for any benefit they have conferred, but a bad memory for those they have received (since the recipient of a benefit is the inferior of his benefactor, whereas they desire to be superior); and to enjoy being reminded of the former but to dislike being reminded of the latter.[18]

In the context of exchanging favors, the disposition to compare himself with others transforms the exchange, in the megalopsychos's mind, into a rivalry for superiority, a jockeying for dominance. Seneca the Stoic says, "The rule for a favor between two people is this: the one should promptly forget that he did it; the other should never forget that he received it."[19] In contrast, the megalopsychos long remembers what he has given and quickly forgets what he has received by others' grace. He feels others' generosity to him as an assault on his personal importance, which he can fend off only by an assault (as he sees it) on theirs. Christians will consider this disposition to rivalry a vice, but for Aristotle, it is apparently compatible with virtue. I call this vice of pride "hyper-autonomy," insofar as it's an insistence on being self-made and not dependent on others, and I call it "domination" to the extent that it's an interest in building yourself up by making others dependent on you. As for involving distortion of memory, these vices are also intellectual vices, and their absence, which is a kind of humility, is an intellectual virtue.

Grandiosity

We might think of grandiosity as an exaggerated seeking of your own excellence, of thinking yourself capable of greatness that you are not capable of; while pusillanimity is the under-seeking of your own excellence. The corresponding humility would be the neither exaggerated nor under-seeking of your own excellence, and the virtue of pride that I call aspiration (see Table 1) would be the same as humility, perhaps differentiated by being thought of with a different contrasting case.[20]

But this will not do. If grandiosity is supposed to be a vice of pride, then the mere exaggerated seeking of your own excellence isn't grandiosity. You might, merely by mistake, seek an excellence for yourself that is in fact beyond you; indeed, you might do so while exhibiting the virtue of aspiration, if you do so out of a pure desire for excellence and with no non-instrumental motive of making yourself important. For example, you might aspire to play the guitar better than John Williams out of a sheer desire to make beautiful music, where this is utterly beyond your talents. Perhaps, in some sense, you are grandiose in this, but your grandiosity will not count as a vice of pride. On the other hand, if you aspire to this level of performance with a non-instrumental desire of making yourself more important than (or just as important as) John Williams, then your grandiosity is a vice of pride. It qualifies as such not simply in virtue of its exaggerating your capacities but in virtue of the reason for which you overreach.

In fact, you might exhibit something like grandiosity without actually overreaching. Let's say that you are in fact a raw talent who could be the next John Williams, but you come from a backwoods community where playing music like Williams is beyond anybody's fondest dream. (No one's even heard of Williams.) You dream, instead, of playing better than Mops Moseley, who is legendary in your Appalachian valley as the all-time greatest. According to local lore, it's utterly impossible to be better than Mops, who is regarded as the beneficiary of a unique divine gift to which no rational person could aspire. Nevertheless, you aspire to best him, to usurp the position of Appalachian demi-god that he currently enjoys, and you are in fact talented enough to make good on this aspiration. So despite not overreaching for excellence, you suffer from a vice of pride motivationally similar to grandiosity. It is certainly in the spirit of grandiosity, psychologically indistinguishable from it, prescinding from historical context. On the other hand, if you had equally high musical aspirations—for the sake of the music—you might still count spiritually as humble, despite your high ambitions. Again, we see that the reason for the desire or action—a love of music or a desire to be greater than Mops—makes the difference between vicious pride and virtuous humility. The reason that is definitive of the vices of pride is self-importance.

We have looked at conceit, hyper-autonomy, domination, and grandiosity, four of the vices of pride. Each is a way of being preoccupied with your own self-importance.

Conceit is a preoccupation with your already established (high) degree of excellence (whether or not you actually possess such excellence), where the supposed excellence grounds such pseudo-importance. Preoccupation with your self-importance, where it is a wished-for rather than current attainment, is not called conceit (though perhaps it's called ambition), but it is a variant of conceit. And the corresponding humility is a kind of unconcern for, and thus inattention to, such importance. This humility allows you to pay attention to other people and things; it is thus a kind of freedom that paves the way for other virtues such as generosity, gratitude, compassion, forgiveness, and justice, virtues in which conceit tends to disable you. It also increases the visibility, for you, of excellence in other people and other things.

Hyper-autonomy is a concern to be the chief or sole contributor to your own being and accomplishments, also for the sake of your self-importance, and it obstructs the recognition of your debts to other people and God. The corresponding humility is a freedom from hyper-autonomy, a kind of relaxation about the attribution of your good being and accomplishments. It thus opens the way for gratitude to others and cognitive clarity about attributions.

Domination is a concern to be the author of other people's excellences and goods for the sake of your self-importance. It can thus masquerade as generosity while undermining or threatening interpersonal affection and forestalling friendships. The corresponding humility is the absence of a concern to be the author of other people's goods and excellences for the sake of your self-importance, and thus a willingness to let their agency have play. This kind of humility allows interpersonal relationships to flower, largely because it gives others room for their own agency and the credit for it.

Grandiosity is a concern with achievement beyond your potential, for the sake of your self-importance. The corresponding humility is the absence of the concern with self-importance in connection with achievement; it is compatible with the virtue of pride that I call aspiration (see below), and it facilitates practical wisdom about goals.

Conceit, hyper-autonomy, domination, and grandiosity are distinct members of the vices-of-pride family. Each is a different concern for self-importance: conceit an excluding interest in your own excellence or superiority, hyper-autonomy an insistence on authoring or originating yourself and your achievements, domination a desire to be the controller or creator of other people's selves and lives, and grandiosity a self-inflating and overreaching ambition. Humility, as the absence of this or that dysfunctional self-concern, has at least four distinct dimensions. These dimensions are unified by being the absence of what unifies the vices of pride: the desire for self-importance. Humility is a sort of servant-virtue, inasmuch as it serves and facilitates more substantive virtues. The different dimensions of humility facilitate the functioning of somewhat different groups of other virtues. Thus, humility as the absence of conceit opens the way for generosity of spirit and the epistemic virtue of wonder; humility as the absence of hyper-autonomy opens the way for gratitude; humility as the absence of domination opens the way to a happier mutuality and the sincere promotion of others' potential; humility as the absence of grandiosity opens the way to virtuous aspiration and achievement; humility as the absence of arrogance removes an obstacle to justice and the respect of others.

The philosophy of virtue aims, among other things, to delineate, distinguish, and trace the interrelations of the virtues. They work together in the moral life, so that any given excellent action or reaction is likely to exemplify more than one of them; but if the task is to say what each of them contributes to the action, we must try not to attribute to one virtue the special contribution of another. If we feed on too narrow a diet of more or less concrete cases, we may be tempted to include in the analysis of humility the functions of other virtues that humility enables. Thus, we might think that humility, as such, is motivated by a concern for others, or by a desire to reciprocate benefits or treat others fairly, or by an appreciation of the wonders of the natural world, or whatever. In the picture I'm promoting, these concerns and the freedom to express them are all benefits and reasons that humility has the status of a virtue. But I think it would be sloppy philosophy to attribute such functions to humility as such, since these functions all belong essentially to other virtues, such as generosity, justice, and wonder. Unless we accept a very strong version of the unity of the virtues, in which each has all or many of the properties of the other virtues, we will want to individuate the virtues by the function(s) that each uniquely contributes. My proposal here is that humility, simply as humility, has the function(s) of subtracting the vices of pride from the structure of human character.

The Vices of Humility and the Virtues of Pride

When David Hume speaks of humility in his *Treatise*, he has in mind an emotion very much like what we call shame. In Hume's vocabulary, humility and pride are strongly contrasting passions: pride is a good feeling about yourself because of your association with something excellent (say, your beautiful house, a record of achievements, or good qualities of mind), while humility is a bad feeling about yourself because of your association with something that seems dishonorable (say, a dirty, decaying house in a slum neighborhood, a criminal record, or a lack of good mental qualities and skills). Thus, he says the following:

> Every valuable quality of the mind, whether of the imagination, judgment, memory or disposition, wit, good-sense, learning, courage, justice, integrity; all these are the cause of pride: and their opposites of humility.[21]

And this:

> Thus *Pride* is a certain satisfaction in ourselves, on account of some accomplishment or possession, which we enjoy: *Humility*, on the other hand, is a dissatisfaction with ourselves, on account of some defect or infirmity.[22]

Hume thinks of humility as a painful emotion—an emotion that you feel at a given moment and then possibly don't feel again for a long time.

But we are now reflecting about virtues and vices, and these are dispositions, not passions or feelings. The first definition of humility in the Oxford English Dictionary treats it as a disposition. Humility is "the quality of being humble or having a lowly opinion of oneself; meekness, lowliness, humbleness: the opposite of pride or haughtiness." This is not a very good definition of humility in general, and certainly not of humility as a virtue, but it does put into words one of the concepts of humility as a vice, and it connects nicely with the passion that Hume mentions. If you have a low opinion of your value, you're likely to be susceptible to feelings of shame. A sense of shame can be a virtue, or at least a trait that's morally good to have. To be incapable of feeling shame, when what you have done is shameful, is vicious. To be shameless is itself shameful. But the vice of humility is an indiscriminate disposition to feel shame, a pervasive disposition to think and feel yourself to be worthy of dishonor and unworthy of respect. It is a chronic and implicit sense of being, in the words of the homie Bandit, *bueno para nada*, or "good for nothing" (see more on Bandit later). This soul-theme, this *basso ostinato* of self-contempt, may be overlaid by posturing and bravado, but these are really expressions of despair.

So I call this vice "deep shame." Some may find the word "vice" unnecessarily harsh, feeling a diagnosis of pathology more compassionately appropriate. But I want to use the language of virtue and vice quite inclusively. It is not a necessary condition of a trait's being a vice that its possessor be blameworthy for having acquired it. We can distinguish vices that invite anger from ones that invite pity, and deep shame belongs clearly to the latter group. The virtue of pride that corresponds to deep shame (see Table 1) is self-respect; it is in the same mode (perceived value of self) as the vice of pride that we call conceit.

Gregory Boyle is a Jesuit priest who works with gang members in Los Angeles. He is the founder of Homeboy Industries, a group of businesses expressly created to provide jobs for former gang members. Boyle sees the intimate connection between self-respect and another virtue of pride that I call "secure agency"—an implicit and explicit sense of one's ability to act well and effectively. He tells a story about Bandit, the homie I just mentioned. Bandit's daughter is going off to college to study forensic psychology, and he is concerned about her and asks Father Greg (known as "G-Dog" to the homies) to give her a send-off blessing. After the ceremony, when everybody is preparing to go home, Bandit hangs back in the parking lot. Boyle says to him,

> "Can I tell you something, dog? . . . "I give you credit for the man you've chosen to become; I'm proud of you."
>
> "*Sabes qué*?" he says, eyes watering. "I'm proud of myself. All my life, people called me a lowlife, a *bueno para nada*. I guess I showed 'em."
>
> I guess he did.
>
> And the soul feels its worth.[23]

"The soul feels its worth" is a line from the Christmas carol "O Holy Night," sung by G-Dog's mother in another part of the story: "Long lay the world in sin and error pining—'til He appeared and the soul felt its worth."[24]

Bandit suffered from the kind of "humility" I'm calling deep shame, and through the work of G-Dog and the community at Homeboy Industries, began to get free of this vice and has made something of himself, even to the point that he has a daughter going to college—a first in the entire known history of the family and the neighborhood. In his book of stories about the homies and his ministry to them, Boyle emphasizes the role of unwavering, welcoming, loving regard for these people, a number of whom are very tough criminals and even murderers. The usual reaction to them by "respectable" people is fear and loathing, as if they were dangerous and hideous members of an alien species and not really human beings. That deep shame takes root in their souls should come as no surprise.

The vice of pride that we call vanity is a concern with being adulated, admired, and celebrated; it fails to appreciate the appointed admirer's claim to personhood. As such, it's a socially isolating state of mind. (Perhaps it's called vanity because the sought relation to the other is empty of human excellence or spiritual value.) It is true that, to satisfy the vain person's appetite for admiration, the admirer must be perceived as having status, but status is not the same as humanity. Consider Rosamond Vincy in George Eliot's *Middlemarch*. In the following description, she is thinking about Tertius Lydgate, a handsome young physician who has recently arrived in town and whom Rosamond takes to be of higher social rank than any of the eligible bachelors of Middlemarch:

> Rosamond, in fact, was entirely occupied not exactly with Tertius Lydgate as he was in himself, but with his relation to her; and it was excusable in a girl who was accustomed to hear that all young men might, could, would be, or actually were in love with her, to believe at once that Lydgate could be no exception. His looks and words meant more to her than other men's, because she cared more for them: she thought of them diligently, and diligently attended to that perfection of appearance, behavior, sentiments, and all other elegancies, which would find in Lydgate a more adequate admirer than she had yet been conscious of.[25]

So Rosamond exemplifies a vice that consists of an intense concern ("need"?) for being the subject of positive regard (to use a conveniently reductive term that possibly obscures an important distinction), and she has this in common with Bandit. Bandit's deep shame is also a need for positive regard, though when in the depths of his pathology, he might not admit the need.

Note Boyle's generosity; it contrasts with a kind of stinginess with credit that is associated with arrogance and hyper-autonomy; if arrogance involves a preoccupation with one's own entitlements, such generosity is an attentiveness to others' entitlements. Boyle's concern reaches out, takes the initiative, lights up with the joy of pride in Bandit's entitlement to credit, and performs the pleasurable action of giving him that credit. Note how the word "chosen" stresses Bandit's entitlement. Humility is at work supporting Boyle's generosity, as his attention points away from himself and toward Bandit. And supporting this humility is Boyle's virtue of pride that I call "entitlement serenity." Contrast cases of concern with getting credit and cases of competition with others for it, which we so frequently see. In Father Boyle, the notions of entitlement and credit are subordinated to a project of fellowship, a communing of spirits.

Boyle's unwavering compassionate regard for Bandit and others like him aims to help them feel their worth and so become more human, more excellent, and more responsive. It aims to elicit from them a reciprocating respect and love similar to the respect and love that elicits it. By contrast, the admiration and adulation that Rosamond hungers for will not have such an effect on her, and her vanity is such that even if she met with real love, she would probably construe it as the kind of self-importance-conferring admiration that her vanity seeks. (This seems to be, in fact, the way she responds to Lydgate's love.) Thus, her vanity makes her resistant to love—even more resistant, one might think, than the criminals with whom Gregory Boyle works. This contrast is reminiscent of the Gospels. Vanity's constitutive concern is for praise and admiration that are "empty" of mutuality, reciprocity, gratitude, and the bond of friendship; and it aims at a kind of personal importance that is similarly void—what this chapter calls "self-importance." That's what sets the vicious concern of vanity apart from Bandit's craving for affirmation and credit. The concern that is satisfied in the virtues of self-respect, self-confidence, and secure agency is for an intrinsically social kind of importance, a concern with being included in a fellowship where there is no thought of excluding or possessing comparatively greater importance than others.

Boyle's interaction with Bandit in the parking lot is emblematic of his ministry: "I give you *credit* for the man you've *chosen* to become; I'm *proud* of you." And Bandit accepts the credit and affirms that he's proud of himself. This pride is an expression and instigator of the virtue of self-respect rather than of the vice of vanity or conceit. At least that is so from all that we know. Bandit is very glad to have been credited, by someone who knows him, with having done something important and good. But as far as we know, his pride is not a preoccupation with his own self-importance, as in the case of the great-souled man, and, above all, it doesn't involve his feeling contempt for others. I think that, in some people, what begins as a humanizing pride transmogrifies, with time and neglect of moral self-vigilance, into vanity and other vices of pride. But that deplorable development is not necessary, and the difference is stark between the virtue of self-respect or secure agency and the vices of conceit, vanity, or hyper-autonomy.

David McCullough reports of President Harry Truman a generous humility similar to Greg Boyle's: "More than once in his presidency, Truman would be remembered saying it was remarkable how much could be accomplished if you didn't care who received the credit."[26]

McCullough reports this in the context of Truman's insisting that the European Recovery Plan to rebuild the economies of Europe after World War II be named after George Marshall rather than himself. Truman was a pretty self-confident person, someone who had a good sense of his own worth and ability to do things, and so had the virtue of pride that I call entitlement serenity—a strong enough sense of himself that he did not need to seek credit and other entitlements, and thus an ability to keep his eye more on what needed to be done than on his own glorification because of what he got done. It seems to me that such inattention to self is characteristic of the virtues of self-respect, self-confidence, independence, entitlement serenity, and other virtues of pride in their most mature forms. Mature pride is self-secure but not self-preoccupied. This is what enables virtuous pride to support humility and even to look like it. Each of these virtues of pride is a disposition to construe oneself in a complimentary and satisfying way: as honorable, as competent, and as entitled to this or that. But the construal is dispositional—not often reflectively exemplified—and submerged by other concerns, for example, Boyle's concern for the homies and Truman's concern to help the world run smoothly and avert further human disaster in Europe.

Greg Boyle's encouraging words to Bandit about the credit he deserves and Bandit's joy in receiving that credit are contextually justified. Presumably, Bandit's self-concept remains fragile, so it's a good pastoral practice to reinforce what entitlement serenity he has by stressing to him the credit he's entitled to. A person with deeper serenity in this regard wouldn't need this particular pastoral attention. The pastor might then focus with Bandit on his daughter's achievements.

Deep shame is closely connected with the vice that I call "defeatist lethargy," and also with pusillanimity. Tara Smith has defeatist lethargy or pusillanimity (small-mindedness) in mind when she writes of humility, "Typically, the humble person does not want very much. She is content with a minimal standard of living, or job, or romance, and satisfies herself with relatively low-level needs and aims."[27]

The pusillanimous person is short on aspiration, and the lethargic defeatist feels powerless to do anything worthwhile. The Reverend Camden Farebrother of Eliot's *Middlemarch* is a nice example of these defects. He is a minor clergyman, reputed by the liberal-minded to be good moral preacher and an excellent man, but thought by the evangelicals to insist too little on Christian doctrine. He supports himself, his mother, his elder sister, and his mother's sister on a small income, so he is often in need of the money that he wins at whist or billiards, though he doesn't feel right about supplementing his income in these ways. Farebrother has shown Lydgate, the new doctor in Middlemarch, his fine collection of fauna. An anencephalous monster in Farebrother's collection catches Lydgate's eye, and he trades it to him for some sea-mice in spirits.

Nicolas Bulstrode, the domineering evangelical banker in town, wants Lydgate to manage a new hospital that he's building. Lydgate very much wants to do it, but Bulstrode insists that he support the election of an evangelical preacher against Farebrother as salaried chaplain of the hospital, thus depriving Farebrother of a nice opportunity for financial relief and consequent improvement in his pastoral behavior. Thus, in the interest of his medical mission, Lydgate reluctantly casts the decisive vote for the evangelical Tyke. The next time they meet,

> Mr. Farebrother met him with the same friendliness as before. . . . the Vicar of St. Botolph's had certainly escaped the slightest tincture of the Pharisee, and by dint of admitting to himself that he was too much as other men were, he had become remarkably unlike them in this—that he could excuse others for thinking slightly of him, and could judge impartially of their conduct even when it told against him.
>
> "The world has been too strong for me, I know," he said one day to Lydgate. "But then I am not a mighty man—I shall never be a man of renown. The choice of Hercules is a pretty fable; but Prodicus makes it easy work for the hero, as if the first resolves were enough. . . . I suppose one good resolve might keep a man right if everybody else's resolve helped him."
>
> The Vicar's talk was not always inspiriting: he had escaped being a Pharisee, but he had not escaped that low estimate of possibilities which we rather hastily arrive at as an inference from our own failure. Lydgate thought that there was a pitiable infirmity of will in Mr. Farebrother.[28]

Farebrother seems to be a forgiving person. A kind of humility frees him not to be alienated from Lydgate by Lydgate's giving their friendship little weight in the election. This manifestation of humility is virtuous if it is enabled by a relative unconcern about his self-importance as indicated by support from friends. But Eliot and Lydgate think Farebrother's humility is to be attributed, instead, to his defeatist shortfall of aspiration. The consequent low estimation of his own worth makes it appear to him, justly and fairly, that Lydgate not take him much into consideration. The case is ambiguous, I think. If Farebrother understood that the very existence of the hospital would have been jeopardized by Lydgate's voting for him, then he would see the vote as a case of justice, and a virtuous humility would allow him to see this clearly—to set personal disappointment aside and not let Lydgate's vote stand irrationally in the way of their friendship. In this case, he would be overlooking the "slight" without slighting his own self-respect. On the other hand, if his thought was that he isn't worth standing up for, and so it doesn't matter that Lydgate "betrayed" him, then his "forgiving" attitude is really a condoning attitude, and his humility is the kind of vice that Tara Smith thinks humility is. I think we would need to know more than we do about Farebrother's heart to decide which of these possibilities is actual.

In the finale of *Middlemarch*, we learn that the proud Lydgate succumbs, under the pressure of social circumstances created by his wife's vanity and snobbery, to an infirmity of will like the one he rues in Farebrother; he succumbs to a similar smallness of mind or pusillanimity as he advances toward the age of Farebrother and as we meet the latter in this passage. Both men, otherwise quite virtuous enough, fail in the end to exemplify steadfastly the virtue of pride that I'm calling aspiration. And Eliot's novel is a masterful depiction of the difficulties that life throws in the way of those who would exhibit that virtue over the long haul.

The gang members, both former and potential, with whom Father Boyle works come from homes and neighborhoods that tend to breed not just pusillanimity but deep shame and defeatist lethargy. Youth workers and teachers have nominated Vanessa, a teenager from such a neighborhood who is clearly escaping the grip of these vices of humility, as a moral exemplar and community leader. She has cofounded an intramural basketball league for adolescent peers. Kevin S. Reimer and M. Kyle Matsuba quote Vanessa in an interview:

> I recently began to realize that I'm significant to society. I don't want to be like, "Ooh, I'm great," but it's nice to know that I matter and people care about me and I can pass that down. All the blessings I've been given, I can give to others and I think that's pretty cool. It says that I pretty much care about people and I care about who they are. . . . I wouldn't have realized who I am if someone hadn't signaled that I was special, that God loved me. It's this chain of reactions—if you become aware of other people, then it's beneficial to everyone. It makes a big difference and it's so important, because if you're not noticing what other people are doing, it's like living time bombs; they don't realize how wonderful they are and how important they are to other people. If no one took the time to tell me, I'd be the same way. . . . I'm proud of the fact that I'm thankful for what I have. That

> I've gone through what I have, even when I have struggles. There are so many things I don't like about myself, but I do like how I'm positive. I would not appreciate things if I didn't. That says that I'm pretty caring and compassionate to others. If you aren't, you're wasting your time and energy. No matter what happens, it gives you the encouragement to go on.[29]

Vanessa here construes herself and speaks about herself in very positive terms, against a background of Christian metaphysics. She is moving toward mature self-respect and secure agency. She has a strong sense of her own value and of her ability to affect the world she lives in for good, and she conceives that good, in part, as lifting some of her community members out of deep shame: "they don't realize how wonderful they are." She aspires to make something of herself; she's neither grandiose nor small-minded, but expresses the virtue of pride that I call "aspiration" in the Table of Vices and Virtues. She is not conceited like Aristotle's *megalopsychos*. Her speech is permeated with expressions of gratitude, which presupposes the humility that is the absence of hyper-autonomy; her newfound sense of her importance is generous and socially qualified. She is very self-focused in this speech, but she expresses no contempt for anybody, and, if she thinks herself superior to others who are less self-confident or grateful, she doesn't stress it or seem to get satisfaction from her superiority as such. Her pride seems to be entirely of the virtuous kind. Vanessa is a fine exemplar of virtuous adolescent pride.

I would stress its adolescence. If at the age of fifty, she were as excited and voluble about herself as in this speech, I think we'd worry about her maturity. As Greg Boyle ministered to Bandit's fragile pride with explicit crediting, Vanessa ministers to her own fragile pride in this speech. We hope that, at age fifty, her self-admiration will have quieted down and become implicit self-respect, self-confidence, and secure agency, a family of submerged complimentary self-construals. If she has matured in her virtues of pride, she will not be less knowledgeable about her virtues, but she'll be less focused on them. Her focus will be on her projects, on other people's improvements, and on the glory of God, to whom she expresses such gratitude even in her adolescence.

Conclusion

Virtues and vices are connected with and distinguished from one another in a variety of ways—ways that come to light often only when we expressly treat them together and insist on making clear to ourselves their relations to one another. It's very unlikely that a deep understanding of them will emerge from studies that treat virtues individually and in isolation. This chapter is only a rough sketch with a few areas filled in with a bit more detail. But I have begun to sketch connections and distinctions among the members of the humility-pride family, a very important family of traits for moral and epistemic psychology.[30]

Chapter 8

Intellectual-Virtue Terms and the Division of Linguistic Labor

Linda Zagzebski
University of Oklahoma

The work of Hilary Putnam and Saul Kripke on natural kind terms in the seventies led to a revolution in semantics. For a long time before that, the dominant theory of meaning maintained that the meaning of a term is a description in the head. What a term refers to is whatever fits that description. Putnam argued in an important paper that meaning cannot be both a description in the head and such that it fixes the reference of a term. Since Putnam continued to accept the connection between meaning (intension) and reference (extension), he concluded that "Meanings ain't in the head."[1]

The key to the new semantics was the idea that many terms refer indexically. The primary focus of the theory was natural kind terms.[2] Briefly, water is whatever is the same substance as that, gold is whatever is the same element as that, human is whatever is the same species as that, and so on. A second important feature of the theory was its assertion that it takes observation to find out what makes that substance (element, species) what it is, so empirical observation was woven into the semantics of natural kind terms.

A third interesting feature in Putnam's version was his proposal that natural kind terms function semantically through a network that links users to the extension of the term in a way that privileges certain users. He called this the Division of Linguistic Labor. Speakers do not all have the same function in the linguistic network. Ordinary speakers defer to experts to both identify the objects in the extension and find out what the deep structure of a given kind is. In this way, ordinary speakers are dependent on others in the network for their semantic success.

Putnam concluded that what we mean is determined by something outside of us in two ways. First, it is partly determined by the world, because the indexical feature of meaning has the consequence that a difference in extension is sufficient for a difference in what we mean in the use of a term. Second, what we mean is partly determined by a social linguistic network that links us to the extension of the term. A description in the head is not necessary to fix the extension and is far from sufficient. In short, what we mean is not up to us.

I have been developing a moral theory I call Exemplarist Virtue Theory, in which a "good person" functions semantically in the same way natural kind terms function in the theories of Putnam and Kripke. I propose, first, that "good person" refers indexically. A good person is a person like that, where we pick out good persons directly through the experience of reflective admiration. Second, we discover what makes good persons good in a way that is roughly parallel to the way we find out what makes water water and what makes gold gold. We observe them and test what we observe by our responses of admiration or dis-admiration. Observation of natural kinds is empirical; observation of admirable persons may include controlled empirical studies, but it more commonly comes in the form of narratives. I think that what we discover when we read or watch narratives of paradigmatically good persons is that we admire certain patterns of emotions, perceptions, ends, and behaviors. We call these virtues. So what "virtue" means is not a description in the head but is what makes persons like that admirable. What makes persons like that admirable is discovered by observation and reflection upon our responses of admiration to what we observe.

I conjecture that it will turn out that this approach to virtue excludes natural talents from the category of virtues, but it includes a wide range of traits acquired through human agency, including intellectual virtues. So it excludes natural musical ability, physical strength, good memory, and native intelligence, but it includes open-mindedness, courage, intellectual courage, perseverance, intellectual perseverance, humility, and intellectual humility. I say this under the hypothesis that we do not admire natural talents in the same way we admire the moral traits, but we admire open-mindedness, intellectual courage, and intellectual humility in the same way we admire the moral traits. I propose, then, that the most important division in the set of admirable qualities is not the division between moral and intellectual virtues, but the division between acquired traits like the moral and intellectual virtues mentioned above and natural talents that do not involve agency. We discover that by reflecting upon what we admire and how we admire it. This proposal can be empirically tested.

If I am wrong about what we reflectively admire, then I am wrong about the set of virtues, but I maintain that a virtue is what we reflectively admire in persons who are picked out directly through the experience of reflective admiration.

The third feature of direct reference theory I mentioned is Putnam's Division of Linguistic Labor. I think that this also is a feature of moral terms, like "good person" and "virtue," and of terms for particular virtues, like "courage" and "open-mindedness." Putnam says that natural kind terms are externalist in two ways, and I think that "good person" and virtue terms are externalist in the same two ways. They are externalist because what "good person" refers to is partly determined by the way the world is—by the features of good persons awaiting our discovery. It is also externalist because there is a division of moral linguistic labor. We all succeed in referring to good persons, virtue, and particular virtues because we are connected to the extension of these terms through a linguistic network in which different persons have different roles. Externalism in moral semantics therefore leads to externalism in moral philosophy of mind. What we mean by "good person," "virtue," "generosity," "open-mindedness," and "fairness" is not up to us.

In what follows, I will focus on the division of moral linguistic labor and then discuss the way it applies to names of intellectual virtues. I think that this way of looking at the semantics of these terms illuminates the use of virtue theory for the practical purposes of moral education and civic discourse, and it explains some of the particular challenges that arise in the use of the intellectual virtue terms.

The Division of Linguistic Labor

Putnam's principle of the division of linguistic labor gives certain individuals the role of expert in identifying the objects in the extension of the term. We can identify diamonds and tigers and elm trees as a collective body because some of us can do so, and the rest of us rely upon the experts for success in referring to the objects in the extension. Individual users also have a role to play in using a term correctly, according to Putnam. In order to know what "elm tree" or "diamond" means, it is not enough to speak English and be willing to defer to experts in identifying diamonds and elm trees. There is a linguistic obligation to have a certain minimal competence in the use of a term in order to count as knowing what the term means; and roughly, that means we need to grasp what Putnam calls the "stereotype," a description that aids the user in connecting to the linguistic network and effectively communicating with others. A stereotype is not a set of necessary and sufficient conditions for the application of a term; the idea is not a return to the descriptive theory of meaning. But Putnam thinks the stereotype is usually roughly correct, even though it is usually vague. So we need to know something about stereotypical tigers in order to count as having acquired the word "tiger," we need to know something about stereotypical elm trees in order to count as having acquired the world "elm tree," and so on.[3] Interestingly, Putnam conjectures that it is linguistically obligatory to be able to tell tigers from leopards in order to know what "tiger" means, but it is not required that one be able to distinguish elm trees from beech trees in order to know what "elm tree" means.[4]

As far as I know, Putnam does not explain why the stereotype of a tiger distinguishes it from a leopard, whereas the stereotype of an elm tree does not distinguish it from a beech tree. My view is that since a linguistic network links individual users with the extension of a term through other speakers, that means that pictures and descriptions produced by other speakers are part of the network. If these pictures and descriptions are common enough, some of them become part of the stereotype that every competent user of the term is expected to grasp. A competent speaker should have seen many pictures of tigers or heard them described. That would explain why ordinary speakers who know what "tiger" means must know that tigers have stripes. If they do not know that, they are not properly connected to the network with respect to that word. But pictures of elm trees do not function the same way as pictures of tigers, at least not in the part of the world I live in. We teach children "a tiger looks like that," but even those of us who can say "an elm tree looks like that" do not expect others to remember what is distinctive about that species of tree, and the stereotype of an elm tree includes no details about the leaf shape or the appearance of the bark. I could be wrong about that, of course, in which case maybe neither Putnam nor I has properly acquired the use of the word "elm tree." But even if "elm tree" is more like "tiger" after all, there are still words like "magnesium," "oryx," and "dendrobium," which are such that only a minority of the language users can give any descriptive details about the designated kind or reliably identify its members.

I think, then, that Putnam is right that an ordinary speaker can succeed in referring to the members of a kind with only the vaguest idea of what the kind is like, and I think he is also right that a competent speaker must be properly connected to a linguistic network that privileges certain users, but I believe that the privileged users need not be experts in the sense of having a commonly recognized authority, and I will say more about that below. I also think that there is more in the network than speakers who adequately grasp a stereotype and who are causally connected to the objects in the extension of a term through the privileged speakers. Since speakers are aware that they all have the same referential intentions, they are causally connected both to the referent of the term and to each other. The stereotype is a compilation of what many other speakers say about the kind, and I have suggested that it can include pictures. The reason a speaker must grasp the stereotype is that the speaker is not properly connected to other speakers without being aware of what is widely said or shown by speakers in the network about the kind in question. When most other speakers have very little to say about the kind, an individual speaker can acquire the word for the kind without knowing much at all about it. In other cases, speakers say quite a lot, and an individual speaker has not properly acquired the word for the kind without knowing what is commonly said. That would explain why individual speakers should be able to distinguish tigers from leopards, but not elm trees from beech trees.

The causal connection to other speakers allows an individual user of a term to enhance her grasp of the kind under their influence. If a speaker has only a minimal grasp of the stereotype, but she is properly connected to the linguistic network, she will be willing to adopt the richer descriptions of others in the network, and she will be willing to defer to others who are better than she is at identifying the objects to which the term refers. When appropriate, she will recognize experts who make the final determination of the extension of a term, but for the most part, she will defer to anybody who knows more than she does about the kind in question. (Few speakers are connected to experts directly or pay much attention to experts.)

I think there can be practical reasons for the fact that stereotypes of different kinds have different levels of precision. Ordinary speakers need to be able to distinguish water from other clear liquids, but they do not need to have the same level of competence in identifying non-poisonous plant species. So we all need to be able to grasp a stereotype of water that allows us to reliably identify water, to distinguish it from harmful substances, but it does not matter if each of us can reliably identify the different species of orchids and distinguish them one from another. Since there are important practical reasons for every speaker to be able to identify water, the network includes numerous pictures and information about water, which contribute to both a richer stereotype and a better grasp of the stereotype by individual members of the network. Anybody who does not grasp a reasonable part of that information is not properly connected to the network of speakers and does not know what "water" means. The function of experts in the network is to determine what it takes to be "really" water and to make distinctions such as identifying the different isotopes of water, but ordinary speakers cannot simply hand over the job of identifying the water in our ordinary environment to the experts. A term like "tiger" also has a reasonably robust stereotype, but the reason is probably cultural. We enjoy stories and pictures of tigers, even though few of us will ever encounter a tiger outside of a zoo. But if we are properly connected to our linguistic network, we know that tigers are striped.

Putnam says that, although the stereotype, typically, is roughly correct, it is not a necessary truth that the stereotype accurately describe the members of the extension of a term. Since the stereotype can change, this must be correct. Putnam thinks that it is part of the stereotype of gold that it is yellow in color (I think he means golden), but if jewelry made of white gold, pink gold, and green gold became more common in the experience of the users in a linguistic community, the stereotype could change without a change in referential intentions and without any change in the meaning of "gold." It is not a necessary truth that gold is golden, and the stereotype can change because of a cultural accident, without any change in what the experts believe.

We also like to think that, as the experts find out more about the kinds they investigate and spread their knowledge throughout the community, the stereotype of those kinds becomes more accurate. That assumes, of course, that the experts are good at their job and that communication through the network works well. Individual speakers do a better job of identifying the members of the kind partly because the experts are doing a better job, but it is partly due to the proper function of the network that allows the stereotype to become more accurate.

I think that the division of linguistic labor applies to many other terms besides natural kind terms. Artifact terms like "kilim rug," "mass spectrometer," and "fuel-injection system" are all terms whose users refer through other speakers, some of whom are experts, although these terms do not all require the same level of expertise to identify the objects in the extension. For instance, rug buyers can learn what a kilim rug is without extensive training, but even before they acquired that ability, they could refer to kilim rugs for the same reason they could refer to dendrobiums before they took up a career in botany. Other terms refer in such a way that, although some persons are experts in them, expertise is not necessary for identifying members of the extension. "Automobile" might be such a term. There are also cases in which the privileged users are not experts in the sense that a scientific expert or an expert in automobile mechanics would be. Some users might be privileged because they were among the early users of a term, but it is a stretch to call them "experts" because they do not have specialized training. This happens a lot with slang terms like "tacky" or "nerd," which at some point become part of wider usage. So twenty years ago, if you wanted to know whether somebody was a nerd, you would ask a teen. You knew who the privileged users were.

My claim, then, is that in each case of a linguistic network, (a) speakers refer to the extension through other speakers; (b) some speakers are recognized as having greater competence than others in the use of the term and have a specialized role in the network; and (c) every speaker is expected to grasp a stereotype, which varies from term to term in its level of richness and precision, and may be contained in stories or pictures as well as in verbal descriptions.

The Division of Moral Linguistic Labor

I propose that there is a division of linguistic labor for moral terms such as "good person" and terms for individual virtues. We refer to good persons through a network that connects us to admirable persons through other users, some of whom have a privileged function. Each user of the term "good person" needs to be able to grasp the stereotype of a good person. Virtue terms function as descriptors that are part of the stereotype of a good person, and they are important for communication among the members of a community, but they do not provide necessary and sufficient conditions for membership in the kind. An ordinary speaker should be aware that good persons have certain traits like generosity, honesty, and courage, but it is not necessary that she can give an account of these traits or of a virtue in general in order to acquire the use of a virtue term.

Virtue terms also refer indexically. They are the traits we admire in persons like that. The stereotype of a virtue term is not just a set of adjectives; it is also likely to be expressed in narratives and pictures of virtuous actions. These stories and pictures serve a linguistic function in connecting the users of moral terms to a causal network linking them to the extension of the term. The stereotype associated with a virtue term or the term "good person" includes narratives about the virtues, so the stereotype is fairly robust—more like "water" than "cadmium." No one has properly acquired the use of a virtue term or the term "good person" without the ability to refer to descriptions and narratives. The function of narratives in the stereotype means that an ordinary user of the term "good person" needs to be able to identify some good persons in order to count as having acquired the term "good person," but there is no linguistic expectation that a member of the network can recognize all good persons.

In contrast, I believe that there is a social obligation to know the members of the extension of the deontic terms "wrong act" and "duty," and the linguistic community is much more demanding of competent users of these terms than of the virtue terms. A speaker who fails to recognize many wrong acts is deemed linguistically incompetent in the use of the word "wrong" and may be called a sociopath. "Wrong" and "duty" connect individuals to act categories that are learned in a variety of ways. Stories can be useful in giving the extension of "wrong," but wrong acts can usually be adequately identified in a list of prohibitions. In contrast, a story is more useful in explaining what loyalty and disloyalty are. If so, the virtue terms are part of a different type of linguistic network than the deontic terms. In this chapter, I am focusing on the virtue terms, not the deontic terms.

The function of privileged users in the division of linguistic labor is different for moral terms than for scientific terms. We expect ordinary users of "diamond" or "gold" to be able to describe a stereotypical diamond or piece of gold and perhaps pick out some examples, but we defer to the experts to tell us what is really gold or a diamond, and the experts are even more important for kinds that we do not regularly encounter in ordinary life, like cadmium or oryxes. In contrast, most of us probably think we are pretty good at identifying exemplars, probably as good as we are at identifying water, but as is the case with water, it would be a serious mistake to think that our community is irrelevant to our ability to identify exemplars and to teach us the stereotype of a good person. The extension of "good person" is not determined privately or determined by democratic vote. Some members of the social linguistic network are linguistically privileged.

I mentioned above that for some terms, like "automobile," there are specialized functions in the network that do not involve special privilege in identifying the members of the extension. An auto mechanic, for example, has a special role in explaining the proper functioning of an automobile, but almost anybody can identify an automobile. I think we see a variety of special roles in the network for virtue terms. There are psychologists who have the role of finding out how widespread the extension of a virtue term is, how changeable the extension is (e.g., whether virtuous persons tend to remain virtuous), and whether there are any connections between the extension of one virtue term and another. I surmise that philosophers also have a specialized function that includes making the functioning of the network clearer and pointing out inconsistencies in the stereotype, in addition to contributing their powers of abstract reasoning about virtue to the community.

The people who deserve to be linguistically privileged are the persons who are good at distinguishing true exemplars from the counterfeits and at spotting counterfeit virtues. Unfortunately, the people who have great influence in determining both the stereotype and the extension of moral terms often have that influence because of their political power or media presence rather than because of their wisdom. Miranda Fricker has made an important contribution to social epistemology in her work on ways in which the use of language can be unjust. Her general point can be extended to a problem in the division of moral linguistic labor.[5] There are people who have a great deal of influence over the stereotype of a good person and the individual virtues, and their judgments affect the use of terms by the people in their community. If the opinion-makers do not have good judgment, the result can be confusion about the meaning of these terms.

Imagine what it would be like to live in a community in which the "experts" at identifying certain natural kinds start to misidentify the members of the kind, then put out an inaccurate stereotype to the public. Assume that the experts and ordinary users have the right semantic intentions but they start to lose their causal connection to the extension of the term. The result would be semantic confusion. I think that this has happened in the use of moral terms when the opinion-makers have misidentified the persons, traits, or acts to which we refer in our moral vocabulary, thereby leading those they influence to misidentify the members of the extension of these terms, and thereby further leading to a change in the stereotype that is less accurate than it was previously. I am not sure what is included in the current stereotype of a good person in the United States, but it seems to me that it includes more elements of bravado, incivility, and lack of self-control than in the past, and it lacks elements of intellectual humility and open-mindedness. If so, it seems to me that the stereotype has become less accurate.

A virtue term can fall out of use when people no longer admire a person who fits the stereotype, and that is more likely to happen when the stereotype changes. I think this happened with the word "chastity." In Christian moral theology, chastity is the virtue that governs sexual desire and behavior. In that sense, it is a virtue everyone needs. But many people identify chastity with sexual abstinence. Obviously, people are not going to think of sexual abstinence as a generally admirable virtue, and if the stereotype of chastity is a person who does not engage in sexual acts, it is no wonder the word has gone out of common usage.

There is another reason a virtue term can go out of use. When Simon Blackburn writes that he has no use for the word "chastity," it appears that it is not because he is using a new stereotype of a chaste person, but because he does not admire the chaste person as described in the original stereotype.[6] That suggests something very interesting about virtue and vice terms. Even when there is no change in the descriptive part of a stereotype, if the emotional reaction to that stereotype changes, the word no longer has any meaning. Admiration for virtue and contempt for vice is imbedded in the referential intentions of words for virtues and vices. Members of a linguistic network understand that. If a member of the network does not admire people described in the stereotype of a virtue term, that person will cease using the term, except perhaps in an ironic way. If most members of the network cease to admire people who fit the stereotype, the word goes out of use.

I think that loss of words for many of the virtues like gratitude and civility is partly driven by a theoretical stance that these traits are not admirable, but the decline of usage can also be partly driven by general inattentiveness that makes the stereotype thinner and vaguer than it was before.[7] Eventually, people become unable to grasp the stereotype at all, and this can lead to a situation in which there is no longer any stereotype to grasp. That can happen even when the majority of people in a community would, upon reflection, judge that a trait like gratitude or civility, as formerly described, are good traits. And once the word disappears, it is very difficult to make a conscious improvement in the behavior the word describes without reintroducing the word.

Sometimes we cannot improve the stereotype of a good person without adding a word to our vocabulary that did not previously exist. As Miranda Fricker points out, there are wrong acts that are not noticed until someone invents a word for it—e.g., "sexual harassment." Sexual harassment was virtually invisible when there was no word for it in the common vocabulary, and the stereotype of a good person did not include anything that expressed the full range of the value of respect for women. The stereotype changed for the better when words like "sexist" and "sexual harassment" became commonplace, and it is very difficult to see how that change could have happened without the change in vocabulary.

Words are not added to the common vocabulary until they become used by people with the greatest linguistic influence. If I am right that moral critique sometimes requires critique of a linguistic network, that would include critique of the claims of people who are most influential in the network. Fortunately, we are in a better position to critique opinion-makers than we are scientific experts, as long as we become reflective about our emotions of admiration and its opposite, contempt. It can be hard for a non-expert to know if someone is a climate expert or an expert economist, but we have ways to identify those whose moral judgment is most trustworthy. We can do that through reflection on our moral emotions, particularly the emotion of admiration. These emotions can be used to critique moral discourse. When we do so, we may need to invent a new term like "sexual harassment" or reintroduce an old one like "civility." We can also change a stereotype for the better without changing a word. For instance, we may want to eliminate the inclusion of vengeance in the stereotype of justice without eliminating the words "justice" or "vengeance."[8] These changes can be effected by extended reflection on what we admire as a community. A moral linguistic network can therefore change by internal critique, not just by the accident of political power and cultural influence.

Another way in which a linguistic community can change is by expanding under the influence of an encounter with other moral linguistic communities. A linguistic community expands as the causal connections between communities expand. To see the simplest case, let us go back to natural kinds and consider two independent communities that both have words for the same kind. Call it K1. We can imagine that we know the words are inter-translatable because the extensions of the terms coincide and the stereotypes are similar. Each community has its own linguistic network and its own experts. But suppose that community A is more scientifically advanced than community B, and community B realizes that. Community B might then come to acknowledge the experts in community A as their own experts. In order to do that, they would need to recognize that the experts in community A have the same intentions as the experts in community B: to find out the deep structure of K1 and to distinguish K1 from distinct kinds. But even if they are unwilling to go that far, they might still acknowledge that the experts of community A are more expert than the ordinary speakers of community B. In either case, linguistic community B expands, at least with respect to one word.

In the case of moral communities, we get blended linguistic communities when one community's stories and literature about exemplars become available to another. Westerners who read the *Analects* are automatically causally connected to the Chinese readers (and writers) of the *Analects*. Obviously, the connection is weak, but it exists. The same thing happens when Western readers read Viking tales or the *Bhagavad Gita*, and it is bound to happen if they spend any amount of time in a foreign country. The changes can be profound when especially admirable and influential persons change something in the stereotype they use for "good person" or a virtue term.

The acceptance of the Universal Declaration of Human Rights is an especially vivid example of the expansion of a moral linguistic community, especially when we look at the signatories that did not already have a word for "rights" in their linguistic community. One possibility is that they added a word translated "rights" to their vocabulary, in which case their linguistic community expanded to include the linguistic community of people using the term "rights."[9] It is more likely that they signed the document not because they were willing to add a term to their vocabulary, but because they decided that what the drafters of the declaration meant by "rights" was close enough to terms already in use in their vocabulary that they could accept the declaration. But even in that case, it seems to me that the act of signing the declaration put them into a causal network with the drafters of the declaration and its other signatories, thereby expanding the linguistic community they were a part of and inevitably changing their use of moral terms.

I think that the expansion of causal linguistic networks is not only the best way to alter the usage of moral terms; it is also the best way to get moral agreement. In fact, I think that such expansion is a necessary condition for agreement. There are examples of that in contemporary cross-cultural moral discourse. I have been told that one translation of "sexual harassment" in Arabic (التحرش الجنسي) would probably be unintelligible to most Arabic-speaking people, other than intellectuals familiar with contemporary Western thinking.[10] This is a case in which Arabic speakers who are knowledgeable about Western views of sexual respect have a weaker connection with ordinary Arabic speakers in some part of their vocabulary than they have with most speakers of European languages. The Arabic speakers who have adopted terms for Western values are connected to a different linguistic network than ordinary speakers of Arabic. If that is right, it is hopeless to change the views of ordinary Arabic speakers about sexual harassment without a network of Arabic speakers that closely connects ordinary speakers with those who speak Arabic but who also use words for sexual harassment.[11]

I think this shows the importance of dialogue among morally admired people in different communities. That kind of dialogue is an important impetus for linguistic expansion, because people have effects on each other, and that, in turn, has an effect on their respective linguistic networks. This makes it all the more important that we solve the problem that admirable people are often not the most influential. I think that when the wisest people are sidelined in public discussion and non-admirable people take center stage, it is difficult for us to even formulate the thought that certain good things are good and certain bad things are bad.

Intellectual Virtue Terms

I have said that I believe intellectual virtue terms operate the same way as moral virtue terms. Roughly, I think that any kind of virtue is a trait we admire in people like that, where "that" refers directly to those individuals we admire as people. We identify what we admire in them by observing them and testing our reactions. I hypothesized that we do not admire natural talents the same way we admire acquired traits that engage a person's agency, and that the latter group includes intellectual virtues such as open-mindedness, intellectual courage, intellectual perseverance, intellectual generosity, and intellectual humility, as well as the standard moral virtues. These are the traits that are central in civic life. I want to conclude by applying the points I have made about the division of moral linguistic labor to terms for intellectual virtues.

Like moral virtue terms and the term "good person," I propose that intellectual virtue terms refer indexically, and not through a description. Open-mindedness is one of the features we admire in admirable people like that. It is that disposition of motivation and behavior. There is a shared set of referential intentions in the use of intellectual virtue terms that connects users of those terms to the extension of the term through a linguistic network. When we investigate the intellectual behaviors we admire in narratives or personal experience, we can identify the deeper admirable features of the people we admire for their intellectual behavior. Cognitive psychologists and philosophers have a role to play in the network for these tasks. What the specific psychological features of an intellectual virtue consist in—emotion dispositions, behavioral dispositions, etc.—is a matter for investigation, both through the kind of moral psychology done by philosophers and the kind of controlled psychological studies conducted by psychologists and neuroscientists.

Competent users of intellectual virtue terms must grasp the stereotype of the intellectual virtue in order to be competent users of the term. The stereotype can be expressed in narratives, and it includes descriptions, but these descriptions are not necessary and sufficient conditions for the accurate application of an intellectual virtue term. Stereotypes differ from one another in their levels of richness and precision, and it seems to me that the stereotype associated with most intellectual virtue terms is vague. Intellectual virtue terms that have the same names as moral virtues—such as intellectual courage, intellectual humility, intellectual honesty, and intellectual generosity—and probably borrow most of their stereotype from the stereotype of the parallel moral virtue, with the proviso that it is in the domain of intellectual inquiry or belief. But I believe that the lack of narratives about intellectual virtues in common discourse is a problem.[12] Think of how difficult it would be to understand courage without stories of courageous heroes. The lack of stories about intellectually courageous people puts us in that situation with respect to the virtue of intellectual courage. The same point applies to other intellectual virtue stereotypes. They are deprived of the vividness and motivational power they would have if they were directly linked with well-told stories.

I proposed above that a virtue term can go out of use either because people change their attitude of admiration toward the stereotype or because the stereotype itself gets distorted and no longer expresses something that the community finds admirable. I said that I think both of these situations happened with the word "chastity." I suspect that these two processes are connected because the fading of a term from common usage hastens the distortion of the stereotype. That is happening with the stereotype associated with the term "virtue." As "virtue" has faded from use, the stereotype has altered. In my experience, people associate "virtue" with religious and political conservatism. If they do not admire the values of religious and political conservatives, they lack the admiration for what is expressed in the stereotype of virtue, and since admiration is an intrinsic component of virtue, the word "virtue" quickly disappears.

The suspicion of the idea of truth was a social force that undermined intellectual virtue terminology for decades, and it no doubt contributed to the distortion of the stereotype of intellectual virtue. I think, however, that the almost complete lack of well-known narratives depicting intellectual virtues is an even greater problem. Civic discourse requires participants not only to possess intellectual virtues but also, importantly, to understand what the intellectual virtues are—not by having the ability to give an account of an intellectual virtue but by associating intellectual virtue terms with people they admire in a certain way. They need to grasp a stereotype of an intellectual virtue and admire people who fit the stereotype. But to do that, they need access to exemplars of the intellectual virtues.

Unfortunately, we live in a society in which people in the public eye get away with close-mindedness, intellectual stubbornness, intellectual sloth, intellectual cowardice, and a general disvaluing of truth. There is little connection between what they say and what they believe, or between what they believe and what they should believe. Although many people detect something wrong, most lack the vocabulary to express it, and if I am right, they have trouble even forming the thought that the intellectual virtues are worthy of their admiration and the intellectual vices deserving of scorn. That is precluded by the lack of a common word with a commonly grasped stereotype, and a network that links the users to people exhibiting the virtue or vice. But the indexicality of virtue and vice terms is good news because it gives us the opportunity to invent words: "X is stuff like that." In a sense, Harry Frankfurt did that with his best-selling little book *On Bullshit*, but, of course, "bullshit" was a word that already had a meaning. Still, the popularity of the book made the stereotype of a person who is careless about the truth clearer and more widely grasped, and that was an important contribution to the linguistic network.

I mentioned the merging or expanding of linguistic networks in the use of moral terms, which I believe happened with the adoption of the Universal Declaration of Human Rights, and I think that the same points apply to the domain of intellectual virtue. Human rights documents typically recognize the right to the free expression of opinion, but we need words for the right to be told what the informant conscientiously believes to be the truth. We need words that express the idea of intellectual or epistemic abuse, and we need words for the social commitment to contributing to the intellectual well-being of the community, which underlies most of the intellectual virtues. The greater the awareness of the social effects of intellectual vice and virtue, the more likely it will be that we get attention from influential participants in our linguistic network about these vices and virtues.

I also said that I think that participation in a common moral linguistic network is a necessary condition for getting moral agreement. The same condition applies to getting agreement about the ethics of belief and testimony. Fortunately, if I am right about the semantics of direct reference as applied to virtue terms, we would not have to have a common concept associated with these terms for us to be linked to the same network. So the good news is that it is not necessary that the work of philosophers on intellectual virtues permeates the network sufficiently to affect the stereotype of an intellectually virtuous person. It is enough to have common words, with some images and stories that ordinary people associate with these words. But the bad news is that we have not even done a very good job of creating stereotypes of intellectual virtues through stories and examples. I believe that civic discourse will be impoverished until we do so.

Chapter 9

Virtues and Vices of Civility

Michael Pace
Chapman University

People have radically diverging attitudes toward civility. Many complain about a "breakdown of civility" that they regard as one of the worst problems for our society. The problem, they contend, is moral as well as epistemic: people don't treat others with the respect they morally deserve. And the breakdown of civil discourse is a main barrier to our being able to make intellectual progress on important issues that affect us all. "More concern for civility!" they cheer.

Others complain that civility is dangerous, and they worry that there is too much concern about it in our culture. Again, for these people, the worry is moral as well as epistemic. Too much concern about civility, they claim, threatens people's moral right to free speech and disproportionately harms those whose speech is deemed uncivil. And they worry that labeling certain speech as "uncivil" can too easily be used as an excuse to sideline the voices of minorities or those with unfashionable opinions, leaving us all worse off intellectually. "Less concern for civility!" they recommend.

These competing attitudes toward civility are prominent in several different arenas, perhaps most obviously in American politics. Calls for more civility and less incivility in public discourse are commonplace among politicians from both parties who declare the breakdown of civility as a main reason for legislative gridlock. On the other hand, some of those suspicious of civility see political demands for more of it as a tool to suppress strongly divergent voices. Others worry that people are too concerned with "political correctness" or even with possibly offending others to be able to speak their minds.

The differing attitudes toward civility are perhaps currently at their most extreme in American universities. On the one hand, prominent cases of hate speech on college campuses have made some worry that campuses are unsafe places for racial minorities. An epidemic of sexual assault on campuses (affecting one in six women, by some estimates) suggests to some that we need stricter standards for speech that are sensitive to the ways words might trigger strong emotional attitudes to past traumatic experiences. Others worry about students from marginalized groups being targeted by "microaggressions," a type of uncivil speech defined as "the everyday verbal, nonverbal, and environmental slights, snubs, or insults, whether intentional or unintentional, which communicate hostile, derogatory, or negative messages to target persons based solely upon their marginalized group membership."[1] Many college administrators, worried in part by parallels between the current political culture and the unrest of the sixties, have called on faculty and students to engage civilly in dealing with disagreements.

From the perspective of those who stress the dangers of civility, many current trends on college campuses for responding to perceived incivility are overreaches that pose a threat to the free expression of ideas. Faculty members have expressed concerns about universities that have fired tenured staff for speech deemed uncivil, and they have interpreted calls for more civility by college administrators as thinly veiled attempts to violate academic and expressive freedoms and keep certain viewpoints from being heard. Others worry that student responses to perceived microaggressions—along with expectations that professors will include "trigger warnings" on course content that might be construed as offensive—have produced a climate in which controversial topics can no longer be addressed in the classroom. Prominent comedians have publicly announced that they refuse to perform on college campuses, claiming that today's students are too easily offended by humor that is satirical in nature. Some sociologists have gone so far as to claim that there has been a major cultural shift toward a "victimhood culture" among college students who demand that universities protect a spurious "right not to be offended."[2]

What exactly is it that people are lamenting the loss of when they complain about a breakdown of civility? What is it that others fear when they worry that civility is potentially harmful? In this chapter, I argue for a philosophical account of civility that can help us make sense of the truth in both attitudes. I attempt to give an account of civility, with particular attention to its potential moral and epistemic value and its potential dangers. Rules of civility, I argue in the next section, are social norms that allow us to communicate respect or disrespect for others. In the section "Civility and Respect," I argue that having such norms can be of great moral and epistemic value, as they help us treat others with the respect that we morally owe them and to promote good intellectual inquiry. However, the fact that civility rules are very often determined by social convention also makes them potentially dangerous, morally and epistemically. In the section "The Potential Value of Norms of Civility," I argue that rules of civility can be skewed in different ways, so that they run counter to our intellectual goals. Rules of civility can discourage us from engaging with each other in inquiry and can even be skewed to the extent that they require intellectual vice and prohibit displays of intellectual virtue. Moreover, the danger of skewed norms is a real, practical problem that is not confined to far-off-possible worlds of the sort that often concern philosophers.

Setting the Stage

Two very different uses of "civil" and "civility" have the potential to cause confusion. Phrases such as "civil rights" and "civil unrest" employ an older use, meaning "of or relating to citizens and their concerns." A newer use, developed sometime in the sixteenth century, is (to quote the *Merriam-Webster* definition) "polite, reasonable, and respectful behavior."[3] It is often perfectly obvious which of these two uses is intended. (When a divorced couple attempts to be civil, they are obviously attempting to treat each other politely and with some respect—not to be better citizens or to talk politics; and the Civil War was a war among U.S. citizens, not an especially polite war!) Phrases such as "civil discourse" and "civil disagreement," however, are potentially ambiguous in whether they connote citizenship or polite and respectful action, and they can even be used to connote both senses (that is, discourse or disagreement about specifically political matters, which is also polite or respectful).

My topic is the polite or respectful sense of civility, which can also be applied to discourse or disagreement about controversial issues that are not political in nature. It is worth noting, though, a connection between the two senses that suggests how the present discussion might be relevant to both. The connection I have in mind is emphasized by sixteenth- and seventeenth-century philosophers, who regarded civility as a set of virtues or qualities that equip people to be good citizens. Among these qualities are tolerance, politeness, and mutual respect, which allow for people to structure and pursue a shared life together as citizens despite deep differences in values and beliefs. These qualities are especially important in a pluralistic democratic society, where the success of the nation depends on people making decisions that affect the whole population. As we will see, a main function of the "polite or respectful" sense of civility is to allow us to work through or in spite of our disagreements, in order to pursue a common goal. When the common goal is to make political decisions, then civility is most closely linked to its etymological origin. But rules of civility can have the function of making possible other shared, non-political projects, by keeping people pursuing these projects together despite disagreements. Some projects are social in nature. (For example, norms of civility constrain speech at a dinner party or at the Thanksgiving table, so that people can jointly pursue the goal of having an enjoyable time, or at least preserve some shred of familial goodwill.) In other cases, the common goal is epistemic, such as discerning as a group what course of action is best. A main function of rules of civility, at their best, is to help us manage actual or potential disagreement so that we can achieve shared goals.

Still, what is civility that allows it to have this function? What important properties, if any, do the words "civil" and "uncivil" allow us to pick out and track? Notice, first, that we use these words to label people as well as behaviors. Behaviors that we describe as civil or uncivil are sometimes relatively simple actions (a tip of the hat, a refusal to shake hands, a derogatory remark, etc.), and sometimes they are more complex events that include multiple actions (a conversation, a debate, etc.). To say that a person is civil or uncivil is to describe a character trait that disposes them to behave civilly or uncivilly. Thus, a civil or uncivil person is one who usually treats people civilly or uncivilly.

A second important point to notice about civility is that it is what philosophers sometimes call a "normative" category. It involves an evaluation of a behavior or a person as good or bad in some respect, and there are rules (norms) that determine whether an action counts as civil or uncivil, how serious its violation is, and what sanctions are appropriate for someone who has violated it. In this respect, rules of civility are like rules of law, grammar, and morality. The rules of civility are widely understood in a culture, at least implicitly, although they may be difficult to articulate explicitly.

Common dictionary definitions connect civility with behavior that is polite and respectful. Dictionary definitions are often good places to start in thinking about a concept, but they typically lack the precision and insight that we need. It will be beneficial to consider in more detail the connection between civil behavior and behavior that is polite and respectful.

Civility is closely connected with politeness. Even so, not all rules of politeness or etiquette have to do with civility. Civil and uncivil behaviors are ways of treating other people or groups, but not all rules of politeness or etiquette have to do with how we treat others. The rule that one ought to eat one's multi-course meal with utensils, beginning from the outside and working inward, for example, does not seem to be a rule aimed at encouraging proper treatment of others; it seems, rather, to be aimed at demonstrating social status. Violating this rule does not constitute treating anyone uncivilly. Thus, rules of civility are, at best, a subclass of rules etiquette, namely ones having to do with how we are to treat others.

* * *

Thinking of rules of civility as just rules for polite treatment of others suggests a challenge to the idea that civility is morally important. Unlike moral rules (e.g., don't lie, don't steal, etc.), rules for polite treatment (e.g., greet people with a handshake, say "please" when you make requests of others, etc.) seem to be arbitrary social conventions, and they can seem trivial in importance compared to genuine moral rules. Below I will argue that there is something to the objection that rules of civility can be dangerous, in that they are social conventions that can conflict with moral norms. However, here I want to stress that the idea that rules of civility are trivial and thus morally unimportant is too quick.

As Richard Boyd has stressed, norms of politeness have an important moral function to play when we interact often with strangers:

> As trivial as they may seem . . . casual signifiers of human respect such as "please" or "thank you", "excuse me" or "how's it going", serve to awaken a sense of sympathy and to breed an easy spontaneity among urban-dwellers whose primary interactions with others are both fleeting and superficial. Despite their evanescence, however, they are not devoid of moral significance. Insofar as they communicate to others a basic and elemental respect, these ritualized practices and everyday formalities are the cement that makes modern society possible.[4]

Likewise, as Boyd also notes, being uncivil can be quite morally serious:

> [T]o fail to be civil to someone—to treat them harshly, rudely or condescendingly—is not only to be guilty of bad manners. It also and more

> ominously signals disdain or contempt for them as moral beings. Treating someone rudely, brusquely or condescendingly says loudly and clearly that you do not regard her as your equal.[5]

Boyd here emphasizes a connection between civility and the morally important category of respect. Even though rules of civility may involve arbitrary social conventions, these rules nevertheless can play an important moral function in that they help us treat each other with appropriate respect. This connection between civility and respect deserves more attention.

Civility and Respect

Might we think of civil behavior as a kind of respectful behavior and uncivil behavior as a kind of disrespectful behavior? I will argue that being civil or uncivil is not the same as being respectful or disrespectful, although the concepts are closely linked. To better see the connection and the difference, though, it will be helpful to digress to say a few words about what respect is.[6]

We can distinguish, first, between respectful attitudes and actions.[7] To have an attitude of respect or disrespect is to have a relatively high or low assessment of a person's worth in some capacity or role. One might respect or disrespect another person as an artist, a comedian, a conversationalist, a tennis player, or (perhaps most importantly) a human being. One can have competing attitudes toward the same person, respecting the person in one capacity while disrespecting them in another.

However, it is not only attitudes that can be respectful or disrespectful; for instance, we can easily recognize when people have been *treated* with respect or disrespect (especially when we have been treated these ways). As such, many actions have what Nicholas Wolterstorff helpfully calls "respect-disrespect import." They involve treating someone as being of relatively high or low worth. Respectful or disrespectful behaviors, like their corresponding attitudes, are directed toward a person in some capacity or role. Wolterstorff gives the following examples:

> The disrespect I show the king, when I refuse to pay him respect by kneeling before him, is focused on his social rank; I belittle him as king. The disrespect shown Lance Armstrong, by those who cast aspersions on his record of winning the Tour de France seven times in a row by

> suggesting that he must have been taking performance-enhancing drugs, is focused on his achievement as a cyclist; they belittle him as a competitive cyclist. The [Croatian] rapist demeans his victim as a Bosnian, say, or as a woman—and in any case, as a human being.[8]

Why do certain actions have respect-disrespect import? Why do they count as treating someone as having relatively high or low worth? We can distinguish between respect-disrespect import that derives from an action's communicating (or displaying) respect or disrespect and respect-disrespect import that does not. In refusing to follow the convention of kneeling, one can communicate clear disrespect for a king. In a similar way, shaking hands manifests mutual respect in virtue of communicating that one regards the other as one's equal in some sense. The act of shaking hands has acquired this meaning in virtue of old and widespread social conventions. In many contexts, failing to shake hands, likewise, has disrespect import. Thus, Miss Manners says,

> [T]he gesture [of shaking hands] itself has been so well known that a refusal to participate must be explained ("I'm so sorry; but I can't shake hands.") because a refusal to shake hands is a symbolic insult (and thus a handy gesture when faced with tyrants and outlaws).[9]

Bows, handshakes, and their refusals derive their respect and disrespect import from the fact that they communicate respect or disrespect. But although communicating respect or disrespect is one common way of treating people with respect or disrespect, many actions have respect-disrespect import that does not derive from what they communicate or display about the worth of a person or object. Suppose, for example, that you do a good deed for someone in complete secrecy, so that neither the recipient nor anyone else knows that there was even a benefactor (much less that you were the doer). Good deeds like this are clear cases of treating people with respect—treating them as having a high degree of worth—but they do not derive their respect import from communicating anything. On the disrespect side, Wolterstorff's example of the extreme disrespect shown by rape has disrespect import that is non-communicative. A person who commits a rape in complete secrecy (by drugging the victim, for example) has committed a seriously disrespectful action, although not in virtue of an act of communication. To take a less heinous example, if I invade your privacy by secretly reading your diary without your permission, I will have treated you disrespectfully, although I will not have communicated disrespect. As a general rule, when one is morally obligated not to treat things with a certain status (e.g., human beings) in some way, to fail to treat them that way has disrespect import that does not derive from communicating disrespect.

Many actions have both communicative and non-communicative respect-disrespect import. Purposefully and publicly causing serious pain or injury to someone, for example, communicates or displays the perpetrator's disrespect for the victim to everyone who knows about it, including the victim. Such an act has both communicative and non-communicative disrespect import, and each may be quite serious. In other cases, the communicated disrespect is more important. For example, a slap on the face has some disrespect import in virtue of the deliberate pain it causes, but more disrespect import in virtue of the disdain it communicates.

In an insightful article to which I am indebted, Cheshire Calhoun points out that cases such as these, of secretly benefiting or mistreating someone, are cases in which civility and respectful behaviors come apart. They are respectful or disrespectful behaviors (respectively), but they do not count as civil or uncivil. For example, secretly reading someone's diary is a disrespectful violation of the person's privacy, but it does not seem right to say that it is uncivil (or civil—neither category seems to apply). Calhoun's plausible diagnosis of why secret mistreatments are not properly considered uncivil (or civil) is that they do not communicate disrespect. She says,

> [W]hat makes being civil different from being respectful, considerate, or tolerant, is that civility always involves a *display* [italics added] of respect, tolerance, or considerateness. Thus civility is an essentially *communicative* form of moral conduct.[10]

Notice that, so far, Calhoun's argument is compatible with the idea that civility is a kind of respectful behavior; namely, behavior that is respectful because it communicates respect. However, Calhoun argues against the idea that civility is a kind of respectful behavior by giving examples that she takes to show that there can actually be respectful behaviors that are uncivil, and civil behaviors that are disrespectful. Her cases of respectful behavior that is uncivil include

> a person who carefully skirts his neighbor's lawn while sarcastically declaring, "Don't worry, I won't step on your precious grass;" the employer who carefully follows affirmative action guidelines but who tells the new employee, "You know you only got this job because you're black;" or the partygoer who rues his own self-restraint by announcing, "I guess I won't tell that (sexist) joke since I know you gals don't have a sense of humor."[11]

Although I will suggest below that there are genuine cases of uncivil but not disrespectful behavior, these examples are not convincing. The behavior of the sarcastic neighbor, for example, involves two distinct actions: the walk around the yard and the sarcastic remark. Walking around the yard is respectful to some degree, perhaps, although its status as a respectful action is arguably canceled by the remark that follows, which has the force of making clear that walking around should not be interpreted as respectful. But the snide remark is both uncivil and disrespectful. (Similar remarks reply to Calhoun's other examples, none of which involves a single action that is at once respectful yet uncivil.) One might reply that civility and respectfulness are not best evaluated in these cases by focusing on each event singly, but rather by evaluating the longer episode of interaction. What we most care about is not that an individual comment, action, or the like is civil, but rather that conversations or interactions, taken as a whole, are civil and respectful. It is not clear, however, that any of these examples involves an interaction that is, on balance, respectful.

Calhoun's central example of an action that is civil and yet disrespectful involves a man in the Deep South, circa 1950, who follows a norm of etiquette that says that he should hold the door open for a woman. Following this rule, according to Calhoun, successfully communicates, in his social context, that the man respects her as a woman, and it thus counts as civil behavior. (Failing to open the door, likewise, might be seen as uncivil.) However, the action also manifests a disrespect for women as being weaker or unequal to men. It is, according to Calhoun, a disrespectful but civil action. To take another example (not one of Calhoun's), suppose that a white shop owner living during the era of Jim Crow laws installs a separate water fountain for black people to use. Insofar as installing the water fountain treats black people as inferior and unequal, the act is a disrespectful one. But the action is arguably a civil gesture, given the prevailing norms at the time (although, of course, it would be extremely uncivil if done today).

I find these examples convincing as cases of civil but ultimately disrespectful behavior. It is not clear, though, that Calhoun correctly diagnoses these with her distinction between manifesting versus communicating respect or disrespect. The reason the relevant actions are ultimately disrespectful to women and to blacks seems equally to involve what the actions communicate or display; namely, that they are inferior or unequal.

A further point about the nature of respect and disrespect will make possible a better diagnosis of cases of disrespectful but civil behavior, and it will allow us to construct better examples than that of the sarcastic neighbor to show that there can be uncivil but respectful behavior. As Wolterstorff notes, "disrespect" is often ambiguous. It can refer to the relatively low worth that a person is treated as having when they are treated disrespectfully (what Wolterstorff calls the "disrespect import" of an action). But it can also refer to a richer moral category of treating someone as having less worth than they actually have. In order not to confuse these, let us follow Wolterstorff in calling the morally richer concept "under-respect." To treat someone with under-respect is to treat the person as having less worth than they objectively have. (Alternatively, "treating a person with [under-respect] is treating her in a way that is incompatible with acknowledgment of her true worth.")[12]

To see the need for the distinction between disrespect import and under-respect, let's consider some examples of behaviors that are disrespectful but not under-respectful. Writing in 2007, Wolterstorff perhaps unintentionally provides a good example in his description of those who disrespect Lance Armstrong. We now know that Armstrong used performance-enhancing drugs, and his athletic feats are of less worth because of it. Thus, those who were showing him disrespect for this reason in 2007 were not, as it turns out, treating him with under-respect as an athlete.[13] Likewise, failing to bow or show formal courtesy to a king might not be a case of under-respect if the king is illegitimate and not worthy of respect as king. Many Christian martyrs in Roman times are said to have similarly refused to pray to emperors who demanded to be treated as divine. In doing so, they were not treating the emperors with under-respect.

The Roman Christian who refuses to worship the emperor is a more compelling case of uncivil but not under-respectful behavior than Calhoun's sarcastic neighbor. Refusing to bow communicates disrespect and counts as uncivil in Roman society, although it is not under-respectful. The reason uncivil and under-respectful behavior come apart in this case seems to turn on the idea that it is actual worth—not the attitude of the culture toward the worth of a person, embodied in civility norms—that determines whether an action is under-respectful. By contrast, it is the attitude of the culture toward the worth of the person that is relevant to whether an action is civil. Let us call this "culturally perceived worth." The culturally perceived worth of a person or member of a group can be inflated above the person's actual worth, so that in order to count as civil, one must communicate what is, in fact, over-respect.

There is another way that rules of civility can require over-respect, even when culturally perceived worth is not higher than actual worth. As David Hume notes, good manners often require going above and beyond what morality obligates us to do:

> [I]n order to render conversation, and the intercourse of minds more easy and agreeable, good-manners have been invented, and have carried the matter somewhat farther [than morality]. . . . [W]herever a person's situation may naturally beget any disagreeable suspicion in him, it is the part of good-manners to prevent it, by a studied display of sentiments, directly contrary to those of which he is apt to be jealous. . . . Strangers and foreigners are without protection: Hence, in all polite countries, they receive the highest civilities, and are entitled to the first place in every company. A man is lord in his own family, and his guests are, in a manner, subject to his authority: Hence, he is always the lowest person in the company; attentive to the wants of every one; and giving himself all the trouble, in order to please, which may not betray too visible an affectation, or impose too much constraint on his guests.[14]

Hume's point here is that rules of civility sometimes require that one display more respect to others than they are strictly owed, for the sake of putting everyone at ease so that we can pursue common goals (have an enjoyable party, for example). Proper manners sometimes mandate actions that the society itself recognizes to be over-respectful, requiring that one demonstrate a humble attitude that puts others' interests ahead of one's own.[15] For example, consider the way that Hume's point about civility rules involving strangers and foreigners is even more exaggerated in gift-giving cultures, in which it is considered rude not to present a visiting foreigner with a gift. It might be that such cultures think that strangers have a worth such that to fail to give them a gift is to undervalue them. More likely, though, the norm mandates what even the culture regards as over-respect for the sake of other goods.

The dependence of norms of civility on culturally perceived worth, rather than on objective worth, also explains why it is possible to have cases of civil but under-respectful behavior, such as Calhoun's case of the chivalrous gentleman and the case of the shop owner in the Jim Crow South. These are examples of actions that are civil in their cultural context but are under-respectful. They involve a society's systematically under-valuing the worth of some minority group in a way that becomes incorporated into conventions of civility. In such contexts, one will still count as civil if one's actions communicate a level of worth that fits with societal standards but is well below their objective worth. Thus, the shop owner who builds a separate water fountain treats black people as having some positive worth that fits the worth the culture perceives them as having, although it fails to befit their actual worth, since it signals that they are separate and so unequal.

Let us sum up the main points about the relation between civility and respect. Civil actions are ones that communicate respect to the recipient, and uncivil actions are ones that communicate disrespect. Norms of civility are socially established rules for what counts as a proper show of respect and what does not in particular circumstances. Civil or uncivil actions can, nevertheless, come apart from actions that are genuinely respectful or under-respectful. One way this can happen is when rules of civility incorporate inaccurate claims about the worth of groups or individuals. When socially perceived worth is lower than actual worth, rules of civility can count behaviors as being civil that are, in fact, under-respectful (as in the cases of the chivalrous gentleman and the shop owner in the Jim Crow South). When socially perceived worth is inflated above actual worth, rules of civility can also require what is, in fact, over-respect (as in the case of Roman Christians refusing to worship the emperor). Moreover, rules of civility can require over-respect relative to socially perceived worth (as in the example of gift-giving cultures).

The Potential Value of Norms of Civility

We are in a position now to see both the potential value that civility has and some potential dangers. Consider, first, the potential benefits of having norms of civility that are widely followed and enforced. First and foremost, if norms of civility embody an adequate sense of the worth of others, civility is an important part of the ethics of treating people with proper respect. When civility norms are good ones, we owe it to each other to be civil. A moral obligation to treat people civilly (and not uncivilly) derives from our moral obligation not to treat people with under-respect.

Second, having norms of civility that are widely followed and enforced can be quite instrumentally valuable, helping us pursue common goals that would otherwise be threatened by the potentially destructive power of disagreements. Here and throughout the rest of the chapter, I will focus on the role of norms of civility in contexts where the most salient goal is an epistemic one—the goal of getting at the truth with respect to some issue or deciding on a best course of action. Some contexts in which the potential value of civility is epistemic are ones in which people have to make a group judgment, such as when a hiring committee must decide together on the best candidate or a jury must decide as a group if the defendant is guilty. Other contexts are ones in which people are trying, in discussion, to discover the truth for themselves. The basic idea behind thinking that norms of civility are potentially epistemically valuable in such contexts is that we will be better positioned to get at the truth—both as individuals and as groups—when we engage civilly with each other. As David Estlund says in discussing the value of civility in deliberative democracies, "The telos of civility is, in part, truth."[16]

What exactly is the contribution that civility can make to our successfully pursuing the truth? My answer is that good rules of civility have the potential to promote two ideals that, in turn, make it more likely that we will get at the truth individually and collectively. The first ideal is widespread engagement: we are more likely to get to the truth when we engage with each other in conversation, pooling information and reasoning with each other. Widespread engagement is epistemically beneficial even (and perhaps especially) when we engage with those with whom we disagree. As J. S. Mill points out in *On Liberty*, his classic argument for free speech, engaging with a diverse set of viewpoints, lessens the chance that we will fail to consider possibilities that turn out to be true and helps us sharpen and improve the reasons we have in cases in which we already hold the correct view.[17]

The second ideal that tends to promote the goal of getting to the truth is that we exercise intellectual virtues in our collective inquiry. Intellectual virtues are character traits that aid inquiry.[18] Especially relevant to our discussion are the virtues of intellectual humility and open-mindedness, which enable us to empathetically understand views we don't hold, recognize our own fallibility and intellectual limitations, and take seriously the idea that others might be right and we might be wrong. (Also relevant is intellectual honesty, a disposition to recognize one's own convictions and the reasons for them, and to be honest about one's assessment of the weight of reasons, including those that one doesn't share.)

The epistemic ideal for deliberation involves a high degree of engagement among people who manifest intellectual virtues, including open-mindedness and intellectual humility. I suggest that the potential epistemic benefits of having civility norms derive from their potential to promote both of these ideals. Let us take these points in turn.

First, norms of civility have the potential to encourage widespread engagement. People are more likely to continue engaging in conversations that are conducted civilly, even when they are disagreeing about highly controversial issues. In a slogan, civility keeps conversations going. Strong norms of civility can also make it more likely that conversations will begin. I am much more likely to begin to engage with you, and you with me, if we know that our conversation will be civil, communicating mutual respect. In some circumstances, rules of civility even preclude disengaging from disagreements, motivating us to face up to our disagreements rather than avoid them. Ignoring someone's point can be an act of incivility, demonstrating disrespect. (In my field of academic philosophy, it is often pointed out that having one's work carefully criticized by someone in person or in writing is the surest sign of respect for one's work; the insult is to have one's work ignored.)

Second, good norms of civility have the potential to encourage exercises of intellectual virtue, especially open-mindedness and intellectual humility. Being open-minded and intellectually humble arguably holds respect import that does not derive from what it communicates, much like secretly benefitting someone. It is a way of treating others with intellectual respect, even apart from what it communicates to them. But if the norms of civility are not skewed, manifesting these virtues in one's conversation will also be a way of communicating or displaying intellectual respect. Engaging in discussion in a way that is intellectually humble and open-minded may thus be required or encouraged by rules of civility.

Potential Dangers of Norms of Civility

As we have seen, rules of civility have the potential to aid us in pursuit of the truth by helping us engage widely with each other in a way that manifests intellectual virtue. However, it is important not to exaggerate the potential contribution civility can make to encouraging widespread engagement and exercises of intellectual virtue. Even very good rules of civility do not always encourage engagement or certain kinds of intellectual virtue. With respect to engagement, norms of civility are sometimes simply neutral as to whether one should engage in conversation or not. A group of highly civil people, who would communicate adequate respect to others if they were to interact, might cloister themselves in isolated communities with like-minded people, without desiring to interact with those with whom they disagree. Further, many norms of civility that promote social goals discourage or prohibit us from engaging with others in certain ways. Norms of civility prohibit us from discussing controversial issues like politics and religion at dinner parties, for example, and they prohibit us from being too nosy in many situations. Many norms of civility fit the aphorism that "good fences make good neighbors" and encourage us to fence off or ignore our potential disagreements rather than confront them.

Furthermore, although civility norms tend to promote open-mindedness and intellectual humility, they tend not to promote a character trait needed to balance these; namely, having the courage of one's convictions. It is possible to show too much intellectual humility or open-mindedness by too quickly conceding to others' points of view. Richard Mouw has suggested that "one of the real problems in modern life is that the people who are good at being civil often lack strong convictions and people who have strong convictions often lack civility."[19] Groups of highly civil people whose civility manifests in their lacking convictions will miss out on the good of robust debate.[20]

The social science literature suggests ways that norms of civility lead away from truth by discouraging engagement and adequate conviction. For example, in one prominent type of experiment on group deliberation, individuals in a group are given different sets of information bearing on some question (which candidate out of several is best for the job, for example), and then they are asked to answer the question as a group. Subjects in the experiment are given information that, if shared among members, points to a clear answer to the question. (Thus, if information about the candidates for the job were combined by the group, they would easily see that there is a unique candidate who is the best qualified for the job.) A key finding of such experiments, however, is that groups do not combine the information that the members have, and the order in which information is presented in the deliberation often leads the group away from the correct answer. Summing up a growing literature on group deliberation, Cass Sunstein describes two influences that keep people from sharing relevant information (and thus lead the group away from the truth):

> The first consists of informational influences, by which group members fail to disclose what they know out of deference to the information publicly announced by others. The second involves social pressures, which lead people to silence themselves in order not to face reputational sanctions, such as the disapproval of relevant others. As a result of these problems, groups often amplify rather than correct individual errors; emphasize shared information at the expense of unshared information[;] . . . and tend to end up in more extreme positions in line with the predeliberation tendencies of their members.[21]

According to Sunstein, one reason people with relevant information tend not to share it involves "social pressures." Those who disagree with the opinions already shared tend not to share their opinions and their evidence out of a desire not to show disrespect to those who have already shared. Social pressures in these studies are magnified when the person in question is from a marginalized group—a woman or a member of a racial minority, for example. Notice that this error seems to be precisely a way that norms of civility prevent group members from adequately engaging with each other and sharing relevant information and opinions. Civility, in these cases, hinders engagement.

In cases involving what Sunstein calls "informational influences," people neglect to share relevant information because they too quickly change their opinions to match the opinions of those who have already expressed opinions and shared information. By the time they have a chance to share the information they have that is relevant to the decision, they regard it as misleading evidence that is not valuable enough to share, since it opposes the opinion that other group members (and they) now share. As a result, their information does not get combined with other information in the group to lead toward the correct conclusion. Arguably, this is a case in which people are too intellectually humble or deferential in their beliefs; a lack of proper conviction leads away from truth. Moreover, norms of civility can exacerbate the problem by implying that it is rude, or communicates intellectual disrespect to those who have already shared, if one does not conform one's view or if one plays "devil's advocate" for a view that is unpopular or does not conform to others' views. In short, civility can lead one to give up one's convictions too easily, leading to epistemic losses rather than gains.

Above, we noted that because norms of civility are influenced by social convention, they can condone what is, in fact, under-respect (as in the case of the shop owner in the Jim Crow South); they can also require what is, in fact, over-respect (as in the case of Christians refusing to worship the emperor). The epistemic dangers involved in civility norms that discourage engagement and certain manifestations of intellectual virtue can be much worse when norms are skewed in these ways.

Norms that condone under-respect and require over-respect carry distinct dangers. One obvious moral danger of skewed civility norms that condone under-respect is that they promote violations of the important moral obligation we have not to treat others under-respectfully. But such norms are also epistemically dangerous in fairly obvious ways, and they can easily lead away from our getting to the truth by precluding or discouraging engagement and open disagreement among people, owing to class, race, sex, etc. It is epistemically detrimental, for example, to have civility norms in play that systematically condone treating women with less intellectual respect than men, with the consequence that treating women as less credible than men, ignoring their opinions, etc., is either not uncivil or is treated as a less serious case of incivility. (The social-psychological studies alluded to above suggest that women are, in fact, less likely to voice dissenting views in group situations, which suggests that these dangers are not mere possibilities.) Such norms discourage widespread and open-minded engagement in a way that is likely to lead away from our getting to the truth about important matters. Other examples that deserve special mention, since they can have especially serious epistemic consequences, are norms of civility that condone intellectual under-respect for experts. Some civility norms might condone under-respect for experts by implying that it is not uncivil at all to denigrate or disregard expertise in some area. Some have argued that such norms of civility are currently in play in some political and religious subcultures in our society, which openly show disrespect for scientific expertise.[22]

Norms that condone under-respect allow those who should have a legitimate voice in the conversation to be ignored and undervalued. They thus encourage the intellectual vices of close-mindedness and intellectual arrogance and discourage widespread engagement in ways that are likely to be barriers to our jointly pursuing the truth.

The epistemic dangers of norms that require over-respect are somewhat less obvious than the dangers of norms that condone under-respect. It might seem that civility norms that require over-respect are relatively benign when compared to norms that condone under-respect, especially since treating someone with under-respect constitutes harm to the recipient, although treating someone with over-respect seldom, if ever, does.[23] Moreover, as we saw from Hume, having norms that require over-respect in some contexts can be valuable for promoting certain kinds of social goals. Nevertheless, civility practices that require over-respect can also serve as barriers to our achieving our shared epistemic goals, and many of the current worries about civility can helpfully be thought of as dangers that derive from a concern that civility norms require too much intellectual respect. This seems an apt diagnosis, for example, of the way civility norms lead away from truth in the social-psychological experiments described above, in which group members feel social pressures not to present evidence or opinions that diverge from the emerging consensus of the group out of a fear that this would convey too little intellectual respect to those who have already expressed views.

Norms of civility can, in principle, be skewed in such a way that it is considered uncivil—a display of intellectual disrespect—even to express disagreement about some topics or to bring them up in conversation. As an extreme example, consider a culture in which relativism about truth has taken hold to such an extent that even to hold or express the idea that there is an objective truth about some domains (such as morality or religion) communicates disrespect. In principle, the norms of civility of a culture might enforce a spurious "right to be right," treating it as disrespectful to imply that others hold views about morality or religion that are incorrect.

In other cultures, it might be widely viewed as communicating disrespect to hold or express particular opinions considered beyond the pale, or to so much as bring up certain topics. One might hope that norms of civility would draw a sharp distinction between the content of a conversation and the mode of conduct of those discussing it. Virtually any topic, one might think, should be fair game for discussion, so long as the mode of conduct of those discussing it is appropriately respectful. But while rules of civility might make such a distinction, in practice, they can fail to distinguish between content and mode of conduct. Rules of civility can preclude some topics from being discussed or opinions from being shared.

Indeed, this seems to be just the worry expressed by those who claim that college campuses are populated by overly coddled students, who mistakenly think that they have a "right not to be offended" by views or topics that they find abhorrent or beyond the pale. As an example of this kind of criticism, consider how a Harvard law professor has suggested that it is difficult in the current academic culture to teach about rape law, since students and teachers are afraid that discussing the topic may cause offense, produce emotional discomfort, and lead to official complaints from students.[24]

It is worth stressing that the mere fact that someone feels offended at something someone else says is not sufficient to show that the speech was uncivil. People can be oversensitive and can misinterpret as disrespectful something that did not, in fact, communicate disrespect. What is actually communicated is determined by social conventions, not directly by the hearer's interpretation. However, the respect or disrespect communicated by an action, and how much respect is required by norms of civility, are matters of convention that can be influenced by widely shared views about what is offensive. Thus, if it is widely agreed upon that bringing up some topic is offensive, doing so will communicate offense and will count as uncivil.

Another way that norms of civility can require too much over-respect is by treating violations of some norms as more serious than they should be treated.

Consider, for example, the culture of Muslim extremism, in which drawing a cartoon depicting Mohammed (an expression which, I would contend, is genuinely uncivil to Muslims) is treated as a justification for killing the artist. A criticism along these lines is also common among those who worry that the response to microaggression and other uncivil speech on many college campuses is too severe. Some colleges have websites aimed at rallying public outcry by recounting detailed stories of perceived microaggressions (complete with names of alleged perpetrators). In other cases, complaints such as these result in Title IX investigations against faculty members. Critics contend that the reactions tend to over-punish some cases of speech that, though uncivil, do not merit the degree of punishment meted out.

My aim in this chapter is not to settle whether these critics are right, but to provide an account of civility and its potential benefits and dangers that might illuminate the debate. It is true in principle, at least, that norms of civility can require too much over-respect in a way that obstructs our epistemic goals by discouraging engagement and encouraging polarization. (If one cannot disagree without offending, one will be tempted to retreat and talk only to people with whom one agrees.) Such norms can also, in principle, discourage people from having the courage of their convictions. Whether critics are correct that the current culture in U.S. universities already exhibits these potential dangers deserves more careful discussion.

At their best, norms of civility can make it more likely that we will reach our epistemic and social goals. At their worst, they can obstruct these goals. It is worth noting, in conclusion, that different norms might be better calibrated for different subcultures or groups that have different epistemic and social goals. There are groups that would not be well-served by having norms that give a long leash for expressions of disagreement. Consider, for example, military groups that must often make quick, life-and-death decisions. Such an organization is served well by a strong chain of command and social norms that discourage disagreement (though even such an organization can go too far in this respect). The goals of such an organization, including winning battles and keeping its soldiers alive, would be ill served by welcoming disagreement at every turn. Prolonged deliberation would mean almost certain death.

By contrast, other organizations would be better served by norms of civility that give a wide berth to disagreement and open challenge. Consider, for example, the New York Fed, the arm of the Federal Reserve tasked with regulating the nation's biggest banks. An external investigation of the Fed in 2009, which aimed to explain why the Fed failed to stop the 2008 financial crisis and to recommend changes, found that the culture of the Fed was partly to blame.[25] According to the report, the culture was such that examiners feared asking difficult questions of banks or speaking out against them in reports, and disagreement with one's supervisors was seen as a show of disrespect. The report suggested that the Fed cultivate different cultural norms according to which expert examiners would be encouraged to be contrarian, and would be professionally rewarded for showing a willingness to speak up and even disagree with superiors. Socrates once described his contribution to society by analogy to a gadfly buzzing in the ear of those in power. Given its regulatory goals, the Fed would be well-served by social norms that value the gadfly.

We could easily multiply these examples of social norms that seem well-suited for different social and epistemological purposes. For example, a rule of civility by which it is extremely impolite for a student to interrupt a professor to explain his or her own take on the subject would be out of place in an introductory chemistry class, where the goal is to impart to students the knowledge of well-established theories. The same rule, though, would not be suitable as a norm in a philosophy classroom, which should encourage students to express opinions and explore ideas that potentially differ from those of the professor.

Chapter 10

Cultivating Intellectual Humility and Hospitality in Interfaith Dialogue

Richard J. Mouw
Fuller Theological Seminary

Simone Weil, one of my favorite spiritual writers, has a provocative way of encouraging Christians to pursue the quest for truth: "Christ likes us to prefer truth to him," she wrote, "because, before being Christ, he is truth. If one turns aside from him to go toward the truth, one will not go far before falling into his arms."[1]

While I have taken personal encouragement from that piece of counsel, whenever I have quoted it in lectures, I have sometimes received mild pushback from Christians who find it a bit too provocative. It is a nice thought, they say, that we can walk into the unknown with the confidence that we can't go very far without meeting the embrace of Jesus. But can't that kind of confidence also set us upon dangerous paths that might even lead us away from Jesus? Don't we at least need to hear a word of warning about the possibility that when we "go toward the truth" we could actually be moving toward the snares of falsehood?

The concern is legitimate, even extremely important. My own proclivity for affirming Weil's word of encouragement without issuing the corresponding warning has to do with my conviction that, in the evangelical community, we have typically needed more encouragement than warning about the intellectual quest. But the requisite nuances should still be acknowledged and explored, and I will do a bit of that here.

* * *

In an often-cited passage in his book *On Christian Doctrine*, St. Augustine encourages Christians to make free use of the ideas of "heathen" thinkers. In doing so, he says, we can follow in spirit the example of the people of Israel when they were leaving Egypt. The Israelites were rightly fleeing the Egyptians' pagan idols and oppressive practices. But they also had the wisdom to take some things with them from Egypt; namely, some of the "vessels and ornaments of gold and silver, and garments," which God's people "appropriated to themselves, designing them for a better use, [and] not doing this on their own authority, but by the command of God."

The same kind of appropriation holds, argues Augustine, for matters of the mind. When "those who are called philosophers, and especially the Platonists," have developed thought that "is true and in harmony with our faith, we are not only not to shrink from it, but to claim it for our own use from those who have unlawful possession of it." The deliverances of these thinkers contain "gold and silver, which they did not create themselves, but dug out of the mines of God's providence which are everywhere scattered abroad." Therefore, Augustine goes on, when the Christian rightly "separates himself in spirit from the miserable fellowship of these men," we ought to take these God-given items with us in order to put them "to a Christian use."[2]

Augustine offered this assessment of "heathen" thought not long after he had become the bishop of Hippo. His views on these matters had undergone a significant change in tone from a half decade earlier when, shortly before becoming priest, he had written *Of True Religion*. In that short treatise, he was much less harsh toward non-Christian thinkers. Indeed, he went so far as to suggest that "[i]f Plato and the rest of them, in whose names men glory, were to come to life again" and to see the flourishing of Christian life and worship, they would rejoice. If, said Augustine, "they really were the men they are said to have been, [in seeing that] the human race was being called away from desire for temporal and transient goods to spiritual and intelligible goods and to the hope of eternal life," they would have to repent of their own timidity regarding teaching truths. "That is what we did not dare to preach to the people. . . . We preferred to yield to popular custom rather than to bring the people over to our way of thinking and living." And then this bold verdict: "So if these men could live their lives again today, they would see by whose authority measures are best taken for man's salvation, and *with the change of a few words and sentiments*, they would become Christians" (emphasis mine).[3]

I describe that as a "bold verdict," and I have to confess that I think Augustine overdoes the boldness. For one thing, he is much too accepting at that stage in his thinking of the actual content of Platonistic thought. There is obviously much disagreement these days in the Christian academy about how much error there is in Plato's philosophical system. I have often, only half-jokingly, made a distinction for my students between a radical de-Platonizing of Christian thought—based on the assumption that if Plato said something, we have to reject it—and a moderate de-Platonizing—which holds that if Plato said something and it is wrong, then we should reject it. But I think that most of us who have thought about such things would agree that the differences between Platonistic philosophy and biblical thought come down to more than a matter of "a few words and sentiments."

Of course, it took only a few years of careful theological reflection on Augustine's part to come to see the seriousness of many of those differences. When he came around to distancing himself from much that he had previously affirmed in Plato's thought, he did not simply reject out of hand all of the content of Platonism. And rightly so. There is much that Plato wrote about, for example, justice and virtue and beauty, that rings helpful for my own efforts to discern the contents of a biblical worldview. There are indeed "vessels and ornaments of gold and silver" that are to be discovered in Plato's writings.

But I am not happy with Augustine's later depiction of how we are to appropriate these positive elements in the works of "heathen" thinkers. When we discover something good in what they have produced, he says, we Christians are to "claim it for our own use from those who have unlawful possession of it," just as the Israelites, as they fled the land, seized valuable things from the Egyptians in order to put those things to a proper use.

I have no complaints against the attitudes and behaviors of the children of Israel as they departed Egypt. They had suffered greatly under their Egyptian oppressors, and they rightly saw much of the wealth of Egypt as having benefited from labors for which they, the Israelites, had not been properly compensated. Furthermore, I'm sure that under the godly leadership of Moses, they exercised some good judgment in deciding what they could legitimately appropriate for their own use as a people dedicated to the service of the God who is the ultimate "owner" of everything in creation.

The important question about Plato, however, is whether the good things that we can discover in what he produced as a philosopher were, as Augustine insists, in Platonism's "unlawful possession." Consider, for example, the passage to follow, which is a favorite of mine from Plato's *Meno*. Socrates has been leading his friends in a discussion of how we are to understand the nature of virtue. After several attempts to come up with an adequate account, his friends become discouraged. They have been looking for a unified definition of virtue, but instead, they complain, all they have come up with is a "swarm" of virtues. Socrates responds by encouraging them to keep at the task. The human soul, he says, is immortal, " having been born again many times." And because the soul has "seen all things that exist, whether in this world or in the world below," it actually possesses a kind of suppressed "knowledge of them all." His friends then press on in the assurance that "all nature is akin," which means, he says, that we can be confident of success, "if a man is strenuous and does not faint."[4]

Now, this passage clearly expresses some decidedly non-Christian thoughts. Reincarnation is not a Christian teaching, nor does coming to "know" something actually a recollecting what we have previously encountered in directly contemplating, in a bodiless condition, eternal Forms. What Plato means by the affirmation that "all nature is akin" is quite different than what I mean when I confess that "all things hold together" in Jesus Christ (Col. 1:17).

But I still find this passage spiritually inspiring. Because God is the creator of all things, and because he watches over every sparrow as well as over his human children, the assurance that "all nature is akin" strikes a positive chord in the deep places. And the words of epistemic hope that Socrates offers to his disciples points me to a similar kind of confidence for the Christian intellectual journey.

In acknowledging my gratitude for this passage authored by Plato, I do not think of myself as seizing something that is in his "unlawful possession." Indeed, it is important that I see it as something rightfully "owned" by Plato. While I can find similar messages of encouragement in uniquely Christian writings, it is precisely the fact that his comments inspire me in the context of his thought, his non-Christian convictions, that they stimulate a special kind of appreciation in my heart and mind. I would not receive the encouragement in the same way if I were to come across exactly the same words, "all nature is akin" in, say, Habakkuk or 1 Timothy or Martin Luther.

Another attractive thing about this passage for me is its literary value. Plato is a wonderful writer, and in these words by Socrates to his friends, he has put together some fine sentences. They express his philosophy well, and they show how that philosophical perspective can inspire and motivate. And in all of that, what Plato says in this instance comports well with the overall literary development of this dialogue.

To put it bluntly, I don't want to "seize" this from Plato. I see no need to rescue it from his possession. I want him to "keep" it. I like the passage precisely because it is an expression of his gifts—gifts that I thank his creator for blessing him with, and talents that Plato has put to such excellent use.

In saying all of that about the passage in the *Meno,* I do not in any way mean to ignore the ways in which I disagree with Plato from a Christian point of view. He is wrong about some matters that are of eternal importance. My assignment as a Christian scholar is to do what I can to help the Christian community to discern the difference between truth and falsehood. But I must not do that in a way that encourages Christians to denigrate the accomplishments of non-Christian thinkers.

I have often found it helpful, especially in addressing orthodox Reformed audiences, to point to the example of John Calvin in this regard. On several occasions, Calvin expressed appreciation for the contributions of non-Christian thinkers. Before his evangelical conversion, he had studied law and cultivated a special gratitude for the insights he had found in Seneca's writings. In his *Institutes*, Calvin explains the theological basis for this positive regard for the "admirable light of truth shining" in the works of pagan thinkers by explaining that "the mind of man, though fallen and perverted from its wholeness," can still be "clothed and ornamented with God's excellent gifts." Indeed, Calvin insists that to refuse to accept the truth produced by such minds is "to dishonor the Spirit of God."[5]

I see no reason why Calvin would not endorse the comments I made above about the passage in Plato's *Meno*. Plato's nicely expressed thoughts about the quest for virtue are an exhibit of the ways in which a pagan thinker can produce something that is "clothed and ornamented with God's excellent gifts." And to recognize this is to honor the workings of God's Spirit beyond the boundaries of the Christian community.

And I don't think I am violating the spirit of Calvin's way of making his point by insisting, as I did with reference to the passage in the *Meno*, that the Spirit of God gave these gifts to Plato. It is not as if Plato was somehow simply "channeling" words and thoughts that the Spirit was transmitting through him, as if Plato were a rather sophisticated version of the ventriloquist's puppet. While the Spirit was mysteriously at work in Plato's intellectual endeavors, he did not produce the good things to be found in his dialogues in spite of himself.

Those good things were genuinely Plato's. We can be grateful to the Spirit for what he empowered Plato to accomplish while also admiring Plato himself for the talents that he put on display in his creative endeavors.

My motivation for belaboring these matters is to counter what I often come across as some—for me—distasteful habits of mind in the evangelical community regarding what can or cannot be learned from engaging non-Christian thought and, more generally, from the broader cultural contributions of unbelievers. The worst-case scenario, of course, is the refusal on the part of some Christians to see any value at all in engaging the intellectual-cultural accomplishments of non-Christians. But if we do get to the point where we find it impossible simply to deny any value in those accomplishments, we often resort to the kind of assessment that we see in Augustine's Egyptian imagery. Anything worthwhile in the thoughts of unbelievers is there in spite of those who have those thoughts. They are unlawful possessors of truth and goodness and beauty. To use a good biblical phrase that is often put to bad use, "we take captive" those things in order to bring them into obedience to Christ (2 Cor. 10:5).

* * *

So now I return to Simone Weil's comment about seeking the truth. When faced with what looks like a choice between staying close to Jesus and stepping out in the direction of something that looks like it may be a manifestation of truth, we should move toward the truth. Jesus is the truth, and if we genuinely seek the truth, we cannot go very far without entering into his embrace.

I repeat: I see the dangers of what she is proposing. I also see the dangers of the views I have just articulated about God's gifts to non-Christian thinkers. I fully endorse the Calvinist doctrine of total depravity, and I take the "holistic" interpretation of the doctrine that holds that our sinful rebellion has touched all areas of our lives: personal relations, spiritual dispositions, political strivings, aesthetic yearnings, intellectual endeavors, and much more. All of these expressions of our humanity flow from our "heart" commitments, and the sinful "heart is deceitful above all things and beyond cure. Who can understand it?" (Jer. 17:9)

This means that we certainly must be careful not to fall into error by uncritically appropriating non-Christian thought. But the deceit to which we are prone in our sinfulness can also tempt us to take false security in an "us" versus "them" polarity, whereby we refuse to accept what the Spirit has accomplished beyond the borders of the Christian community. G. K. Chesterton put it well when he said that "[i]dolatory is committed not merely by setting up false gods, but also by setting up false devils."[6]

One of the factors that has inhibited traditional Christians, especially evangelicals, from freely engaging the ideas of others in a spirit of learning was pointed to by Herman Bavinck in discussing the question of how to engage creatively with non-Christian religions. Bavinck was a nineteenth-century orthodox Calvinist, a younger colleague of Abraham Kuyper. I want to build on an insight of his that I have found helpful in my own participation in interfaith dialogues.

The insight from Bavinck comes up in his *Reformed Dogmatics*, where he criticizes the way that "in the past the [Christian] study of religions was pursued exclusively in the interest of dogmatics and apologetics. The founders of [non-Christian] religions, like Mohammed," Bavinck observes, "were simply considered imposters, enemies of God, accomplices of the devil." This assessment is no longer tenable, however, because, Bavinck argues, those religions "have become more precisely known"; we have been learning more about them, says Bavinck, from "both history and psychology." And then Bavinck offers this theological verdict: "Also among pagans, says Scripture, there is a revelation of God, an illumination by the Logos, a working of God's Spirit."[7]

One important emphasis in his comments is the way he appeals to a rather robust divine "revealing," which supplements the all-important content of biblical revelation. Indeed, his proposal here presupposes an explicit Trinitarian framework. There is the extra-biblical "revelation" on display in the natural realm, along with an "illumination" by the Logos, and the "working of God's Spirit." This suggests a more dynamic character to God's "natural" dealings with other religions than the more static patterns often suggested by the ideas of "general revelation" and "natural law." In citing three different sources of a divine "revealing" to other religions, Bavinck is clearly suggesting that the divine Trinity takes an active interest in their particularities. The way, that the Logos may illuminate, or the Spirit may be at work in, the thoughts of a practitioner of Hinduism, for example, might be very different from the manner in which those divine realities impact the spiritual quest of a Muslim or a Confucian.

The second helpful emphasis in Bavinck's comments is his insistence that it is not enough to approach non-Christian religions within the confines of "dogmatics and apologetics." It is important to stress the fact that Bavinck is not dismissing the concerns associated with dogmatic or apologetic foci in approaching other religious systems. Developing our understanding of the central truths of the gospel and defending those truths against those who reject them are non-negotiable aims for those of us committed to the cause of the gospel. But for a proper understanding and assessment of, for example, Islamic teaching, Bavinck is saying that we cannot proceed "exclusively" with dogmatic or apologetic questions in mind. We can hold fast to our profound conviction that Christ alone can save while acknowledging that it is still legitimate to ask whether we can gain insights into the truth about God and the human condition by attending to the content of, say, Muslim thought.

When the main question is whether we have good reasons to believe that, say, a fully committed Muslim—someone whose understanding of reality is spelled out in consistently Muslim terms—can go to heaven, many of us will have to answer that a person who wants to enter into a saving relationship with the one true God will not achieve that goal by adhering consistently to Muslim beliefs and practices. If, however, we can bracket the dogmatic and apologetic focus on issues about whether Muslims *qua* Muslims can be saved, then we are free to evaluate this or that particular Muslim teaching in terms of whether it illuminates reality, and we may well find many good and true elements in the Muslim worldview. Indeed, we might even find things in the Muslim understanding of spiritual reality that can enrich—perhaps by calling our attention to spiritual matters that we have not thought about clearly—our own Christian understanding of religious truth.

* * *

I turn now to some practical recommendations. What must we cultivate in our spiritual lives in order to foster a healthy Christian intellectual hospitality?

I think John Calvin had it right when he identified humility as basic to Christian spirituality:

> I have always been exceedingly delighted with the words of Chrysostom, "The foundation of our philosophy is humility;" and still more

> with those of Augustine. . . . when asked, What is the first precept in eloquence? answered, Delivery: What is the second? Delivery: What the third? Delivery: so, if you ask me in regard to the precepts of the Christian Religion, I will answer, first, second, and third, Humility.[8]

The writer of Psalm 139 offers strong support for this insistence when he expresses his own humble awareness that because God is all-knowing, the contents of his own consciousness, including his motives and cognitive assessments, are open to the correction of divine scrutiny. The persistent habit of careful self-examination requires a spirit of humility, including in our intellectual lives.

Again, Simone Weil points explicitly to the link between intellectual pursuits and spirituality, specifically with reference to humility:

> [T]he virtue of humility is a far more precious treasure than all academic progress. From this point of view it is perhaps even more useful to contemplate our stupidity than our sin. Consciousness of sin gives us the feeling that we are evil, and a kind of pride sometimes finds a place in it. When we force ourselves to fix the gaze, not only of our eyes but of our souls, upon a school exercise in which we have failed through sheer stupidity, a sense of our mediocrity is borne in upon us with irresistible evidence. No knowledge is more to be desired. If we can arrive at knowing this truth with all our souls, we shall be well established on the right foundation.[9]

Many of us who have been active in interfaith dialogue have been helped in understanding the importance of humility to our efforts by Leonard Swidler's well-known "Dialogue Decalogue," where he sets forth ten principles for constructive interfaith engagement.[10] We need not examine Swidler's "commandments" and his accompanying commentary on each item here, but it is instructive to reflect briefly on some of the spiritual dispositions that those principles point us to in sorting out some issues regarding intellectual hospitality. Swidler emphasizes, for example, the need to approach perspectives different from our own with a humble spirit of learning. Understandably, this does not come easily for evangelicals, especially when the topics have to do with explicit religious beliefs. We have often approached other religious perspectives—Buddhism,

Islam, animism—with an exclusive emphasis on soteriological concerns. We have rightly insisted that human beings can only be reconciled to God through the atoning work of Jesus Christ, and we have resisted any moves in the direction of religious relativism or syncretism.

Again, that soteriological focus is an important one. But we can proclaim clearly our profound conviction that Christ alone can save while at the same time acknowledging that it is still legitimate to ask whether we can gain insights into the truth about God and the human condition by attending to the content of, say, Muslim thought.

It is a little easier to "bracket" the salvific questions, of course, when we move away from explicitly theological matters. We can engage, for example, in Freud's arguments in his *Civilization and Its Discontents*, or in Simone de Beauvoir's *The Second Sex*, without concentrating on whether either of them is going to heaven. What is important for all of these kinds of cases, though, is the willingness to learn and even to admit that we have misunderstood these perspectives in the past. Truthfulness is a key biblical ideal, and it is a sin to bear false witness against our neighbors, whether they are Muslims, Viennese psychoanalysts, or Parisian existentialists.

Another humility-related theme that looms large in Swidler's "Decalogue" is empathy. The ability to see things from the point of view of those whom we are engaging is crucial for better understanding. Here is how Swidler puts it:

> Each participant needs to describe her/himself. For example, only a Muslim can describe what it really means to be an authentic member of the Muslim community. At the same time, when one's partner in dialogue attempts to describe back to them what they have understood of their partner's self-description, then such a description must be recognizable to the described party.[11]

Empathy is experiencing the feelings and concerns of others as if they were our own. Hospitality is a fine image for understanding what this means in the life of the mind. We "make room" for the ideas of a Simone de Beauvoir by attempting to grasp the feelings and concerns that give rise to her ideas about gender. To be sure, attempting to understand the views of a self-professed atheist from the "inside," as it were, can be a special challenge for a Christian. But it is an important challenge.

Indeed, it may be that we Christians have special advantages in nurturing the necessary kind of empathy. The humble awareness of our own sin can lead us, as Simone Weil put it in straightforward terms, "to contemplate our stupidity." We know we are finite creatures. God is God, and we are not, which means that we fall far short of omniscience. And the cognitive defects that stem from finitude are even more greatly exaggerated because of our sinful rebelliousness. This means that what might appear at first glance to be our radical disagreement with a certain point of view might, upon humble reflection, require a confession of sin. A case in point: I hold conservative views about sexuality—but I also have to confess that we traditional Christians have been inexcusably cruel toward people who experience, for example, same-sex attractions. Or, to take another perspective, my disagreements with the Wicca perspective are very real—but I have to remind myself about the witch-burnings of the past. And so on.

But there is more at stake than repentance regarding our own misdeeds and misunderstandings—as important as that is. As already emphasized, a spirit of genuine learning must enter into the picture. Often, there is truth to be culled from serious reflection upon distorted truths. And, as John Calvin rightly insisted in the case of Seneca, there are straightforwardly positive truths to be found outside the boundaries of the Christian community. The Spirit of God is at work, promoting the cause of truth, in the larger world.

* * *

One of the teachers in my undergraduate studies who influenced me the most was a godly Wesleyan professor of literature at Houghton College, Dr. Josephine Rickard. In a seminar for English majors, we engaged in a heated discussion about graphic portrayals of sexuality in fiction. I argued that, as Christians, we should see fictional portrayals of the human condition as an opportunity better to understand the reality of sin in the world. "Doc Jo"—as we called her with fondness—was not happy with my line of argument and finally reprimanded me with these words: "Mister Mouw," she said in a sharp tone, "we can have a perfectly adequate awareness of the reality of trash without having to go around lifting the lids of every trash can in town!"

Her point was well put—and well-taken by me. And I have often thought of it as a necessary warning about my own tendencies to celebrate what I have been discussing here as intellectual hospitality. To make room for others in our homes, for example, is to do so with a necessary awareness of the actual physical conditions. Our homes are physical spaces, with walls and windows and doors. As hosts, we have to plan our invitations to guests in the light of those physical limitations. Genuine hospitality is not properly practiced when we allow thieves to break in and steal.

Similarly, Christian intellectual hospitality must respect appropriate boundaries. Some intellectual "intrusion" can be dangerous. Just as a human invader may corrupt the very spaces that we create in our homes for extending hospitality, so can ideas corrupt our mental and spiritual "spaces."

It may seem counter to my overall purpose in this chapter to make this point as I conclude. But the fact is that intellectual promiscuity is a genuine danger in the broader Christian community, and it can become a danger when evangelicals take on the intellectual challenges that we have been able to avoid in the past, largely because of the heavy dose of anti-intellectualism that we have inherited. My main task here has been to offer thoughts that can counter that anti-intellectualism by encouraging practices of intellectual hospitality, while at the same time recognizing that the alternative to anti-intellectualism is not without dangers of its own.

A healthy evangelical intellectual life must be pursued with the cultivation of the kind of spiritual discernment that equips us to recognize dangers of many varieties. The dangers may be real, but we cannot ignore the way that stepping-into-the-unknown imagery captures something important to intellectual inquiry in particular. The scholarly life is an ongoing series of stepping into the unknown. Every time we pick up a new book to read, or choose a new topic to write about for an essay, or map out a new research project, or agree to take or teach a new course, we are taking steps into uncharted territory. In our intellectual pursuits, we are regularly stepping out on new adventures. And I, for one, am grateful for Simone Weil's reminder that the arms of Jesus are always out there!

Notes

Introduction: Seeking Intellectual Virtue for the Sake of Civil Discourse

[1] "New Survey Shows Americans Believe Civility is on the Decline," The Associated Press-NORC Center for Public Affairs Research, April 15, 2016, http://www.apnorc.org/PDFs/Rudeness/APNORC%20Rude%20Behavior%20Report%20%20PRESS%20RELEASE.pdf; "What Unites and Divides the United States?" The Associated Press-NORC Center for Public Affairs Research, accessed February 28, 2019, http://www.apnorc.org/PDFs/AP-NORC%20Omnibus%20October%202018/Topline_pdf.pdf.

[2] Weber Shandwick, Powell Tate, and KRC Research, "Civility in America 2018: Civility at Work and in Our Public Squares," accessed February 28, 2019, https://www.webershandwick.com/wp-content/uploads/2018/06/Civility-in-America-VII-FINAL.pdf.

[3] "Americans Concerned Lack of Civility Breeds Violence . . . ," Marist Institute for Public Opinion, November 2, 2018, http://maristpoll.marist.edu/wp-content/uploads/2018/11/NPR_PBS-NewsHour_Marist-Poll_USA-Summary_1810311039.pdf#page=1.

[4] Simone Weil, *Waiting for God* (New York: Harper & Row, 1973), 69.

Chapter 1: Intellectual Virtues, Civility, and Public Discourse

[1] My primary focus will be the quality of public discourse in the United States; however, similar points could be made, some with even greater strength, about the state of public discourse in other parts of the world.

[2] For more on the history of civility and how it compares to civility in the present, see Clifford Orwin, "Civility," *The American Scholar* 60, no. 4 (1991): 553–64; Stephen L. Carter, *Civility: Manners, Morals, and the Etiquette of Democracy* (New York: Basic Books, 1998), 9–19, and 117–20; and Os Guinness, *The Case for Civility: And Why Our Future Depends on It* (New York: Harper Collins, 2008), chaps. 2 and 3.

[3] Lenar Whitney, "Campaign 2014: Lenar Whitney 'Global Warming Is a Hoax,'" *The Washington Post*, July 30, 2014, video, 4:45, http://www.washingtonpost.com/

posttv/politics/campaign-2014-lenar-whitney-global-warming-is-a-hoax/2014/07/30/e06388ce-17f8-11e4-88f7-96ed767bb747_video.html.

[4] Jonathan Chait, "Why I'm So Mean," *Daily Intelligencer*, February 8, 2012, http://nymag.com/daily/intelligencer/2012/02/jonathan-chait-why-im-so-mean.html.

[5] My claim is not that de Rugy is right and Chait is wrong. Rather, my concern is with the way in which Chait has gone about responding to de Rugy's argument. For an interesting discussion of the exchange between de Rugy and Chait, see Clive Crook, "U.S. Taxes Are Unusually Progressive," *The Atlantic*, February 10, 2012, http://www.theatlantic.com/business/archive/2012/02/us-taxes-really-are-unusually-progressive/252917.

[6] For a general overview of virtue epistemology, see Heather Battaly, "Virtue Epistomology," *Philosophy Compass* 3, no. 4 (2008): 639–63; and Jason Baehr, "Virtue Epistomology," *Internet Encyclopedia of Philosophy*, 2004, http://www.iep.utm.edu/virtueep/.

[7] As this list suggests, I am thinking of intellectual virtues along "responsibilist" versus "reliabilist" lines. Virtue reliabilists like Ernie Sosa, *A Virtue Epistemology: Apt Belief and Reflective* Knowledge, Vol. 1 (Oxford: Oxford University Press, 2007) and John Greco, *Achieving Knowledge* (Cambridge: Cambridge University Press, 2010) think of intellectual virtues on the model of cognitive faculties, like memory, vision, and introspection, *not* as good intellectual character traits. For more on the distinction between these two approaches, see Jason Baehr, "Educating for Intellectual Virtues: From Theory to Practice," *Journal of the Philosophy of Education* 47, no. 2 (2013): 248–62.

[8] On a broader conception of "smarts," they are partly constituted by intellectual habits or virtues. See Ron Ritchhart, *Intellectual Character: What It Is, Why It Matters, and How to Get It* (San Francisco: Jossey-Bass, 2002) for a development of this point.

[9] Lists like these raise the obvious question of how intellectual virtues (and vices) are related to what we ordinarily think of as *moral* virtues (and vices). Oversimplifying a bit, we can think of intellectual virtues as the character traits of a good *thinker, learner, or truth-seeker* and moral virtues as the character traits of a good *neighbor* (in the biblical sense). For a more precise and complex account of this relationship, see Jason Baehr, *The Inquiring Mind: On Intellectual Virtues and Virtue Epistemology* (Oxford: Oxford University Press, 2011), appendix.

[10] For an instructive discussion of some specific forms of reasoning that are common in public discourse, the intellectual vices they manifest, and the intellectual practices and virtues that can remedy them, see Robert Garcia and Nathan King, "Toward

Intellectually Virtuous Discourse: Two Vicious Fallacies and the Virtues that Inhibit Them," in *Intellectual Virtues and Education: Essays in Applied Virtue Epistemology*, ed. Jason Baehr (New York: Routledge, 2016), 202–20.

[11] As noted earlier, there may be other aspects of incivility, even incivility in public discourse, that are not very well captured by intellectual-vices terminology; for instance, aspects having to do with etiquette or manners. For an account of civility that focuses primarily on these aspects, see P. M. Forni, *Choosing Civility* (New York: St. Martin's Press, 2002), 9 which includes the following statement: "Whatever civility might be, it has to do with courtesy, politeness, and good manners."

[12] One might even wonder whether this is a dangerously mistaken diagnosis because it (apparently) lays the blame on people's character rather than on broader societal or situational factors. This worry might arise from either of two deeper doubts: one about the very existence of character (see John M. Doris, *Lack of Character: Personality and Moral Behavior* [Cambridge: Cambridge University Press, 2002]) and the other about whether the specific sorts of behaviors in question really can be attributed to the manifestation of intellectual vices. On the latter point, I wish to remain neutral. As will become clearer below, I am not wedded to the view that familiar manifestations of incivility in public discourse are the result of intellectual vices. What I am committed to is the claim that these are manifestations of the actions and attitudes *characteristic* of intellectual vices. (One can, of course, engage in vicious behavior, even if such behavior is not habitual or otherwise "second nature" in the way that is characteristic of the possession of a vice.) On the former point, for an argument against the situationist claim that most people don't possess intellectual virtues or vices, see my *Intellectual Virtues and Education: Essays in Applied Virtue Epistemology* (London: Routledge, 2016).

[13] Mill also describes problematic public discourse using the language and concepts of intellectual character. See, for example, John Stuart Mill, *On Liberty*, ed. Elizabeth Rapaport (1859; Indianapolis: Hackett, 1978), 50–52. Citations refer to the Hackett edition.

[14] Of course, some uncivil behaviors in this context (e.g., name-calling) do have considerable moral significance. However, my immediate focus is on certain, more purely epistemic manifestations of civility. At a certain level, given the simultaneously epistemic and interpersonal nature of public discourse, it will be impossible to disentangle considerations of intellectual virtues and vices from their moral counterparts (e.g., it may be that the shortcomings in question are at once epistemic *and* moral). At present, my point is that intellectual-vice concepts appear to be uniquely well suited to

capture certain prominent aspects of incivility in this domain. Thanks to Jim Taylor for feedback on this point.

[15] Or, at any rate, it is to suggest that the person is *acting like* a person with such vices, which is also personally indicting. For a full account of how or why intellectual virtues and vices (and not just moral virtues and vices) bear on personal worth, see Jason Baehr, *Inquiring Mind*, chaps. 6–7.

[16] A related point is that intellectual vices tend to block access to the truth and other epistemic goods. This provides a further explanation of why the behavior in question is objectionable. However, this feature is not unique to intellectual virtues. Mishandling of evidence, bad reasoning, and the like also block access to the truth.

[17] This is the flipside of the familiar claim that intellectual *virtues* are character traits rooted in a "love" of epistemic goods. See James A. Montmarquet, *Epistemic Virtue and Doxastic Responsibility* (Lanham, MD: Rowman and Littlefield, 1993); Linda Trinkaus Zagzebski, *Virtues of the Mind: An Inquiry into the Nature of Virtue and the Ethical Foundations of Knowledge* (Cambridge: Cambridge University Press, 1996); Robert C. Roberts and W. Jay Wood, *Intellectual Virtues: An Essay in Regulative Epistemology* (Oxford: Clarendon Press, 2007); and Jason Baehr, "Educating for Intellectual Virtues: From Theory to Practice," *Journal of the Philosophy of Education* 47, no. 2 (2013): 248–62.

[18] While not typically using the words "intellectual character" or "intellectual virtue," many who write about the nature of civility use language that is rich in intellectual virtues and vices terminology. See, for example, Mill, *On Liberty*, chap. 3; Kristin Schaupp, "Epistemic Peers and Civil Disagreement," in *Civility in Politics and Education*, ed. Deborah Mower and Wade L. Robison (New York: Routledge, 2013), 23–43; Robert F. Ladenson, "Civility as Democratic Civic Virtue," in *Civility in Politics and Education*, ed. Deborah Mower and Wade L. Robison (New York: Routledge, 2013), 207–15; Forni, *Choosing Civility*, chaps. 1, 4, 10, 23; Carter, *Civility*, chaps. 8–9, 12; Richard J. Mouw, *Uncommon Decency: Christian Civility in an Uncivil World*, 2nd ed. (Downers Grove, IL: InterVarsity Press, 2010), chap. 5; Amy Gutmann and Dennis Frank Thompson, "Moral Conflict and Political Consensus," *Ethics* 101, no. 1 (1990): 77–78; Herbert Marcuse, "Repressive Tolerance," in *A Critique of Pure Tolerance*, ed. Robert Paul Wolff, Barrington Moore, Jr., and Herbert Marcuse (Boston: Beacon Press, 1965), 94–95, 106, 112; Albert O. Hirschman, "Having Opinions—One of the Elements of Well-Being?" *The American Economic Review* 79, no. 2 (1989): 77–78; and Richard C. Sinopoli, "Thick-Skinned Liberalism: Redefining Civility," *The American Political Science Review* 89, no. 3 (1995): 612–15, 618–19.

[19] The idea is that if the suggested antidote can be shown to be promising or to be in a good position to successfully address the problem, this will be sufficient to show that it is substantive and worth taking seriously (even if it also, in some sense, is a fairly obvious solution).

[20] This includes, of course, ancient philosophers like Plato and Aristotle, modern philosophers like Descartes and Locke, contemporary virtue ethicists (e.g., Nancy Sherman, *The Fabric of Character: Aristotle's Theory of Virtue* [Oxford: Clarendon Press, 1989]), and positive psychologists (e.g., Christopher Peterson and Martin E. P. Seligman, *Character Strengths and Virtues: A Handbook and Classification* [Oxford: Oxford University Press, 2004]), among others. For a recent collection of perspectives on cultivating virtue from the standpoints of philosophy, theology, and psychology, see Nancy E. Snow, ed., *Cultivating Virtue: Perspectives from Philosophy, Theology, and Psychology* (Oxford: Oxford University Press, 2014).

[21] Indeed, what little research there is on "intellectual character formation" suggests that there is substantial overlap between practices aimed at fostering moral virtues and those aimed at fostering intellectual virtues like curiosity, open-mindedness, and intellectual courage. See especially Ritchhart, *Intellectual Character.* Central to Ritchhart's account of how teachers can help their students grow in intellectual virtues or "thinking dispositions" is the claim that teachers must create structures and opportunities for their students to *practice* (the actions characteristic of) intellectual virtues, which, of course, echoes Aristotle's famous claim in Book II of the *Nicomachean Ethics*: that we become (morally) virtuous by performing (morally) virtuous actions.

[22] For more on the connection between intellectual virtues and civic engagement, see Harry Brighouse, "Civility, Citizenship, and the Limits of Schooling," in *Civility in Politics and Education,* ed. Deborah Mower and Wade L. Robison (New York: Routledge, 2013): 192–93; Ladenson, "Civility," 207–15; Jeff Buechner, "Authentic Civic Participation Requires Critical Thinking Methods that Work," in *Civility in Politics and Education*, ed. Deborah Mower and Wade L. Robison (New York: Routledge, 2013), 222–30; Carter, *Civility*, 25–28, 108–12); Mark Button, "'A Monkish Kind of Virtue?' For and Against Humility," *Political Theory* 33, no. 6 (2005): 840–68; Marcuse, "Repressive Tolerance"; and Allan Hazlett, "Skepticism and Intellectual Humility as Civic Virtues," in *Intellectual Virtues and Education: Essays in Applied Virtue Epistemology*, ed. Jason Baehr (New York: Routledge, 2016), 71–92.

[23] Brighouse, "Civility, Citizenship," 192.

[24] For defenses of this claim, see Brighouse, "Civility, Citizenship"; Ladenson, "Civility," 215–19; Paul Gaffney, "Competition in the Classroom: An Ideal for Civility," in *Civility in Politics and Education*, ed. Deborah Mower and Wade L. Robison (New York: Routledge, 2013), 250–54; and Baehr, "Educating for Intellectual Virtues."

[25] Again, for an idea of what this might look like, see especially Ritchhart, *Intellectual Character*, but also Ron Ritchhart, *Creating Cultures of Thinking* (San Francisco: Jossey-Bass, 2015) and Baehr, "Educating for Intellectual Virtues."

[26] For a discussion of this objection, see Guinness, *Case for Civility*, 153.

[27] For a similar point, see Guinness, *Case for Civility*, 153–58, and Mouw, *Uncommon Decency*, 22–24.

[28] One recent event that led to objections of this sort was the statement by the University of California, Berkeley's chancellor that "we can only exercise our right to free speech insofar as we feel safe and respected in doing so, and this in turn requires that people treat each other with civility"; Colleen Flaherty, "The Problem with Civility," *Inside Higher Ed*, September 9, 2014, https://www.insidehighered.com/news/2014/09/09/berkeley-chancellor-angers-faculty-members-remarks-civility-and-free-speech. Another was the rescinding of a job offer to Steven Salaita by University of Illinois on the basis of a series of anti-Israel tweets made by Salaita that were deemed by the university to violate a principle of civility that applies to matters of academic and political dispute. Joseph Levine, "Did Salaita Cross the Line of 'Civility'?" *The New York Times Opinionator*, December 14, 2014, http://opinionator.blogs.nytimes.com/2014/12/14/did-salaita-cross-the-line-of-civility/?_r=0.

[29] For more on the distinction between a legal call to civility and one that is normative but not legal (e.g., moral or civic), see Gutmann and Thompson, "Moral Conflict," 85, and Carter, *Civility*, 69–71, 84–85, 161–64, 209–12.

[30] While the first three objections are similar to one another, the thrust of the first one is epistemic, the thrust of the second is legal, and the thrust of the third is social or moral.

[31] See David Estlund, *Deliberation Down and Dirty: Must Political Expression Be Civil* (Bloomington, IN: Poynter Center for the Study of Ethics and American Institutions, 2005), 1.

[32] For discussions that draw a sharp distinction between civility and politeness, see Chesire Calhoun, "The Virtue of Civility," *Philosophy and Public Affairs* 29, no. 3 (2000): 252; Timothy C. Shiell, "Debunking Three Myths about Civility," in *Civility in Politics and Education,* ed. Deborah Mower and Wade L. Robison (New York: Routledge, 2013), 6; Schaupp, "Epistemic Peers," 25; and Guinness, *Case for Civility*, 3. For a

conception of civility that is closely aligned with politeness and manners, see Forni, *Choosing Civility.*

[33] That is, provided that the *epistemic* credentials of these views meet certain minimal standards. More on this below. For a similar point, see Carter, *Civility*, 108–10.

[34] This suggestion is further supported by the fact that there doesn't seem to be a single determinate and univocal concept of civility that answers to all of our rather diverse ways of thinking and speaking about civility. It may be, then, that there are, in fact, *varieties* of civility, some that are important with respect to certain contexts and priorities and others that are important with respect to other contexts and priorities.

[35] For defenses or discussions of one or more versions of this objection, see Benjamin DeMott, "Seduced by Civility: Political Manners and the Crisis of Democratic Values," *Nation* 263, no. 19 (December 1996): 11–19; Carter, *Civility*, 110–11; Mouw, *Uncommon Decency*, 50–53; and Mill, *On Liberty*, 50–52.

[36] One's treatment of an opposing view might be *reasonably* or *minimally* (even if not fully or perfectly) intellectually careful, open, or honest. If so, it will not be intellectually *vicious*. In certain contexts, meeting this relatively low, but not insignificant, standard may be sufficient for achieving some good that a more robustly intellectually virtuous course of action would preclude.

[37] Thus, I suspect that when we find ourselves thinking that (or acting as if) "I can't be civil or intellectually virtuous in this situation; otherwise, I'll lose this argument or others will think I'm a fool or I'll lose the election or my cause won't prevail," we are often overvaluing the good of winning the argument, saving face, winning the election, or having our cause prevail.

[38] For further remarks on and discussion of the challenge here, see Mill, *On Liberty*, 50–52; Calhoun, "Virtue of Civility," 269–72; Estlund, *Deliberation*, 8–9; Gaffney, "Competition," 243–44; and Mouw, *Uncommon Decency*, 50–51, 144–45.

[39] I have been thinking of the competing goods in question as moral, social, or political in nature. But could they also be epistemic? I see no reason to think not; that is, I see no reason to doubt that there could be cases in which a person's intellectually vicious behavior in the context of a public debate, say, could lead to superior epistemic goods (e.g., to a greater number of true beliefs) that couldn't be achieved in the absence of such behavior (e.g., because the audience wouldn't be convinced by a more virtuous communication style). However, again, I think cases of this sort are very rare and that it is often tempting to think one is in such a situation when, in fact, one is not. Such cases raise tricky issues that do not arise in the cases already considered;

for example, whether the behavior, if done *knowing that* and *because* it would have the best epistemic outcome, would be intellectually vicious. I won't stop to pursue this question here.

[40] For more on the claim that a civility principle admits of exceptions, see Shiell, "Debunking," 16–17; Howard Curzer, "An Aristotelian Account of Civility," in *Civility in Politics and Education*, ed. Deborah Mower and Wade L. Robison (New York: Routledge, 2013), 92–94; Calhoun, "Virtue of Civility," 265–72; and Marcuse, "Repressive Tolerance," 83–85.

[41] For defenses or discussions of this objection, see Gutmann and Thompson, "Moral Conflict," 64–65; Shiell, "Debunking," 12; Curzer, "Aristotelian Account," 89–90; and Carter, *Civility*, 122–26, 132–36, 141–45.

[42] Baehr, *Inquiring Mind*, chap. 8.

[43] Note that this is different from saying that some views, once under consideration, can justifiably be assessed in ways that are intellectually vicious. Though I will not take up the issue here, I will note in passing that this strikes me as implausible. Put positively, I think there is a wide constraint on our consideration of other views, such that if and when we engage in such consideration, it should always—barring the sorts of exceptional, high-stakes cases noted above—meet certain standards of intellectual care, honesty, etc. Put yet another way, the fact that a particular view has extremely poor epistemic credentials, while perhaps freeing us from the need to consider it, does not justify considering it in a way that is sloppy, careless, unfair, dishonest, or the like. For similar points, see Estlund, *Deliberation*; Mouw, *Uncommon Decency*, 142–47; and Carter, *Civility*, 213–19.

[44] Much more could be said in explanation and defense of this principle than I can say here. For a related discussion, see my *Inquiring Mind*, 157–62. I will note briefly that a person may have legitimate *practical* reasons for not giving her mind to opposing or foreign views, engagement with which "might" prove epistemically beneficial. The main point of EP is to rule out cases in which it is clear enough that an opposing view is an epistemic dead end.

[45] For similar (but not identical) "exception principles," see Curzer, "Aristotelian Account," 89; Estlund, *Deliberation*, 7; and Gutman and Thompson, "Moral Conflict," 75.

[46] I insert "apparently" because if the views in question really are extremely implausible, then at least some of the behavior in question (e.g., not giving the view a serious hearing) might not be intellectually vicious.

[47] The plausibility of this conclusion depends in part on an issue raised in n. 42 above. If giving *no* consideration to certain extremely implausible views can be

consistent with intellectual virtue, but (barring the extreme cases discussed earlier) giving *hasty, careless, dishonest, or otherwise intellectually vicious* consideration to these views is always impermissible, then it may be that only a subset of the relevant (apparently) vicious actions and attitudes would be justified (namely, those that involve the former but not the latter kind of intellectual activity).

[48] The belief also seems dubious given that it is often held by people on opposing sides of a single debate! That is, each side believes that the other's position is epistemically beyond the pale. But, of course, it is extremely unlikely that both perspectives are correct (unless, of course, the belief in question is held only by extremists and the truth always lies somewhere in the middle—a possibility I will not stop to consider here).

[49] Mill, *On Liberty*, 17.

[50] See, for example, Raymond S. Nickerson, "Confirmation Bias: A Ubiquitous Phenomenon in Many Guises," *Review of General Psychology* 2, no. 2 (1998): 175–200; Ulrich Hoffrage, Ralph Hertwig, and Gerd Gigerenzer, "Hindsight Bias: A By-Product of Knowledge Updating?" *Journal of Experimental Psychology* 26, no. 3 (2000): 566–81; Justin Kruger and Thomas Gilovich, "'Naive Cynicism' in Everyday Theories of Responsibility Assessment: On Biased Assessments of Bias," *Journal of Personality and Social Psychology* 76 (1999): 743–53; Emily Pronin, "Perception and Misperception of Bias in Human Judgment," *Trends in Cognitive Sciences* 11 (2007): 37–43; Emily Pronin, Daniel Y. Lin, and Lee Ross, "The Bias Blind Spot: Perceptions of Bias in Self versus Others," *Personality and Social Psychology Bulletin* 28 (2002): 369–81; Richard Nisbett and Timothy Wilson, "Telling More than We Can Know: Verbal Reports on Mental Processes," *Psychological Review* 84 (1977): 231–59; Timothy Wilson and Nancy Brekke, "Mental Contamination and Mental Correction: Unwanted Influences on Judgments and Evaluations," *Psychological Bulletin* 116 (1994): 117–42; Daniel Kahneman, "A Perspective on Judgment and Choice," *American Psychologist* 58 (2003): 697–720; Thomas E. Nelson, Zoe M. Oxley, and Rosalee A. Clawson, "Toward a Psychology of Framing Effects," *Political Behavior* 19, no. 3 (1997): 221–46.

[51] The commendation of this principle presupposes that we are sometimes able to recognize that another person can reasonably disagree with us about a given matter, *even though* from our own immediate epistemic standpoint, the evidence seems clearly to support our own position. While this strikes me as plausible (and important), there is no question that people are sometimes so wrapped up in or attached to their own perspective that they lack the kind of recognitional ability just noted. This underscores the fact that the application of PRD will sometimes (maybe often) need to be

supplemented by additional measures, some of which I will describe momentarily. Thanks to Jim Taylor for suggesting this point.

[52] Of course, if, upon looking for what is plausible in an opposing view, I find counter-evidence to my own position, then—if I am practicing intellectual virtues—I will revise my position accordingly. But this is unobjectionable.

[53] See Baehr, *Inquiring Mind*, chap. 8 for a chapter-length discussion of open-mindedness thus conceived.

[54] For discussions connecting open-mindedness to civility in public discourse, see Mill, *On Liberty*, chap. 3, esp. 19–21, 43; Gutmann and Thompson, "Moral Conflict," 80–82; Hirschman, "Having Opinions," 77; John Rawls, *A Theory of Justice* (Cambridge, MA: Harvard University Press, 1971), 337–38; John Rawls, *Political Liberalism* (New York: Columbia University Press, 1993), 217–18; Schaupp, "Epistemic Peers," 38–41; Curzer, "Aristotelian Account," 81–82, 85–89; Gaffney, "Competition," 243–44; Carter, *Civility*, 136–40; Mouw, *Uncommon Decency*, 53, 61–64, 118–20; and Button, "A Monkish Kind," 851–56.

[55] For an account of intellectual humility thus conceived, see Dennis Whitcomb et al., "Intellectual Humility: Owning Our Limitations," *Philosophy and Phenomenological Research* 94, no. 3 (May 2017): 509–39.

[56] For discussions that connect intellectual humility (or something like it) to civility, see Mill, *On Liberty*, chap. 3, esp. 17–21, 41; Schaupp, "Epistemic Peers," 24–28, 38–41; Carter, *Civility*, 136–40; Guinness, *Case for Civility*, 108, 156–57; Mouw, *Uncommon Decency*, 52, 61–64; and Button, "A Monkish Kind," 851–56.

[57] See esp. Nisbett and Wilson, "Telling More"; Wilson and Brekke, "Mental Contamination"; and Kahneman, "Perspective."

[58] We would also do well to pay attention to some of the recent literature on "debiasing" (e.g., Roy Baumeister and Brad Bushman, *Social Psychology and Human Nature* [Belmont, CA: Wadsworth, 2010]).

[59] This work benefitted from the generous support of the John Templeton Foundation and the Center for Christian Thought at Biola University. Thanks to several CCT fellows and to Jim Taylor for helpful feedback on an earlier draft.

Chapter 2: It's Good to Be Humble: An Empirical Account

[1] Frank P. McKenna and Lynn B. Myers, "Illusory Self-Assessments—Can They Be Reduced?" *British Journal of Psychology* 88, no. 1 (1997): 39–51.

[2] David Dunning, Dale W. Griffin, James D. Milojkovic, and Lee Ross, "The Overconfidence Effect in Social Prediction," *Journal of Personality and Social Psychology* 58, no. 4 (1990): 568–81.

[3] Joachim Krueger and Russell W. Clement, "The Truly False Consensus Effect: An Ineradicable and Egocentric Bias in Social Perception," *Journal of Personality and Social Psychology* 67, no. 4 (1994): 596–610.

[4] Thomas Gilovich, Victoria Husted Medvec, and Kenneth Savitsky, "The Spotlight Effect in Social Judgment: An Egocentric Bias in Estimates of the Salience of One's Own Action and Appearance," *Journal of Personality and Social Psychology* 78, no. 2 (2000): 211–22.

[5] W. Keith Campbell and Constantine Sedikides, "Self-Threat Magnifies the Self-Serving Bias: A Meta-Analytic Integration," *Review of General Psychology* 3, no. 1 (1999): 23–43.

[6] Shana Lebowitz, "A Psychologist Says a Disorganized Email Inbox Can Be a Sign of Intelligence," *Business Insider*, April 27, 2015, https://www.businessinsider.com/disorganized-inbox-means-youre-smart-2015-4.

[7] Stephen T. Pardue, *The Mind of Christ: Humility and the Intellect in Early Christian Theology* (London: Bloomsbury, 2013), 1.

[8] C. S. Lewis, *The Screwtape Letters* (Oxford: ISIS Large Print Books, 1990), 117.

[9] Julia Driver, *Uneasy Virtue* (New York: Cambridge University Press, 2001).

[10] Robert E. Emmons, *The Psychology of Ultimate Concern* (New York: Guilford Press, 1999), 171.

[11] See June P. Tangney, "Humility: Theoretical Perspectives, Empirical Findings, and Directions for Future Research," *Journal of Social and Clinical Psychology* 19, no. 1 (2000): 70–82, https://doi.org/10.1521/jscp.2000.19.1.70; and June P. Tangney, "Humility," in *Handbook of Positive Psychology*, 2nd ed., ed. C. R. Snyder and Shane J. Lopez (New York: Oxford University Press, 2009), 483–90.

[12] See Don E. Davis et al., "Relational Humility: Conceptualizing and Measuring Humility as a Personality Judgment," *Journal of Personality Assessment* 93, no. 3 (2011): 225–34, https://doi.org/10.1080/00223891.2011.558871; and Bradley P. Owens, Michael D. Johnson, and Terence R. Mitchell, "Expressed Humility in Organizations: Implications for Performance, Teams, and Leadership," *Organization Science* 24, no. 5 (2013): 1517–38.

[13] Wade C. Rowatt et al., "A Social-Personality Perspective on Humility, Religiousness, and Spirituality," *Journal of Psychology and Theology* 42, no. 1 (2014): 31–40.

[14] See Aiden P. Gregg and Nikhila Mahadevan, "Intellectual Arrogance and Intellectual Humility: An Evolutionary-Epistemological Account," *Journal of Psychology and Theology* 42, no. 1 (2014): 7–18; and Elissa Woodruff et al., "Humility and Religion: Benefits, Difficulties, and a Model of Religious Tolerance," in *Positive Psychology of Religion and Spirituality across Cultures*, ed. Chu Kim-Prieto (New York: Springer, 2014), 271–85.

[15] Joshua B. Grubbs and Julie J. Exline, "Humbling Yourself before God: Humility as a Reliable Predictor of Lower Divine Struggle," *Journal of Psychology and Theology* 42, no. 1 (2014): 41–49.

[16] Richard A. Bollinger et al., "Validation of a Measurement of Dispositional Humility" (poster presentation, 114th Annual Meeting of the American Psychological Association, New Orleans, LA, August 2006); and Julie J. Exline et al., "Not So Innocent: Does Seeing One's Own Capability for Wrongdoing Predict Forgiveness?" *Journal of Personality and Social Psychology* 94, no. 3 (2008): 495–515, https://doi.org/10.1037/0022-3514.94.3.495/.

[17] Jordan P. LaBouff et al., "Humble People Are More Helpful than Less Humble Persons: Evidence from Three Studies," *Journal of Positive Psychology* 7 (2012): 16–29, https://doi.org/10.1080/17439760.2011.626787.

[18] Michael C. Ashton and Kibeom Lee, "Honesty-Humility, the Big Five, and the Five-Factor Model," *Journal of Personality* 73, no. 5 (2005): 1321–53, https://doi.org/10.1111/j.1467-6494.2005.00351.x/.

[19] Carissa Dwiwardani et al., "Virtues Develop from a Secure Base: Attachment and Resilience as Predictors of Humility, Gratitude, and Forgiveness," *Journal of Psychology and Theology* 42, no. 1 (2014): 83–90; and Julie J. Exline, "Humility and the Ability to Receive from Others," *Journal of Psychology and Christianity* 31, no. 1 (2012): 40–50.

[20] Julie J. Exline and Peter C. Hill, "Humility: A Consistent and Robust Predictor of Generosity," *Journal of Positive Psychology* 7, no. 3 (2012): 208–18, https://doi.org/10.1080/17439760.2012.671348.

[21] Peter J. Jankowski, Steven J. Sandage, and Peter C. Hill, "Differentiation-Based Models of Forgiveness, Mental Health, and Social Justice Commitment: Mediator Effects for Differentiation of Self and Humility," *Journal of Positive Psychology* 8, no. 5 (2013): 412–24.

[22] Benjamin E. Hilbig and Ingo Zettler, "Pillars of Cooperation: Honesty-Humility, Social Value Orientations, and Economic Behavior," *Journal of Research in Personality* 43, no. 3 (2009): 516–19, https://doi.org/10.1016/j.jrp.2009.01.003.

[23] Tangney, "Humility."

[24] Julie J. Exline and Anne L. Geyer, "Perceptions of Humility: A Preliminary Study," *Self and Identity* 3, no. 2 (2004): 95–114, https://doi.org/10.1080/13576500342000077.

[25] Dwiwardani et al., "Virtues."

[26] Exline, "Humility."

[27] Jim Collins, "Level 5 Leadership: The Triumph of Humility and Fierce Resolve," in *Leadership: Understanding the Dynamics of Power and Influence in Organizations*, 2nd ed., ed. Robert P. Vecchio (South Bend, IN: University of Notre Dame Press, 2007), 394–406; and Megan K. Johnson, Wade C. Rowatt, and Leo Petrini, "A New Trait on the Market: Honesty-Humility as a Unique Predictor of Job Performance Ratings," *Personality and Individual Differences* 50, no. 6 (2011): 857–62, https://doi.org/10.1016/j.paid.2011.01.011.

[28] Jennifer E. Farrell et al., "Humility and Relationship Outcomes in Couples: The Mediating Role of Commitment," *Couple and Family Psychology: Research and Practice* 4, no. 1 (2015): 14–26.

[29] Owens, Johnson, and Mitchell, "Expressed Humility."

[30] Farrell et al., "Humility and Relationship Outcomes."

[31] Jankowski, Sandage, and Hill, "Differentiation-Based Models,"

[32] Neal Krause, "Religious Involvement, Humility, and Self-Rated Health," *Social Indicators Research* 98, no. 1 (2010): 23–39, https://doi.org/10.1007/s11205-009-9514-x.

[33] Kathleen A. Lawler-Row et al., "Forgiveness and Health: The Role of Attachment," *Personal Relationships* 18, no. 2 (2011): 170–83, https://doi.org/10.1111/j.1475-6811.2010.01327.x; and Michael E. McCullough, Robert A. Emmons, and Jo-Ann Tsang, "The Grateful Disposition: A Conceptual and Empirical Topography," *Journal of Personality and Social Psychology* 82, no. 1 (2002): 112–27, https://doi.org/10.1037//0022-3514.82.1.112.

[34] Jankowski, Sandage, and Hill, "Differentiation-Based Models."

[35] Exline, "Humility,"

[36] Dwiwardani et al., "Virtues."

[37] Peter J. Jankowski and Lisa M. Hooper, "Differentiation of Self: A Validation Study of the Bowen Theory Construct," *Couple and Family Psychology: Research and Practice* 1, no. 3 (2012): 226–43.

[38] Peter Hill and Elizabeth K. Laney, "Beyond Self-Interest: Humility and the Quieted Self," *The Oxford Handbook of Hypo-egoic Phenomena*, ed. Kirk Warren Brown and Mark R. Leary Print (New York: Oxford University Press: 2016), 243–56.

[39] Dennis Whitcomb et al., "Intellectual Humility: Owning Our Limitations," *Philosophy and Phenomenological Research* 94, no. 3 (May 2017): 509–39.

[40] Driver, *Uneasy Virtue.*

[41] Owen Flanagan, "Virtue and Ignorance," *Journal of Philosophy* 87, no. 8 (1990): 420–28.

[42] Allan Hazlett, "Higher-Order Epistemic Attitudes and Intellectual Humility," *Episteme* 9, no. 3 (2012): 205–23, https://doi.org/10.1017/epi.2012.11; and Peter L. Samuelson et al., "The Science of Intellectual Humility White Paper" (unpublished manuscript, 2013), http://trebuchet.fuller.edu/wp-content/uploads/2013/09/IH-White-Paper.pdf.

[43] Robert C. Roberts and W. Jay Wood, "Humility and Epistemic Goods," in *Intellectual Virtue: Perspectives from Ethics and Epistemology*, ed. Michael DePaul and Linda Zagzebski (New York: Oxford University Press, 2003), 257–79.

[44] Dennis Whitcomb et al., "Intellectual Humility: Owning Our Limitations," *Philosophy and Phenomenological Research* 94, no. 3 (May 2017): 509–39.

[45] Roberts and Wood, "Humility," 250.

[46] The components listed are distillations of discussions of a working group convened by the John Templeton Foundation in March 2010, on the campus of Princeton University.

[47] The concept of intellectual servility in relation to intellectual humility originated from a discussion among researchers and other scholars associated with the John Templeton Foundation, Grant No. 29630: The Development, Validation, and Dissemination of Measures of Intellectual Humility and Humility.

[48] Joseph Chancellor and Sonja Lyubomirsky, "Humble Beginnings: Current Trends, State Perspectives, and Hallmarks of Humility," *Social and Personality Psychology Compass* 7, no. 11 (2013): 819–33, https://doi.org/10.1111/spc3.12069.

[49] Jack J. Bauer and Heidi A. Wayment, "The Psychology of the Quiet Ego," in *Transcending Self-Interest: Psychological Explorations of the Quiet Ego*, ed. Heidi A. Wayment and Jack J. Bauer (Washington, DC: American Psychological Association, 2008), 12.

[50] Stacey E. McElroy et al., "Intellectual Humility: Scale Development and Theoretical Elaborations in the Context of Religious Leadership," *Journal of Psychology and Theology* 42, no. 1 (2014): 19–30; and Owens, Johnson, and Mitchell, "Expressed Humility."

[51] McElroy et al., "Intellectual Humility."

[52] Cameron R. Hopkin, Rick H. Hoyle, and Kaitlin Toner, "Intellectual Humility and Reactions to Opinions about Religious Beliefs," *Journal of Psychology and Theology* 42, no. 1 (2014): 50–61.

[53] Roberts and Wood, "Humility."

[54] Kent Dunnington, "Intellectual Humility and the Ends of the Virtues: Conflicting Aretaic Desiderata," *Political Theology* 18, no. 2 (2017): 95–117.

[55] Woodruff et al., "Humility and Religion."

Chapter 3: Civil Discourse at the Table of Reconciliation

[1] Allan Boesak and Curtiss DeYoung, *Radical Reconciliation: Beyond Political Pietism and Christian Quietism* (Maryknoll, NY: Orbis Books, 2012), 10.

[2] Jean Zaru, *Occupied with Nonviolence: A Palestinian Woman Speaks* (Minneapolis, Fortress Press, 2008), 77.

[3] Samuel L. Gaertner and John F. Dovidio, "Understanding and Addressing Contemporary Racism: From Aversive Racism to the Common Ingroup Identity Model," *Journal of Social Issues* 61, no. 3 (2005): 628.

[4] Zaru, *Occupied with Nonviolence*, 78.

[5] C. Wright Mills, *The Sociological Imagination*, Fortieth Anniversary Edition (New York: Oxford University Press, 1959, 2000).

[6] Miroslav Volf, *Exclusion and Embrace: A Theological Exploration of Identity, Otherness, and Reconciliation* (Nashville: Abingdon Press, 1996), 181.

[7] Volf, *Exclusion and Embrace*, 148.

[8] Herbert C. Kelman, "Reconciliation as Identity Change: A Social-Psychological Perspective," in *From Conflict Resolution to Reconciliation*, ed. Yaacov Bar-Siman-Tov (New York: Oxford University Press, 2004), 119.

[9] Volf, *Exclusion and Embrace*, 188.

[10] Hazel Rose Markus and Shinobu Kitayama, "Culture and the Self: Implications for Cognition, Emotion, and Motivation," *Psychological Review* 8, no. 2 (1991): 224–53.

[11] Patrick Cheng, *From Sin to Amazing Grace: Discovering the Queer in Christ* (New York: Seabury Books, 2012).

[12] John F. Dovidio and Samuel L. Gaertner, "Categorization, Recategorization, and Intergroup Bias," in *On the Nature of Prejudice*, ed. J. F. Dovidio, P. Glick, and L. A. Rudman (Oxford: Blackwell, 2005), https://doi.org/10.1002/9780470773963.ch5.

[13] Elizabeth A. Johnson, *She Who Is: The Mystery of God in Feminine Theological Discourse* (New York: Crossroad, 1992), 196.

[14] Volf, *Exclusion and Embrace*, 180.

Chapter 4: Rationality and Rightly Ordered Affections: C. S. Lewis on Intellectual Virtue and Civil Discourse

[1] Harry Blamires, "Teaching the Universal Truth: C. S. Lewis among the Intellectuals," in *The Pilgrim's Guide: C. S. Lewis and the Art of Witness*, ed. David Mills (Grand Rapids, MI: William B. Eerdmans, 1998), 16.

[2] C. S. Lewis, "Rejoinder to Dr. Pittenger," in *God in the Dock,* ed. Walter Hooper (Grand Rapids: Eerdmans, 1970), 183.

[3] C. S. Lewis, "Priestesses in the Church?" in *God in the Dock,* ed. Walter Hooper (Grand Rapids: Eerdmans, 1970), 237.

[4] C. S. Lewis, *Mere Christianity,* The Complete C. S. Lewis Signature Classics (San Francisco: HarperOne, 2002), 81.

[5] C. S. Lewis, *The Abolition of Man,* The Complete C. S. Lewis Signature Classics (San Francisco: HarperOne, 2001), 16, 24–25. Lewis uses only the term "sentiments" in the latter passage, but in the former passage he ties together "sentiments," "affections," and "loves." He says, for example, that St. Augustine defines virtue as *ordo amoris,* the ordinate condition of the affections in which every object is accorded that kind or degree of love which is appropriate to it. He goes on, citing Aristotle, to speak about the need for training in "'ordinate affections' or 'just sentiments'" (16). He also observes that Plato had said the same thing.

[6] C. S. Lewis, "On Obstinacy in Belief," *The Sewanee Review* 63, no. 4 (October–December 1955): 33.

[7] Jonathan Edwards, *A Treatise Concerning Religious Affections*, ed. John E. Smith (1746; rept., New Haven: Yale University Press, 1959), 95, 272.

[8] Edwards encapsulates this view in his sermon "A Divine and Supernatural Light" (1734), available online and in many editions of his works.

[9] Alvin Plantinga, *Warranted Christian Belief* (New York: Oxford University Press, 2000), 294–309. Plantinga shows that Edwards himself is not entirely consistent in explaining the relationship.

[10] Lewis, *Abolition of Man*, 24–25. In relation to his discussion of Edwards, Plantinga makes a point very similar to Lewis's about beauty as an objective property (*Warranted Christian Belief*, 309).

[11] Edwards, *Treatise*, 117. Plantinga quotes the passages from Edwards used here, as well as others (*Warranted Christian Belief*, 294–309).

[12] C. S. Lewis, "Bluspels and Flalansferes: A Semantic Nightmare," in *Selected Literary Essays,* ed. Walter Hooper (Cambridge: Cambridge University Press, 1969), 265.

Also quoted in Michael Ward, "The Good Serves the Better and Both the Best: C. S. Lewis on Imagination and Reason in Apologetics," in *Imaginative Apologetics: Theology, Philosophy, and the Catholic Tradition*, ed. Andrew Davison (Grand Rapids: Baker Academic), 61–62; cf. 59–78.

[13] Alister E. McGrath, in *The Intellectual World of C. S. Lewis* (Oxford: Wiley-Blackwell, 2014) offers helpful insights into these issues, especially in his essays "Arrows of Joy: Lewis's Argument from Desire," 105–28, and "Reason, Experience, and Imagination: Lewis's Apologetic Method," 129–46.

[14] In what follows, I make a number of points that are very similar to those found more extensively in the chapter "The Lasting Vitality of *Mere Christianity*" in my book, *C. S. Lewis's* Mere Christianity: *A Biography* (Princeton, NJ: Princeton University Press, 2016), but here I reflect on how Lewis's intellectual virtues bear specifically on the question of promoting civil discourse.

[15] C. S. Lewis, *Surprised by Joy: The Shape of My Early Life* (London: Collins, Fontana Books, 1959), 167. Lewis learned the term from Owen Barfield.

[16] C. S. Lewis, "Learning in Wartime," in *The Weight of Glory: And Other Addresses* (San Franscisco: HarperOne, 1980), 58–59.

[17] In one of his rare political commentaries, in an invited symposium in 1958, "Is Progress Possible?" he entitled his contribution as "Willing Slaves of the Welfare State." Despite that title, Lewis was a bit nuanced. He recognized that it would be hard to reverse the rise of the large state. He also acknowledged that the freedoms he wanted to protect had never existed for more than the privileged few. But he also worried, as quite a few did at the time, that the modern technocratic state and its experts would inevitably lead to regulation of almost all of life—and he considered such a threat to be, more than the H-bomb, "the extreme peril of humanity at present." *God in the Dock*, 315.

[18] C. S. Lewis, *The Screwtape Letters, C. S. Lewis Signature Classics* (San Francisco: HarperOne, 2001), 205.

[19] This paragraph depends closely on Joel D. Heck's "*Praeparato Evangelica*," in *Lightbearer in the Shadowlands: The Evangelistic Vision of C. S. Lewis*, ed. Angus J. L. Menuge (Wheaton, IL: Crossway Books, 1997), 235–58, which uses the same quotation on page 240 from *Voyage of the Dawn Treader* (New York: Macmillan, 1952), 75–76.

[20] Book One of *Mere Christianity* is built around this principle. Lewis explains his purpose in a letter to Sister Penelope dated May 15, 1941, published in "Books, Broadcasts, and the War, 1939–1949," vol. 2, in *The Collected Letters of C. S. Lewis*, ed. Walter Hooper (New York: Harper Collins, 2004), 484–85.

[21] C. S. Lewis, "The Weight of Glory," in *The Weight of Glory and Other Addresses* (San Francisco: HarperOne, 1980), 31.

[22] C. S. Lewis, *The Magician's Nephew* (New York: HarperCollins, 2000), 137.

[23] Lewis, "Preface," in *Mere Christianity,* 6 and 8. Lewis often presents Augustine as the best representative of this perennial Christianity, as, for instance, when he says, "Milton's version of the Fall story is substantially that of St. Augustine, which is that of the Church as a whole"; C. S. Lewis, *A Preface to Paradise Lost* (New York: Oxford University Press, 1961), 66.

[24] Lewis, *Mere Christianity,* 42.

[25] C. S. Lewis, "The Personal Heresy in Criticism," in *The Personal Heresy: A Controversy,* ed. C. S. Lewis and E. M. W. Tillyard (London: Oxford University Press, 1939), 11.

[26] Lewis, *Mere Christianity,* 103–8, quotations from 105.

[27] See Lewis, *Preface to Paradise Lost,* where pride is central to the rebellion of Satan and "Eve fell through pride." (125).

[28] Lewis to Sister Penelope, October 24, 1940, *Books, Broadcasts, and the War,* 452.

[29] Eric Fenn to Lewis, March 23, 1944, quoted in Justin Phillips, *C. S. Lewis in A Time of War* (San Francisco: Harper San Francisco, 2002), 254.

[30] Lewis to Fenn, March 25, 1944, *Books, Broadcasts, and the War,* 608–9.

Chapter 5: Respect as an Intellectual Virtue

[1] Pelser discusses the moral virtue of respect in "Respect for Human Dignity as an Emotion and Virtue," *Res Philosophica* 92, no. 4 (2015): 743–63.

[2] Our distinction between an egalitarian respect for human dignity and special esteem for distinctive excellence should not be confused with Stephen Darwall's influential distinction between recognition respect and appraisal respect (see Stephen L. Darwall, "Two Kinds of Respect," *Ethics* 88, no. 1 [1977]: 36–49). Darwall defines "recognition respect" as "a disposition to weigh appropriately some feature or fact in one's deliberations [concerning how one ought to act]. . . . Thus to have recognition respect for persons is to give proper weight to the fact that they are persons" (39). By contrast, appraisal respect "consists in a positive appraisal of a person or his qualities." He continues, "Unlike recognition respect, one may have appraisal respect for someone without having any particular conception of just what behavior from oneself would be required or made appropriate by that person's having the features meriting such respect. Appraisal respect is the positive appraisal itself" (39). On our view, both

egalitarian respect for intellectual dignity and special esteem for intellectual distinction can involve elements of both recognition respect and appraisal respect.

[3] Robert C. Roberts, *Emotions: An Essay in Aid of Moral Psychology* (Cambridge: Cambridge University Press, 2003), 266–67.

[4] Robert C. Roberts and W. Jay Wood, *Intellectual Virtues: An Essay in Regulative Epistemology* (Oxford: Oxford University Press, 2007), 73; italics original.

[5] Doris Kearns Goodwin, *Team of Rivals: The Political Genius of Abraham Lincoln* (New York: Simon & Schuster, 2005), 551–52. Thanks to Paul Carrese for pointing us toward Goodwin's book.

[6] As Miranda Fricker points out, societal prejudices can push even non-racists toward unjust underestimations of the epistemic credibility of members of another race. See her *Epistemic Injustice: Power and the Ethics of Knowing* (Oxford: Oxford University Press, 2007).

[7] Goodwin, *Team of Rivals*, 553.

[8] Tom Morris, *If Aristotle Ran General Motors: The New Soul of Business* (New York: Henry Holt, 1997), 27.

[9] Roberts and Wood, *Intellectual Virtues*, 206.

[10] Jason Baehr, "The Structure of Open-Mindedness," *Canadian Journal of Philosophy* 41, no. 2 (June 2011): 202.

[11] This paragraph was inspired by thoughts expressed on "Quiddity," the podcast of the Circe Institute.

[12] Charlotte Mason and Karen Glass, *Mind to Mind: An Essay Towards a Philosophy of Education* (self-pub., CreateSpace, 2015), 6. Thanks to Karla West for pointing us to this quote.

[13] For further educational implications of the fact that "children are born persons," see Susan Schaeffer Macaulay, *For the Children's Sake: Foundations of Education for Home and School* (Wheaton, IL: Crossway Books, 1984), chap. 2.

[14] Robert Merrihew Adams, *A Theory of Virtue: Excellence in Being for the Good* (Oxford: Oxford University Press, 2006), 15–16.

[15] Roberts, *Emotions*.

[16] Compare Pelser, "Respect for Human Dignity," 746–49.

[17] As Roberts points out in his essay in this volume, some features of the Aristotelian "virtue" of pride actually seem quite vicious.

[18] See Chapter Seven in this volume, "The Virtues of Pride and Humility: A Survey,"

[19] Roberts, "Virtues of Pride."

[20] Aristotle, *Nicomachean Ethics* VI.11, 1143b11–14.

[21] Hilary Putnam, *Reason, Truth, and History* (New York: Cambridge University Press, 1981), 165–66; italics original. Thanks to Michael Pace for bringing this passage to our attention.

[22] Macalester Bell, *Hard Feelings: The Moral Psychology of Contempt* (Oxford: Oxford University Press, 2013).

[23] Bell, *Hard Feelings*, 39.

[24] We cannot be sure, but we suspect Putnam had something like this in mind.

[25] Bell argues that global contempt is compatible with the kind of respect that Darwall has termed "recognition respect," inasmuch as people can "acknowledge the moral and legal rights of those they contemn" (see *Hard Feelings*, 168–77; quote from 171). But even if that is so, global contemnors lack the *emotional* sensitivity to their target's dignity that we've suggested partially constitutes the moral and intellectual virtues of respect. Thus, we think respect for human dignity and global contempt are ultimately incompatible (unless the qualified contempt we mention counts as global).

[26] Thanks to Gregg Ten Elshof for suggesting this objection.

[27] Here again we part ways with Bell, who argues that we ought to *cultivate* global contempt as the best response to certain character failures (*Hard Feelings*, esp. chaps. 3–5). For an analysis of Bell's provocative case and arguments against it, see Ryan West, "Contempt and the Cultivation of Character: Two Models," *Journal of Religious Ethics* 43, no. 3 (2015): 493–519.

[28] On the distinction between "substantive/motivational virtues" and "virtues of will power," see Robert C. Roberts, "Will Power and the Virtues," *Philosophical Review* 93, no. 2 (1984): 227–47.

[29] For a more complete discussion of the way that the wisdoms of the substantive and motivational virtues constitute the virtue of practical wisdom, see Robert C. Roberts and Adam C. Pelser, "Emotions, Character, and Associationist Psychology," *Journal of Moral Philosophy* 14 no. 6 (2017): 623–45, https://doi.org/10.1163/17455243-46810069/.

[30] Of course, in an overreaction against the overemphasis on comparative excellences, some elements of our culture downplay *all* interpersonal comparisons, attempting to promote self-respect (self-esteem) by celebrating mediocrity, or mere participation, as much as real greatness. Just as cultures that measure personal worth in terms of comparative achievements or physical appearance can erode proper respect for human dignity, so too cultures in which everyone gets a trophy can erode a proper

appreciation for *extra*ordinary human excellence, whether physical, moral, intellectual, or spiritual. We should avoid both extremes.

[31] C. S. Lewis, *Mere Christianity* (New York: Touchstone, 1996), 163.

[32] Note that looking again can be an expression of respect. After all, the Latin root of the English word "respect" literally means "to look again" (Bell, *Hard Feelings*, 169).

[33] For specific practical ideas for reshaping educational institutions, see Philip E. Dow, *Virtuous Minds: Intellectual Character Development for Students, Educators, and Parents* (Downers Grove, IL: IVP Academic, 2013), esp. part 3 and the appendices. The websites of the schools mentioned above also provide helpful resources: http://www.tbcs.org, http://www.ivalongbeach.org, and http://rosslynacademy.org.

[34] Aristotle, *Nicomachean Ethics*, IX.

[35] Talbot Brewer, *The Retrieval of Ethics* (Oxford: Oxford University Press, 2009), 242.

Chapter 6: Humanity as Common Ground: Tolerance and Respect as Ideals in Communicative Discourse

[1] William Shakespeare, *The Merchant of Venice*, III.1.58–68.

[2] W. D. Ross, *The Right and the Good* (Oxford: Oxford University Press, 1930).

[3] Detailed discussion of Ross's list is provided in chap. 5 of my *The Good in the Right: A Theory of Intuition and Intrinsic Value* (Princeton, NJ: Princeton University Press, 2004).

[4] Audi, *Good in the Right.*

[5] My most recent treatment of intuition is in "Intuition and Its Place in Ethics," *Journal of the American Philosophical Association* 1, no. 1 (2015): 57–77. For an extensive discussion and many references, see Elijah Chudnoff, *Intuition* (Oxford: Oxford University Press, 2013).

[6] This ethical commonality, amounting to virtually universal acceptance of certain major moral standards, is argued in detail by Brian Lepard in *Rethinking Humanitarian Intervention* (College Park: Penn State University Press, 2002).

[7] Discussion of the possibility of rational disagreement on the self-evident and references to other work on peer disagreement are provided in Audi, "Intuition and Its Place in Ethics."

[8] For explication of Aquinas's view of humility, see Eleonore Stump, *Wandering in Darkness: Narrative and the Problem of Suffering* (Oxford: Oxford University Press, 2012).

[9] I have defended this principle in *Democratic Authority and the Separation of Church and State* (New York and Oxford: Oxford University Press, 2011), esp. chap. 4.

[10] See, for example, Immanuel Kant, *Groundwork of the Metaphysics of Morals*, trans. H. J. Paton (London: Hutchinson, 1948), sec. 408, in which he says, "[W]e cannot do morality a worse disservice than by seeking to derive it from examples. Every example of it presented to me must first be judged by moral principles. . . . "

[11] This formulation comes from my *Religious Commitment and Secular Reason* (Cambridge: Cambridge University Press, 2000), 86, though I presented it earlier in "The Separation of Church and State and the Obligations of Citizenship," *Philosophy & Public Affairs* 18, no. 3 (1989): 259–96. The principle has been widely discussed; for example, by Christopher J. Eberle in *Religious Convictions in Liberal Politics* (Cambridge: Cambridge University Press, 2002), esp. 84–151, and "Basic Human Worth and Religious Restraint," *Philosophy and Social Criticism* 35, no. 1–2 (2009): 151–81. More recent critical discussion is provided in a book symposium on my *Democratic Authority* in *Philosophical Issues* (New Series) 3.2 (April 2014).

[12] The notion of leveraging and the ethics of engaging it are discussed in more detail in Audi, *Religious Commitment,* 109–11. For a recent discussion, from a legal and philosophical point of view, of both leveraging and the associated sociopolitical principles I have defended, see Micah Schwartzman, "The Ethics of Reasoning from Conjecture," *Journal of Moral Philosophy* 9, no. 4 (2012), 521–44; and Schwartzman, "The Sincerity of Public Reason," *The Journal of Political Philosophy* 19, no. 4 (2011), 375–98.

Chapter 7: The Virtues of Pride and Humility: A Survey

[1] **Pro pride:** Aristotle, *Nicomachean Ethics,* 4.3; David Hume, *A Treatise of Human Nature,* ed. L. A. Selby-Bigge (Oxford: Oxford University Press, 1888), bk. II, pt. 1, sec. II; Richard Taylor, *Ethics, Faith, and Reason* (Englewood Cliffs, NJ: Prentice-Hall, 1985), 85–86; Tara Smith, "The Practice of Pride," *Social Philosophy and Policy* 15, no. 1 (1998), 71–90.

Pro humility: *Benjamin Franklin's Autobiography,* Norton Critical Editions, ed. Joyce E. Chaplin (New York: W. W. Norton); Andrew Pinsent, "Humility," in *Being Good: Christian Virtues for Everyday Life,* ed. Michael W. Austin and R. Douglas Geivett (Grand Rapids: Eerdmans, 2012), 242–64; Robert C. Roberts, "Learning Intellectual Humility," in *Educating for Intellectual Virtues,* ed. Jason Baehr (New York: Routledge, 2015); Nancy Snow, "Humility," *Journal of Value Inquiry* 29, no. 2 (1995): 203–16; Norvin Richards, *Humility* (Philadelphia: Temple University Press, 1992);

Jonathan Edwards, *Charity and its Fruits* (Edinburgh: The Banner of Truth Trust, 1852), lecture VII.

[2] Smith, "Practice," 75–76; italics original.

[3] Hume, *Treatise,* bk. II, pt. I, sec. II, 278.

[4] Richard Taylor, *Virtue Ethics* (Interlaken, NY: Linden Books, 1991), 99, quoted in Norvin Richards, *Humility* (Philadelphia: Temple University Press, 1992), 201.

[5] Gregorius Anicius, *Moralia in Iob* 31.45, 87–90, quoted in Kevin Timpe and Craig A. Boyd, "Introduction," in *Virtues and Their Vices*, ed. Kevin Timpe and Craig A. Boyd (Oxford: Oxford University Press, 2014), 17–18.

[6] Edwards, *Charity*, 336–37. Edwards makes humility a low comparative self-assessment. He insists on its being comparative though he does not go on (here) to say that pride can be virtuous. Were it so, it would presumably be a proper comparative self-assessment as well. Perhaps it would consist in glorious and excellent human beings comparing themselves favorably with less glorious and excellent beings among creatures more generally, but perhaps also among human beings. On the view of humility and pride that I promote in this chapter, neither pride nor humility, as a virtue, is essentially comparative. Both are, however, *compatible with* differential self-comparison.

[7] Søren Kierkegaard, *For Self-Examination: Judge for Yourself!*, trans. and ed. Howard V. Hong and Edna H. Hong (Princeton, NJ: Princeton University Press, 1990), 87.

[8] See the third section for elaboration of this concept.

[9] For more on this, see Robert Roberts and Ryan West, "Jesus and the Virtues of Pride," in *The Moral Psychology of Pride*, ed. J. Adam Carter and Emma C. Gordon (Lanham, MD: Rowman and Littlefield, 2017), 99–121; and Robert Roberts and W. Jay Wood, "Understanding, Humility, and the Vices of Pride," in *The Routledge Handbook of Virtue Epistemology*, ed. Heather Battaly (New York: Routledge, 2019), 363–75.

[10] Aristotle, *Nicomachean Ethics*, 4.3.17.

[11] Nicolas Bommarito notes that "a concert cellist's complete and total indifference to the opinions of others is . . . likely to strike us as arrogant and immodest." "Modesty as a Virtue of Attention," *Philosophical Review* 122, no. 1 (2013): 96.

[12] Both are kinds of contempt: either *emotional* contempt, in which one looks down on the other with either the enjoyment of superiority or with disgust (or both), or non-emotional contempt, in which the other is taken to be so unimportant as not even to be worthy of notice.

[13] Aristotle, *Nicomachean Ethics*, 4.3.15.

[14] The visitors had come expecting to be awestruck with the great man and were disappointed to see him in the homely posture of warming himself by the stove. "Oh, he's just an ordinary man," they thought. And he reassured them that great wonders lie just below the surface of the ordinary.

[15] Aristotle, *Generation of Animals*, 645a15–23, quoted in Pierre Hadot, *What Is Ancient Philosophy?* (Cambridge, MA: Harvard University Press, 2004), 83–84.

[16] We might think that if the megalopsychos is conceited because he is so impressed with his own glory, then this scientist is not exactly *conceited*, because she is only anxiously anticipating a glory that she *may* one day have. I grant the difference and the ill-fit of the word, but point out the similar object of their concern: both are preoccupied with their glory, which is understood as a source of self-importance. The megalopsychos is preoccupied with the glory he has achieved, and the scientist with the glory after which she strains. Both, I say, are distracted and thus epistemically disabled.

[17] Gordon Bottomley, "Poetry and the Contemporary Theatre," in *Essays and Studies by Members of the English Association*, vol. 19 (Oxford: Clarendon Press, 1934), 142.

[18] Aristotle, *Nicomachean Ethics*, 4.3.24–25, 1124b10–16.

[19] *Seneca: Moral and Political Essays*, ed. John M. Cooper and J. F. Procopé (Cambridge: Cambridge University Press, 1995), 218.

[20] This account of grandiosity, along with the associated virtues of humility and aspiration and the vice of pusillanimity, bears some resemblance to Aquinas's account of pride/humility/pusillanimity/magnanimity. See Thomas Aquinas, *Summa Theologiae*, vol. 2 (Westminster, MD: Christian Classics, 1981), 129 (magnanimity), 133 (pusillanimity), 161–62 (humility and pride).

[21] Hume, *Treatise*, bk. II, pt. 1, sec. II, 279.

[22] David Hume, *Dissertation on the Passions* (London: A. Millar, 1757), sect. II, https://davidhume.org/texts/p/2.

[23] Gregory Boyle, *Tattoos on the Heart* (New York: Free Press, 2010), 197–98.

[24] Boyle, *Tattoos*, 196.

[25] George Eliot, *Middlemarch: A Study of Provincial Life*, ed. David Carroll (Oxford: Clarendon Press), 163–64.

[26] David McCullough, *Truman* (New York: Simon and Schuster, 1992), 564.

[27] Tara Smith, "The Practice of Pride," *Social Philosophy and Policy* 15 no. 1 (1998): 78.

[28] Eliot, *Middlemarch*, 182–83.

[29] Kevin S. Reimer and M. Kyle Matsuba, "A Modest Polemic for Virtuous Pride," in *Theology and the Science of Morality: Virtue Ethics, Exemplarity, and Cognitive*

Neuroscience, ed. James A. Van Slyke, Gregory Peterson, and Warren S. Brown, vol. 21, *Routledge Studies in Religion* (New York: Routledge, 2012), 61–62. I'm grateful to Reimer and Matsuba for prompting me, by their paper, to begin thinking of virtuous humility in its connection with virtuous pride.

[30] This chapter has profited from comments I received at Fresno Pacific University and especially from conversations with Scott Cleveland. I am grateful for a grant (with Michael Spezio) from the Self, Motivation, and Virtue Project at the University of Oklahoma and its funding source, the Templeton Religion Trust, which encouraged and facilitated the writing of this chapter. Michael's thought also influenced the development of the chapter. The opinions it expresses are mine, however, and not necessarily those of the John Templeton Foundation or the Templeton Religion Trust.

Chapter 8: Intellectual-Virtue Terms and the Division of Linguistic Labor

[1] Putnam said that he thought a meaning was an ordered pair, in which one of the members is the extension of the term and the other a "meaning vector" with a social component. "The Meaning of 'Meaning,'" *Minnesota Studies in the Philosophy of Science* 7 (1975): 131–93. In a similar but shorter paper, he says that meanings "ain't in the head." "Meaning and Reference," *Journal of Philosophy* 70, no. 19 (November 8, 1973): 704.

[2] Putnam said in passing that he thought most terms refer indexically, including artifact terms, verbs like "jumps," and adjectives like "blue."

[3] Putnam, "Meaning of 'Meaning,'" 168.

[4] Since Putnam says it is preferable to speak of acquiring words rather than knowing what they mean ("Meaning of 'Meaning,'" 167), we can make the same point as follows: it is not necessary to be able to distinguish elm trees from beech trees in order to have acquired the term "elm tree," but it is necessary to be able to distinguish tigers from leopards in order to have acquired the word "tiger" (169).

[5] Miranda Fricker, *Epistemic Injustice: Power and the Ethics of Knowing* (New York: Oxford University Press, 2009).

[6] Blackburn focuses on vice terms rather than on "chastity" in Simon Blackburn, *Lust: The Seven Deadly Sins* (New York: Oxford University Press, 2004). See also the exchange between Allan Gibbard and Simon Blackburn, "Morality and Thick

Concepts," Supplement, *Aristotelian Society* 66, no. 1 (July 1992): 267–99, on the example of "lewd" in their discussion of whether there are thick concepts.

[7] However, there is currently a large project, "Expanding the Science and Practice of Gratitude," at the University of California, Berkeley, with funding from the John Templeton Foundation.

[8] My student, Seth Robertson, has a very interesting unpublished paper titled "The Problem of Revenge for Moral Exemplarism" on admirable vengeance, suggesting that we may rightly admire vengeful persons under certain conditions. If so, it may be premature to propose eliminating vengeance from the stereotype of a just person.

[9] For a fascinating story about the writing and adoption of the Universal Declaration of Human Rights and the pivotal role of Eleanor Roosevelt, see Mary Ann Glendon, *A World Made New: Eleanor Roosevelt and the Universal Declaration of Human Rights* (New York: Random House, 2001).

[10] This is the view of my friend, Norman Stillman, a specialist in Arab-Jewish encounters in Arab lands.

[11] Stillman says that he often tells students that when reading some social or political thinker whose Arabic is hard to understand, they should try to go back to the European writer and language that that person must have been reading. In North Africa, most feminists and social scientists write in French, not Arabic, for that reason. There are many ideas that they cannot adequately express in Arabic.

[12] See Jason Baehr, *The Inquiring Mind: On Intellectual Virtues and Virtue Epistemology* (Oxford: Oxford University Press, 2011), 142, which mentions C. P. Snow's novel *The Search* as an example of intellectual virtue, but that is an exception.

Chapter 9: Virtues and Vices of Civility

[1] Derald Wing Sue, "Microaggressions: More than Just Race," *Psychology Today*, November 17, 2010, http://www.psychologytoday.com/blog/microaggressions-in-everyday-life/201011/microaggressions-more-just-race.

[2] Bradley Campbell and Jason Manning, "Microaggression and Moral Cultures," *Comparative Sociology* 13, no. 6 (2014): 692–726, https://doi.org/10.1163/15691330-12341332. For popular-level discussions of these critiques, see Greg Lukianoff and Jonathan Haidt, "The Coddling of the American Mind," *The Atlantic*, September 2015, http://www.theatlantic.com/magazine/archive/2015/09/the-coddling-of-the-american-

mind/399356/. See also Greg Lukianoff, *Freedom from Speech* (New York: Encounter Books, 2014).

[3] This is the sense employed in the title of Erasmus's 1530 Latin book, *De Civilitatis Morum Puerilium,* the first English translation (1532) of which went under the title *A Little Book of Good Manners for Children.* Desiderius Erasmus, *A Handbook on Good Manners for Children: De Civilitate Morum Puerilium Libellus,* trans. Eleanor Merchant (London: Preface Digital, 2011).

[4] Richard Boyd, "'The Value of Civility?'," *Urban Studies* 43, no. 5–6 (2006): 872, https://doi.org/10.1080/00420980600676105.

[5] Boyd, "'The Value of Civility?'," 867.

[6] The account I give is heavily indebted to Nicholas Wolterstorff's excellent discussion in *Justice: Rights and Wrongs* (Princeton, NJ: Princeton University Press, 2007).

[7] In addition to attitudes and behaviors, we also naturally describe people as being respectful or disrespectful. There is a character trait and corresponding moral virtue and vice that is associated with being respectful or disrespectful.

[8] Wolterstorff, *Justice*, 274.

[9] Quoted in Bethanne Patrick, *An Uncommon History of Common Courtesy: How Manners Shaped the World* (Washington, DC: National Geographic Books, 2011), 14. We can further distinguish between actions that are respectful and disrespectful because they communicate respect or disrespect directly to the recipient, others that involve a communication to others, and some that involve both. Handshakes and insults directed to a person communicate respect to the person, as well as to everyone else who is aware of the actions. Singing a person's praises while he is absent, insulting someone behind her back, or publicly dancing on someone's grave communicates respect or disrespect to everyone around but not *to* the recipient. Civil and uncivil behaviors are ones that communicate or display respect or disrespect directly to the recipient.

[10] Cheshire Calhoun, "The Virtue of Civility," *Philosophy & Public Affairs* 29, no. 3 (2000): 251–75, https://doi.org/10.1111/j.1088-4963.2000.00251.x.

[11] Calhoun, "Virtue of Civility," 261.

[12] Wolterstorff, *Justice*, 275.

[13] It may be, however, that they were treating him with under-respect *qua* person, insofar as people deserve the benefit of the doubt when the evidence is mixed. It may even be that people who cast aspersions on Armstrong are now treating him with under-respect as a person. Insults that are true can still manifest under-respect. Is it incompatible with

acknowledging Armstrong's worth as a human being to continue to bring up the most shameful episodes of his life (e.g., by referring to these episodes to make a philosophical point when one could have used a fictional one)? If so, my apologies to Lance.

[14] David Hume, "Of the Rise and Progress of the Arts and Sciences," in *Essays: Moral, Political, and Literary*, ed. Eugene F. Miller (Indianapolis, IN: Liberty Fund, 1985), 137–38, Library of Economics and Liberty, accessed November 4, 2018, https://www.econlib.org/library/LFBooks/Hume/hmMPL.html?chapter_num=19#book-reader.

[15] Thus, in his book on norms of civility for children, Erasmus includes the following rule of thumb: "[R]eadily ignore the faults of others but avoid falling short yourself." *Handbook on Good Manners.*

[16] David Estlund, "Deliberation Down and Dirty: Must Political Expression Be Civil?" in *The Boundaries of Freedom of Expression and Order in American Democracy*, ed. Thomas Hensley (Kent, OH: Kent State University Press, 2000).

[17] Mill, *On Liberty.*

[18] Jason Baehr, *The Inquiring Mind: On Intellectual Virtues and Virtue Epistemology* (Oxford: Oxford University Press, 2011).

[19] Richard J. Mouw, *Uncommon Decency: Christian Civility in an Uncivil World*, 2nd ed. (Downers Grove, IL: InterVarsity Press, 2010) attributes this point to Martin E. Marty.

[20] See Allan Hazlett, "The Social Value of Non-Deferential Belief," *Australasian Journal of Philosophy* 94 no. 1 (2015): 131–51 for a defense of the claim that there is great social value to disagreements in which people do not too quickly defer to the opinions of others.

[21] Cass Sunstein, "Deliberating Groups versus Prediction Markets (or Hayek's Challenge to Habermas)," in *Social Epistemology: Essential Readings*, ed. Alvin Goldman and Dennis Whitcomb (Oxford: Oxford University Press, 2011), 314–37.

[22] For example, Mark Lilla claims that political conservatives in the era of shock radio and Fox News have "created a right-wing media bubble in which not only liberals and moderates are demonized, but also non-partisan experts in economics and science"; "Two Concepts of Civility," in *Civility and American Democracy: A National Forum* (Boston: University of Massachusetts-Boston, 2012), 37–48. Although Lilla concedes that there is a liberal media bubble as well, which may be biased in various ways, he claims that there is a crucial difference: "Within the liberal media bubble there is still respect for expertise and evidence. That is no longer true in the conservative one."

Lack of respect for intellectual expertise has also historically been characteristic of American Christian Evangelicals. See Mark A. Noll, *The Scandal of the Evangelical Mind* (Grand Rapids: Eerdmans, 1995) for a critique along these lines, and a call to action from within the tradition.

[23] Miranda Fricker argues that treating people with too much respect can sometimes harm them. Suppose a young prince is surrounded by sycophants who show him more respect than he deserves. Fricker argues that this can be bad *for the prince* and can also have bad consequences. However, it also seems to be explained by the distinction between under-respect in different roles. To treat someone dishonestly, other things being equal, is to treat him with under-respect as a person. The sycophants arguably treat the prince over-respectfully as a prince, but under-respectfully as a human being. *Epistemic Injustice: Power and the Ethics of Knowing* (New York: Oxford University Press, 2009).

[24] Jeannie Suk Gersen, "The Trouble with Teaching Rape Law," *The New Yorker*, December 15, 2014, http://www.newyorker.com/news/news-desk/trouble-teaching-rape-law.

[25] For further discussion, see Jake Bernstein, "Inside the New York Fed: Secret Recordings and a Culture Clash," *ProPublica*, September 26, 2014, http://www.propublica.org/article/carmen-segarras-secret-recordings-from-inside-new-york-fed.

Chapter 10: Cultivating Intellectual Humility and Hospitality in Interfaith Dialogue

[1] Simone Weil, *Waiting for God* (New York: Harper & Row, 1973), 69.

[2] Augustine, *On Christian Doctrine, in Four Books*, Christian Classics Ethereal Library (397), chap. 40, no. 60, http://www.ccel.org/ccel/augustine/doctrine.xli.html.

[3] Augustine, *Of True Religion*, 7.

[4] Plato, "Meno," in *Plato's Meno, with Text and Essays*, ed. Malcolm Brown (New York: Bobbs-Merill, 1971), 33.

[5] John Calvin, *Institutes of the Christian Religion*, ed. John T. McNeill, trans. Ford Lewis Battles (Philadelphia: Westminster Press, 1960), II, 3, 6, 273.

[6] G. K. Chesterton, "Quotations of G. K. Chesterton," The Society of Gilbert Keith Chesterton, http://www.chesterton.org/discover/quotations.html.

[7] Herman Bavinck, *Reformed Dogmatics*, vol. 1, trans. John Vriend (Grand Rapids, MI: Baker Academic, 2003), 318.

[8] Calvin, *Institutes*, ii, 11, 11, 268–69.

[9] Simone Weil, "Reflections on the Right Use of School Studies with a View to the Love of God," Hagia Sophia Classical Academy, http://www.hagiasophiaclassical.com/wp/wp-content/uploads/2012/10/Right-Use-of-School-Studies-Simone-Weil.pdf.

[10] Leonard Swidler, "The Dialogue Decalogue: Ground Rules for Interreligious, Interideological Dialogue," Dialogue Institute, http://institute.jesdialogue.org/resources/tools/decalogue/.

[11] Swidler, "Dialogue Decalogue."

Selected Bibliography

The following resources complement the ethos and subject matter of the present volume. For a complete listing of references too numerous for a selected bibliography, consult the Notes section of this volume.

Adams, Robert Merrihew. *A Theory of Virtue: Excellence in Being for the Good.* Oxford: Oxford University Press, 2006.

Audi, Robert. *The Good in the Right: A Theory of Intuition and Intrinsic Value.* Princeton, NJ: Princeton University Press, 2004.

Austin, Michael W., and R. Douglas Geivett, eds. *Being Good: Christian Virtues for Everyday Life.* Grand Rapids: Eerdmans, 2012.

Baehr, Jason. *The Inquiring Mind: On Intellectual Virtues and Virtue Epistemology.* Oxford: Oxford University Press, 2011.

———, ed. *Intellectual Virtues and Education: Essays in Applied Virtue Epistemology.* London: Routledge, 2016.

Carter, J. Adam, and Emma C. Gordon, ed. *The Moral Psychology of Pride.* Lanham, MD: Rowman and Littlefield, 2017.

Carter, Stephen L. *Civility: Manners, Morals, and the Etiquette of Democracy.* New York: Basic Books, 1998.

Church, Ian, and Peter Samuelson. *Intellectual Humility: An Introduction to Philosophy and Science.* New York, NY: Bloomsbury Academic, 2017.

DePaul, Michael, and Linda Zagzebski, ed. *Intellectual Virtue: Perspectives from Ethics and Epistemology.* New York: Oxford University Press, 2003.

Dow, Philip E. *Virtuous Minds: Intellectual Character Development for Students, Educators and Parents.* Downers Grove, IL: IVP Academic, 2013.

Driver, Julia. *Uneasy Virtue.* New York: Cambridge University Press, 2001.

Dunnington, Kent. *Humility, Pride, and Christian Virtue Theory.* New York: Oxford University Press, 2019.

Fricker, Miranda. *Epistemic Injustice: Power and the Ethics of Knowing.* New York: Oxford University Press, 2009.

Guinness, Os. *The Case for Civility: And Why Our Future Depends on It.* New York: Harper Collins, 2008.

Mouw, Richard J. *Uncommon Decency: Christian Civility in an Unchristian World.* 2nd ed. Downers Grove, IL: InterVarsity Press, 2010.

Pardue, Stephen T. *The Mind of Christ: Humility and the Intellect in Early Christian Theology.* London: Bloomsbury, 2013.

Patrick, Bethanne. *An Uncommon History of Common Courtesy: How Manners Shaped the World.* Washington, DC: National Geographic, 2011.

Peterson, Christopher, and Martin Seligman. *Character Strengths and Virtues: A Handbook and Classification.* Oxford: Oxford University Press, 2004.

Ritchhart, Ron. *Creating Cultures of Thinking.* San Francisco: Jossey-Bass, 2015.

———. *Intellectual Character: What It Is, Why It Matters, and How to Get It.* San Francisco: Jossey-Bass, 2002.

Roberts, Robert C. *Emotions: An Essay in Aid of Moral Psychology.* Cambridge: Cambridge University Press, 2003.

Roberts, Robert C., and W. Jay Wood. *Intellectual Virtues: An Essay in Regulative Epistemology.* Oxford: Clarendon Press, 2007.

Sherman, Nancy. *The Fabric of Character.* Oxford: Oxford University Press, 1989.

Snow, Nancy, ed. *Cultivating Virtue: Perspectives from Philosophy, Theology, and Psychology.* Oxford: Oxford University Press, 2014.

Timpe, Kevin, and Craig A. Boyd. *Virtues and Their Vices.* Oxford: Oxford University Press, 2014.

Van Slyke, James A., Gregory Peterson, and Warren S. Brown. *Theology and the Science of Morality: Virtue Ethics, Exemplarity, and Cognitive Neuroscience, Routledge Studies in Religion*. New York: Routledge, 2012.

Wayment, H. A., and J. J. Bauer, ed. *Transcending Self-Interest: Psychological Explorations of the Quiet Ego*. Washington, DC: American Psychological Association, 2008.

Zagzebski, Linda. *Virtues of the Mind*. Cambridge: Cambridge University Press, 1996.

About the Center for Christian Thought

Biola University established the Center for Christian Thought in 2012 to advance Christian scholarship on the big questions of human life. Our mission is to reconnect Christian scholarship with the academy and the church by providing financial and scholarly resources for scholars and pastors.

We have two priorities: first, we periodically offer scholars and pastors research grants. Second, we produce articles, videos, podcasts, and community events featuring deep and enriching Christian wisdom for thoughtful Christian leaders.